By Faith Alone

Answering the Challenges to the Doctrine of Justification

Edited by
Gary L. W. Johnson
and Guy Prentiss Waters

Foreword by David F. Wells

CROSSWAY BOOKS

A PUBLISHING MINISTRY OF
GOOD NEWS PUBLISHERS
WHEATON, ILLINOIS

Cover design: Josh Dennis
Cover illustration: Bridgeman Art Library
First printing 2007
Printed in the United States of America

Unless otherwise indicated, Scripture quotations are from *The Holy Bible, English Standard Version*® copyright © 2001 by Crossway Bibles, a publishing ministry of Good News Publishers. Used by permission. All rights reserved.

Scripture quotations marked AT are the author's translation.

Scripture quotations marked KJV are from the King James Version of the Bible.

Scripture quotations marked NASB are from *The New American Standard Bible*,® Copyright ©The Lockman Foundation 1960, 1962, 1963, 1968, 1971, 1972, 1973, 1975, 1977, 1995. Used by permission.

Scripture references marked NIV are from *The Holy Bible: New International Version*.® Copyright ©1973, 1978, 1984 by International Bible Society. Used by permission of Zondervan Publishing House. All rights reserved. The "NIV" and "New International Version" trademarks are registered in the United States Patent and Trademark Office by International Bible Society. Use of either trademark requires the permission of International Bible Society.

Scripture references marked NRSV are from *The New Revised Standard Version*. Copyright ©1989 by the Division of Christian Education of the National Council of the Churches of Christ in the U.S.A. Published by Thomas Nelson, Inc. Used by permission of the National Council of the Churches of Christ in the U.S.A.

All emphases in Scripture quotations have been added by the author.

ISBN-10: 1-58134-840-1
ISBN-13: 978-1-58134-840-8

Library of Congress Cataloging-in-Publication Data

Johnson, Gary L. W., 1950-
    By Faith Alone : Answering the Challenges to the Doctrine of Justification / Gary L. W. Johnson and Guy Prentiss Waters.
        p.   cm.
    Includes bibliographical references and index.
    ISBN-13: 978-1-58134-840-8 (tpb)
    1. Justification (Christian theology) I. Waters, Guy Prentiss, 1975- II. Title.
BT764.3.J64 2006
234'.7--dc22   2006026386

For my wife, Sarah, helpmeet and fellow heir of the grace of life

—GUY PRENTISS WATERS

For Rick & Jeri Crawford and Rick & Carol Hudson
Beloved family and friends

—GARY L. W. JOHNSON

Contents

Contributors

C. FitzSimons Allison, bishop of South Carolina (ret.), Georgetown, South Carolina.

E. Calvin Beisner, associate professor of historical theology and social ethics, Knox Theological Seminary, Fort Lauderdale, Florida.

John Bolt, professor of systematic theology, Calvin Theological Seminary, Grand Rapids, Michigan.

T. David Gordon, professor of religion and Greek, Grove City College, Grove City, Pennsylvania.

Gary L. W. Johnson, senior pastor, The Church of the Redeemer, Mesa, Arizona.

R. Albert Mohler, Jr., president, Southern Baptist Theological Seminary, Louisville, Kentucky.

Richard D. Phillips, senior minister, First Presbyterian Church, Coral Gables, Florida.

David VanDrunen, Robert B. Strimple associate professor of systematic theology and Christian ethics, Westminster Seminary California, Escondido, California.

Cornelis P. Venema, president; professor of doctrinal studies, Mid-America Reformed Seminary, Dyer, Indiana.

Guy Prentiss Waters, assistant professor of biblical studies, Belhaven College, Jackson, Mississippi.

David F. Wells, Andrew Mutch distinguished professor of historical and systematic theology, Gordon-Conwell Theological Seminary, South Hamilton, Massachusetts.

R. Fowler White, professor of New Testament and biblical languages; dean of faculty, Knox Theological Seminary, Fort Lauderdale, Florida.

List of Abbreviations

ARCIC   Anglican/Roman Catholic International Commission
BAG   Bauer, Arndt, Gingrich
CTJ   *Calvin Theological Journal*
ECT   Evangelicals and Catholics Together
FV   Federal Vision
LDS   Latter-day Saints
NPP   The New Perspective(s) on Paul
IDB   *Interpreter's Dictionary of the Bible*
WCF   Westminster Confession of Faith
WLC   Westminster Larger Catechism
WSC   Westminster Shorter Catechism
WTJ   *Westminster Theological Journal*

Foreword

DAVID F. WELLS

It is a mark of our times that the language of *sola fide* has become quaint, sometimes incomprehensible, but mostly irrelevant. What once carried the full freight of reformational understanding, today seems like a *shibboleth*, an inconsequential matter, something which is of interest to those with a prickly doctrinal sensibility but of no practical consequence to those busy building the church.

What are we to make of this situation? Evangelical estimates vary all the way from deep misgivings on the one end to yawns or smiles on the other end. There are those who see in this the passing of historical orthodoxy, and this is something which they mourn. There are those who see either a matter of no consequence at all or they see in this their liberation, and this is something which they celebrate.

My own view is that this development is a signpost to a very different future, and it is one that we are going to rue. The evangelical world, in fact, is now coming apart because its central truths, what once held it all together, no longer have the binding power that they once had and, in some cases, are rejected outright with no following outcry.

When I was growing up in Rhodesia where my father was a civil servant and a judge, it never even crossed my mind that before long—in fact, even before I had graduated from university—the whole empire of which it was a part would begin to come tumbling down. But so it was. The British Empire, which, at its height, had spread itself over one-third of the earth, reached the point that all empires eventually reach, and it began to disintegrate. Despite brave words from London, it simply could not resist the centrifugal forces, in country after country, that were pulling away from the center in the name of freedom. In the space of a few years the empire had evaporated, though the former members do get together periodically for fraternal exchanges and, perhaps, to remember old times.

This image of a decaying worldly power has come to my mind from time to time as I have thought about evangelicalism. Despite some rather obvious differences between these two empires, there are nevertheless also some parallels. In both empires—the one purely worldly and the other believing—it was common ideas that held things together. In the case of the British Empire, the bond between its many peoples, willing or not, was notions about law with all of the mechanisms to make that law work and ideas about civilization, and these were not always bad. In this other empire, this post-World War II evangelical world, what has held things together amidst its rambunctious, enterprising, and entrepreneurial movers and shakers—not to mention its churches and a multitude of quite ordinary believers—has been a core of beliefs that has been taken with sufficient seriousness until relatively recently. This moderated what possibilities might be tolerated in the ways in which evangelical belief was expressed, and it moderated centrifugal forces intent upon pulling away from the center. This core was what had been secured and defined at the Reformation as it sought to reclaim biblical truth. In the post-World War II period and until relatively recently, evangelicals have followed in this tradition of belief, at least to the extent that they have been committed to the high functional authority of Scripture—*sola Scriptura*—and to the necessity and centrality of the death of Christ understood in a substitutionary way—*solo Christo*. It is believing these doctrines that has defined them as evangelical, held them together, and given them their agenda.

Of course it is also the case that these commitments have been held alongside, and together with, a welter of competing and conflicting views of a secondary order. Evangelicals have taken different positions on church government, baptism, the work of the Holy Spirit, the future of Israel, how election works out, politics and many, many other issues. However, as long as the center held, things evangelical also held together; once that center began to disintegrate, evangelical believing splintered away in all directions, losing conviction along the way or, alternatively, developing misplaced passion and intensity in the secondary matters that now fill the vacated center. What was once an extremely effective coalition of believers that drew into working partnerships people from around the world, people from many different cultures and countries during the twentieth century, has now lost its cohesion, coherence, and direction. Evangelicalism as both a movement and as a significant doctrinal position is in disarray.

There are, no doubt, many different ways in which we might lay out the new topography following this disintegration. Sketches as to where things are and as to how the land now lies might change depending on whether one were looking strictly from within the academy or more broadly in the churches. I want to look more broadly. What I suggest is that there are currently three main constituencies in evangelicalism. There is one in which the historical doctrines of evangelical believing are still maintained and even treasured. There is one that is oblivious to these doctrines and considers them an impediment to church growth. Finally, there is one that is thumbing its nose at both of these first two constituencies, in the one case because its orthodoxy is too confining and in the other because its church life, glitzy as it may be, is too empty.

The reformational doctrines, part and parcel of which is *sola fide,* are still preserved among churches and by individuals in the first major church constituency. This understanding about faith and its function does not, of course, stand alone but has a doctrinal context, and it has connections in the Word of truth which God has given us. The reason that people believe, and the reason that the New Testament affirms, that faith is the sole means of receiving God's saving grace is because of its connections to two other beliefs: *sola gracia* and *solo Christo,* to use the language of the Reformation.

In the sixteenth century, Luther stood his ground where Paul, many centuries earlier, had done so. Despite the light that the New Perspective claims to have cast on Paul's doctrine, I am still persuaded that Luther actually got it right and that Paul thought about justification as the church, following Luther, has always judged that he did and not as the New Perspective now imagines. The Judaizers then and the medievals in Luther's day alike thought that by the keeping of the law, salvation could be merited. Paul first, then Luther later, rejected this, and Luther rejected it because Paul had done so. The reason, quite simply, was their far deeper, far more realistic, and, indeed, far more biblical reckoning with the depths of human sin, its pervasiveness, and the innate corruption it has wrought throughout human nature. How, then, are humans to render up an obedience to the law which is not itself corrupt? The apple of our best works, while rosy and attractive on the outside, is always inhabited by a worm that has destroyed it from within.

So it was that Paul, and indeed the New Testament, led us to see that we contribute nothing to our salvation except, as Archbishop William Temple would later say, the sin from which we need to be redeemed. We are as paupers who stand empty-handed and gratefully accept whatever kindness is offered to us. That kindness comes in the form of Christ's substitution on our behalf, in our place, dying the death that we deserve, bearing in himself God's righteous judgment for our sin, and clothing us in a righteousness not our own. That is the New Testament gospel. That is what Paul calls God's "inexpressible gift," one received by the empty hand of faith alone, and that has always been the evangelical message. Believing this gospel, believing it in its New Testament formulation, is what evangelicalism has always been about.

In the last few decades, however, a second church constituency has been emerging, first in America, and now, like so many other things American, it is being exported overseas. It is made up of a generation of pragmatists, initially Baby Boomers but now spilling out generationally, who have lived off this reformational understanding as does a parasite off its host, separate but surreptitiously using its life and slowly bringing about the death of its host. These pragmatic entrepreneurs, these salesmen of the gospel, may not always deny reformational understanding overtly, but even if they do not, they always hide it from view. They shuffle off this orthodoxy into a corner where they hope it will not be noticed. To the seekers who are so sensitive and who are their target audience, this orthodoxy would be quite incomprehensible, not to say off-putting. So, it is covered up because it is judged to be irrelevant to what is of interest to them and to those who are in the business of selling Christianity; it is likewise judged to be irrelevant to their work.

They want to reconfigure their churches around the marketing dynamic, and that is something quite different. It is this experiment of borrowing off the mechanisms of capitalism, this skimming off of business savvy and the niche-marketing that follows, that makes up the second major constituency in evangelical faith, as I see it.

However, let it be said immediately that this is only second on my list of enumeration. In fact, it is the *dominant* constituency in American evangelicalism today, which is why it is pandered to so shamelessly by *Christianity Today*. And that is also why it passes unchallenged by many evangelical leaders who might know better. Its stunning success has placed it beyond accountability or criticism. Its success has made it invulnerable and impervious.

The idea at the heart of this experiment was always rather simple. If Coca-Cola can sell its drinks, if Lexus can market its cars, why can't the church, using the same principles, the very same techniques, market its message? After all, this is the language that all Americans understand because all Americans are consumers. And so it was that the seeker-sensitive church emerged, reconfigured around the consumer, edges softened by marketing wisdom, pastors driven by business savvy, selling, always selling, but selling softly, alluringly, selling the benefits of the gospel while most, if not all, of the costs were hidden. Indeed, it got worse than this. Sometimes what was peddled was a gospel entirely without cost, to us and apparently also to Christ, a gospel whose grace is therefore so very cheap. And it has gotten even worse. Just as often, the gospel has vanished entirely and been replaced only by feel-good therapy. The message has been about a God without wrath, bringing man without sin, into a kingdom without a judgment, through a Christ without a cross . . . all that we might feel good about ourselves and come back to "church" next week. This, actually, is how Niebuhr described the old, defunct Liberal gospel! But, never mind. Buoyed by George Barna's statistics and flushed with success, seeker-sensitive pastors have sallied forth into the consumer fields in ever more inventive and extraordinary ways to bring in the harvest now ripened, now ready to be gathered and fetched into their auditoriums.

But to what are these seekers coming? Gone are all the signs of an older Christianity. Churches that once looked like churches, symbols of a message transcendent in origin, have now been replaced by auditoriums, and some of them might even be mistaken as business convention centers. Indeed, they might even pass as showrooms—boats and home appliances on display during the week and Jesus on the weekend. And why not? Gone, after all, is the transcendent message, and what remains, really, is quite this-worldly. And this is subtly broadcast visually. Pews have been replaced by chairs, the pulpit by a stage or, maybe, a plexiglass stand, the Scripture reading by a drama group, the choir by a set of sleek and writhing singers who could be straight out of a show in Vegas, and everywhere the Jumbotrons, the technology, the wizardry of a control so complete that it all comes off as being super-casual. This church stuff is no sweat; it's fun! It is to *this* that seekers are coming. Indeed, far more frequently than we might wish to know, it is *only* to this that they are coming.

Barna, at least, is now dismayed. His assiduous polling, which initially launched this experiment in how to "do church," has now been following behind it and churning up some truly alarming findings. You see, none of this pizzazz and glitz has made an iota of difference to those who have been attending. They have been living on our postmodern "bread," on technology and entertainment alone, and not on the Word of God. The result is that they are now living no differently from those who are overtly secular, he says. They have no Christian worldview, they exhibit no Christian character, and they show no Christian commitment. Their pastors, he says, measure their own success by the number of attendees and the square footage of the building, but the people who attend, those who are born again, show none of the signs of the radical discipleship that Jesus demanded. Am I just old-fashioned when I wonder to myself whether there might be a causal connection between this flagging discipleship and the abandoned biblical concerns about truth, the irrelevant orthodoxy, in these seeker-sensitive churches?

The Emergent church, the third of these church constituencies in evangelicalism, is a reaction which, in effect, is saying to the other two constituencies, "a pox on both your houses!" This pox is being pronounced on the one because of its conception of truth and, on the other, because of its emptiness. However, while it expresses its double disaffection with an "in-your-face" attitude, it is most coy about what it is actually for.

To start with, the Emergent church is *not* a movement. No, no. It is only a conversation. Furthermore, it is *not* against historical orthodoxy, it says, well, not really; it just is not particularly for it and, besides, it thinks that the kind of doctrinal clarity and precision which the Reformation yielded is a figment of the "modern" imagination, forgetting that this modern Enlightenment world had not even been born when Luther and Calvin were struggling with Rome and produced such clarity and precision! The Emergent church is evangelical, of course, but it is also many other things too. Why be obnoxiously narrow in this age of wide-open acceptance? The categories in which evangelicalism has thought about itself, you see, came out of the *modern* world which has now collapsed. The Emergent are *postmodern* and that means that being evangelical, along with being everything else, must mean being different from what evangelicals always have been . . . if you are still following me.

The way the Emergent leaders make this distinction between being modern and postmodern is as fatuous as it is convenient. They have borrowed this from their academic gurus—people like Stanley Grenz, Len Sweet, Roger Olson, and John Francke—as a way of upending historical Christian faith. Historical orthodoxy was modern, you see; we, happily, have no option but to be postmodern, thereby allowing us to jettison the truth question that was at the heart of historical Christianity. In Brian McLaren's *A New Kind of Christian,* Neo, the hip, with-it, cool, cutting-edge, suave, slick, postmodern pastor—in short, McLaren himself!—who was once himself benighted but now is wide awake to how things really are, observes that the old question was: which religion is true? The new question is: which religion is good?

Are we really to suppose that when we read the Bible, what we will discover is that the prophets and apostles actually said that whom we worship is not a matter of concern to God provided we are nice about it? But, of course! Here I am thinking that the words about absolute truth used in the Bible had specific meanings, whereas those who live in postmodern times as we do and are "with it" linguistically know that words are only self-referential. They know that words only tell us what some person was thinking at the moment in which the words were used, that these words do not correspond to anything outside that person, that their meanings are not self-contained, and that we who live so much later quite properly must understand them in ways diametrically opposed to what they appear to mean in their context! How silly of me to have thought that the God of the Bible demanded exclusive loyalty, or that he has given us his truth in languages in which that truth has a fixed cash value when, of course, all of this was just a cultural way of looking at things, and one now quite obsolete and useless as we sashay through our postmodern moment.

It has always been the case that the church has had to struggle with aberrant views in its midst. Indeed, the apostle Paul goes so far as to say that "there must be factions [heresies] among you in order that those who are genuine among you may be recognized" (1 Cor. 11:19). What is different, when compared with our more recent history, is that these aberrant views on matters so central and fundamental are not outside the evangelical church but inside it. Not only so, but today these views are masquerading as something that they are not. They are offered in all innocence as Christian orthodoxy, whereas, in fact, they come out of a different universe. What we have is church practice that obliterates the underlying understanding of truth, a methodology for success without too many references to any truth, and a sense that what was once so important in the life of the church can be left behind, unexplored, unappropriated, and without consequences.

That, it seems to me, is a rather different situation from what the Reformers faced, who at least held in common with their Catholic opponents the idea that orthodoxy was important. The argument was over what constituted that orthodoxy.

When all is said and done, Christianity is about *truth* and at the heart of that truth is the gospel, *sola gratia, sola fide, in solo Christo*. If Christianity is not about what is enduringly, eternally true, in all places of the world, in every culture, in the same way, in every time, then there is no reason to strive to find the most accurate ways of stating what it is, nor in other parts of the world would there be any reason to face persecution for it. But across time people have struggled to know it, because in knowing it they have come to know the God whose truth it is and some have had to die for it. Who, one wonders, would want to die for something that was only true at some point in time, to some person, and not for all people in all places and times, or who would want to die for something that actually is not that important to the life of the church, which can be quite successful without it?

I am grateful for this book because I am grateful for any clarity, any light, that can be brought to bear on our situation in the evangelical world, and this particular book brings a lot. This desire for doctrinal clarity that I share with all of these authors, this yearning for biblical truth, makes me hopelessly "modern" as it does them. However, I comfort myself with the thought that perhaps we all just might be "modern" enough to have caught some of the same deep truth-concerns that we also find in the prophets and apostles! And that is no small thing.

Introduction

Whatever Happened to Sola Fide?

GUY PRENTISS WATERS

I n the sixteenth century, the Reformation thundered across Europe with the soul-abasing and God-glorifying gospel of grace. Today, nearly half a millennium later, the doctrines of grace cherished and proclaimed by the Reformers and their heirs—many of whom have sealed their witness with their own blood—are under renewed assault. From what quarter is this attack coming? Is it a philosophical naturalism that denies the existence of an almighty and sovereign God, who made out of nothing the world and all things therein, and who upholds all things by the word of his power? Is it a renewed paganism that calls men and women to worship the creation and to look for the divine within them? Is it a theological liberalism that denies the wrath of God against sin and that affirms the innate goodness of man?

While each of these remains a threat to the church at the turn of the twenty-first century, the renewed assault upon the doctrines of grace is coming from within the evangelical church itself. In what follows, we want to trace the background and development of two seemingly disparate movements that have surfaced within the evangelical and Reformed church—the New Perspective(s) on Paul and the Federal Vision. It will be the New Perspective on Paul and the Federal Vision that will garner the attention of many of the contributors to this volume. By way of introduction, we will ask and answer a few questions about the New Perspective on Paul and the Federal Vision: What are their origins? What are they saying? What is at stake in all of this?

By Faith Alone

As the title of this volume suggests, the contributors will be addressing the state of *sola fide* (by faith alone) in the evangelical and Reformed church. How have the New Perspective on Paul and the Federal Vision challenged *sola fide*? In order to prepare ourselves to answer this question adequately, let us briefly review the Bible's teaching on the doctrine of justification by faith alone.[1] The Scripture teaches that all mankind descending from Adam by ordinary generation have sinned in Adam. We are guilty of Adam's first sin, and we are born corrupt (Rom. 5:12–20). We are not morally neutral people who commit some deeds that are spiritually pleasing to God and some deeds that are displeasing to God. We are conceived and born in iniquity (Ps. 51:5), and the Scripture likens us, even from the womb, to venomous serpents (Ps. 58:3–5). We are sinful by nature and, as such, the whole bent of our being is not to the good but to evil. We drink iniquity like water (Job 15:16). God's analysis of fallen humanity is devastating, "Then the LORD saw that the wickedness of man was great on the earth, and that every intent of the thoughts of his heart was only evil continually" (Gen. 6:5). As the apostle Paul sets out our common human condition in Romans 1:18–3:20, he comes to the stark and sobering conclusion, "by the works of the law no flesh will be justified in his sight; for through the law comes the knowledge of sin" (Rom. 3:20). The sons and daughters of Adam—Jew and Gentile alike—stand condemned by nature. Even the very best works of a Christian are in themselves as a "filthy garment" in the sight of a holy God whose eyes are too pure to behold evil (Isa. 64:6).

Is there any hope? The Scripture replies with a resounding "yes!" The Lord Jesus Christ, the Son of Man and the Son of God, has obeyed the law, suffered and died, and risen again from the dead for the elect. Christ answers the two problems that his people bear. First, they have failed to obey the whole law. The law says "do this and you will live" (Lev. 18:5; Rom. 10:5). And so God's people look to the Lord Jesus Christ through whose obedience the many will be constituted righteous (Rom. 5:18). Second, they have violated the law of God. "For as many as are of the works of the law are under a curse; for it is written, 'Cursed is everyone

---

1. I wish to extend my thanks to the Rev. James T. O'Brien for his review of and comments on this essay, particularly in this portion of it. His suggestions have strengthened the argument and clarity this introduction, for which I assume full responsibility.

who does not abide by all things written in the book of the law, to perform them'" (Gal. 3:10). Christ, however, has redeemed us from the curse of the law, having become a curse for us (Gal. 3:13).

How does the work of Jesus Christ—his "perfect obedience and full satisfaction" (WLC 70)—come to be the possession of the believer? How does the sinner condemned in Adam come to be pardoned and accepted and accounted righteous in Jesus Christ? In his effectual calling, the believer is united by the Holy Spirit to Jesus Christ by faith (WLC 66). In union with Christ, the believer comes into possession of our Lord's obedience and satisfaction for his justification. Faith is the sole instrument by which he "receives and applies Christ and his righteousness" in justification. By faith alone the believer receives for his justification what Christ has done (Rom. 3:21–26).

Theologians use two important words in connection with our justification. First, justification is *forensic*; that is to say, it is a legal declaration. We see Paul underscoring this very point at Romans 8:33–34, "Who will bring a charge against God's elect? God is the one who justifies; who is the one who condemns?" Second, justification entails the *imputation* of Christ's merits to the believer. We see Paul teaching this point at 2 Corinthians 5:21, "He made him who knew no sin to be sin on our behalf, so that we might become the righteousness of God in him." This passage has been called the double exchange—the Christ who was, is, and ever shall be sinless had the sins of the elect reckoned to him so that in him they might be reckoned righteous.

Justification, therefore, is not God "wiping the slate clean" in the sense that he forgives us and gives us a second chance, an opportunity to earn our acceptance before him. Yes, justification means that our sins are pardoned. But this is not all. Justification also means that we are accepted and accounted righteous because of what our Savior has done. We are clothed with the merits of the Lord Jesus Christ. In the words of a well-known hymn quoted elsewhere in this volume:

> Jesus, thy blood and righteousness
> My beauty are, my glorious dress;
> 'Midst flaming worlds, in these arrayed,
> With joy shall I lift up my head.

Justification, therefore, is not a change that God makes within us (although every justified believer is also and of necessity sanctified). The basis of that declaration is not what God already sees in us, nor what God does in us, nor even what God foresees that we will do or he will do in us. Nor does God accept faith instead of good works as the basis of our acceptance. The sole basis of that declaration is without, or outside,

ourselves. That basis is the perfect obedience and full satisfaction of Jesus
Christ (WLC 70).

What does faith *do* in justification? It receives. It receives the perfect
obedience and full satisfaction of Christ. Could we possibly boast that we
at least have put forward faith? Could we find some kernel of credit here?
Not at all! Faith is the gift of God, lest any man boast (Eph. 2:8–10).

What about our good works? Saving faith, after all, must produce
good works. Do those good works justify us? Are they part of the basis
upon which God pardons us and accepts and accounts us righteous? Not
at all. Those good works simply evidence that faith is genuine (see James
2:14–26). We must never rely upon those good works as even the small-
est part of the basis of our justification. Justification is based entirely on
what Christ has done, and all glory goes to our great God.

This, then, is what the Reformers meant when they affirmed *sola fide.*
It is by faith *alone* that a believer is justified. It is this precious doctrine
that is under renewed attack within the church today.

The New Perspective(s) on Paul

Let us trace, then, the first of two movements that have converged
within the evangelical and Reformed churches—the New Perspective(s)
on Paul.[2] The New Perspective on Paul has its origin within academic
critical circles. In other words, its best-known proponents do not identify
with the creeds and confessions of the Reformation.

It is important to recognize the foundational contribution of a scholar
whose work provided much of the impetus for the New Perspective on Paul.
In two famous lectures, Krister Stendahl argued that the Western church's
understanding of Paul has been skewed by the experience of Augustine and
Martin Luther.[3] Both men were ridden with a guilty conscience. Both men
sought and found relief in their understanding of Paul's gospel. Stendahl
argued, however, that the historical Protestant doctrine of justification by
faith alone owed more to Augustine's and Luther's anguish of soul than it
did to Paul's teaching. Stendahl famously insisted that Paul had a "robust
conscience," that the apostle was not burdened with personal guilt from
which he found release through a forensic justification.

2. The following discussion of the New Perspective is a summarization of the argument set
forth in my book on the subject, *Justification and the New Perspectives on Paul* (Phillipsburg,
NJ: P&R, 2004).

3. Stendahl, "The apostle Paul and the Introspective Conscience of the West," in *Paul Among
Jews and Gentiles and Other Essays* (Philadelphia: Fortress Press, 1976), 78–96; "Paul Among
Jews and Gentiles," in ibid., 1–77. These were first presented in 1961 and 1963, respectively.

This conviction is tied to Stendahl's understanding of Paul's "Damascus Road" experience (Acts 9, 22, 26), historically understood among Christians to be the occasion of Paul's conversion. Stendahl claimed that while Paul experienced a "call" on the Damascus Road, he did not experience "conversion" in the customary sense of the word. Paul was now persuaded that Jesus Christ was the Messiah, and that Christ had called him to be apostle to the Gentiles. Paul did not discover in this encounter forensic justification as the solution to personal guilt. Paul's decisive transition from Judaism to Christianity was not to be explained in terms of "conversion" but in terms of the apostle's newfound call to preach to the Gentiles. Stendahl contends that Paul is not taken up with the question "How do I find a gracious God?" but with the following questions: (1) "What happens to the law (the Torah, the actual Law of Moses, not the principle of legalism) when the Messiah has come?" (2) "What are the ramifications of the Messiah's arrival for the relation between Jews and Gentiles?" and (3) "What is the "place of the Gentiles in the Church and in the plan of God?"[4] Stendahl was advancing an insight that later New Perspective writers would develop at greater length: the burden and genius of Paul's thought fundamentally lies *not* in the realm of soteriology (the doctrine of salvation), but in the realm of ecclesiology (the doctrine of the church).

The New Perspective on Paul properly begins not with questions about Paul but with questions about the Judaism of Jesus' and Paul's day.[5] Historically, Protestants had seen Paul opposing Judaism as a religion of works, i.e., a religion wherein one's works or deeds were understood to render the individual acceptable in God's eyes. Paul, particularly in his letter to the Romans, argues that it is impossible for any ordinary human being to be thus righteous. Rather, Paul announces in the gospel, sinners are justified by faith alone. Paul propounds, then, a gospel of grace.

New Perspective proponents have questioned whether this Protestant analysis of ancient Judaism is accurate. E. P. Sanders, in his epochal work, *Paul and Palestinian Judaism,* argued that ancient Judaism is most properly seen to be a religion of grace, not of works.[6] If this is the case, then Paul is not opposing Judaism because it is a religion of works in opposition to his religion of grace. Yet, the apostle is most certainly opposing something in connection with Judaism. Given that Paul's doctrine of justification by faith alone is integrally tied both to his critique of Judaism and of the

4. Stendahl, quoted at Waters, *Justification,* 24.
5. We should note that many biblical scholars do not properly distinguish biblical religion, which is thoroughly gracious, from post-Old Testament Judaism, much of which was not. In this sense, much of first-century Judaism represents a declension from the Old Testament.
6. See the discusion at Waters, *Justification,* 35–58.

Judaizers within the church, justification has been brought to the forefront of New Perspective scrutiny.

Before we proceed, we should observe that, while Sanders has persuaded many scholars that Judaism is gracious, he has not persuaded all scholars. Sanders has established that Judaism was not a crass religion of "merit-mongering" in the fashion represented by turn-of-the-twentieth-century German scholarship. Judaism was, in fact, conversant with the language and with the concept of grace. Sanders, however, is mistaken in concluding that just because Judaism made room for grace it was a thoroughly gracious religion. One of our Lord's own parables illustrates this point. He introduces the parable of the Pharisee and the publican this way: "He also told this parable to some people who trusted in themselves that they were righteous, and treated others with contempt" (Luke 18:9). Jesus represents two people praying to God. The Pharisee prays: "God, I thank you that I am not like other men: extortioners, unjust, adulterers, or even like this tax collector" (18:11). Jesus acknowledges that the Pharisee admits that God has played some role in his being morally different from the notorious sinners whom he mentions in his prayer ("God, I thank you . . ."). Yet, notice Jesus' verdict on the man: he was not justified at all (18:14). This parable captures the temper of the Judaism of many in Jesus' day. It was conversant with grace. It gave a place to grace. It was not, however, thoroughly and radically gracious. This Pharisee looked to his works and not to divine mercy alone to render him acceptable before God.

If one is inclined, however, to argue that Paul's opposition to Judaism was not because Judaism was a religion of works and Christianity a religion of grace, then he must try to explain how and why Paul opposed Judaism. He must explain what Paul meant by *justification*, how and why justification is not "by works," and how and why justification is "by faith in Christ." He must further do so in the wake of Stendahl's trenchant critique that Paul had not experienced a conversion from one religion to another and of Stendahl's insistence that Paul's fundamental concerns lay in the direction of ecclesiology and not soteriology.

Partly from dissatisfaction with Sanders's own responses to such questions as these, James D. G. Dunn offers an important New Perspective reading of Paul's doctrine of justification by faith alone.[7] Dunn asked and answered the question "to what is Paul objecting in Judaism?" by advancing a certain definition of the "works of the law" that Paul opposed. The "works of the law" were not generic human efforts to earn salvation through law-obedience. They were, rather, preeminently those

7. For Dunn's views on "works of the law" and on justification, see especially "The New Perspective on Paul," *Bulletin of the John Rylands University Library of Manchester* 65 (1983): 95–122; and *A Theology of Paul the Apostle* (Grand Rapids, MI: Eerdmans, 1998).

"boundary-marking" laws within Judaism that served to distinguish Jew from Gentile. Examples of these, for Dunn, include circumcision, the Jewish dietary laws, and the laws governing the Sabbath.

What then is justification? For Dunn, justification does not describe how one enters the people of God. It is a declaration that the believer is already a member of the people of God. The true boundaries, then, of God's people are not defined by these Jewish boundary-marking devices (works of the law). They are defined rather by "faith." This principle of justification by faith and not by works of the law, Dunn insists, is Paul's effort to reclaim a faith—manifested in the biblical testimony concerning Abraham—the importance of which had gone awry among his Jewish contemporaries.

In so defining justification by faith as a doctrine primarily relating to ecclesiology rather than to soteriology, Dunn does not altogether exclude questions of salvation from the doctrine. He contends that the distinction "declare righteous" and "make righteous" often used in attempting to translate the Greek word "to justify" (*dikaioō*) is a false dichotomy. Justification, then, includes the inward transformation of the sinner. Justification therefore is not by faith alone. It is by faith *and* the works that result from the inward transformation of the sinner.

Most influential, perhaps, of all New Perspective proponents within the evangelical and Reformed church is Bishop N. T. Wright.[8] Wright, whose ministerial credentials are in the Church of England, has earned a reputation as a moderate biblical scholar, a concerned churchman, and a winsome and engaging public speaker. As such, his substantial (although unfinished) body of writings on the apostle Paul must be taken seriously. Wright has granted Sanders's basic thesis regarding Judaism and manifests affinities with Dunn's understanding of Paul's phrase "the works of the law."

Wright's understanding of justification is not dissimilar to that of Dunn. Justification is not a declaration of how one becomes a Christian. It is, rather, a declaration that the believer is already in the people of God. Characteristic of Wright is his insistence that Paul speaks both of a "present justification" and a "future justification." In present justification, *faith* is said to be a boundary-marking device. Unlike the works of the law, *faith* delineates the people of God as they are constituted around Jesus the Messiah. Future justification is said to take place at the last day. As in present justification, future justification is by *faith*. Faith, however,

---

8. See N. T. Wright, *What Saint Paul Really Said: Was Paul of Tarsus the Real Founder of Christianity?* (Grand Rapids, MI: Eerdmans, 1997); the unpublished "The New Perspectives on Paul," a lecture given at the 10th Edinburgh Dogmatics Conference (2003); and most recently *Paul in Fresh Perspective* (London: SPCK / Minneapolis: Fortress Press, 2005).

will not function in future justification merely as a boundary-marking device. *Faith*, in final justification, includes one's faithfulness. That faithfulness will constitute at least part of the basis upon which the verdict of (future) justification is declared. We have, in such statements, essential agreement with one of the fundamental principles of justification in the Roman Catholic Council of Trent: justification is based, at least in part, on the work of God *in* the sinner. As with Dunn, Wright has rejected the Protestant doctrine of *sola fide*.

The Federal Vision

In at least one important respect the Federal Vision is radically different from the New Perspective on Paul: The New Perspective has its origins in scholarship that self-consciously opposes itself to the Protestant confessions. The Federal Vision sees itself as calling the Reformed world to a more thoroughgoing commitment to the Reformed tradition. As such its proponents are ministers, elders, and congregants within church bodies that identify with the Westminster Standards and the Three Forms of Unity.

Even so, Federal Vision proponents have expressed appreciation for the New Perspective on Paul.[9] For the most part, Federal Vision proponents believe that certain aspects of the New Perspective and Reformed theology are soteriologically compatible. Some Federal Vision proponents, consequently, have been critical of recent Reformed attempts to emphasize the differences between the New Perspective and Reformed theology. Yet, Federal Vision proponents are not all entirely agreed on which aspects of the New Perspective merit some degree of approval. Nevertheless, Federal Vision proponents have often been supportive of Reformed efforts to embrace Wright's and Dunn's insights on matters related to justification, particularly in their efforts to recast the doctrine as primarily ecclesiological.

Is it true that insights from the New Perspective on Paul can be incorporated into Reformed theology as easily as some Federal Vision writers claim that they can be? Two examples suffice to answer this question in the negative. One Federal Vision writer has expressed appreciation for certain New Perspective(s) definitions of the "righteousness of God" as *covenantal faithfulness* (rather than the righteousness of Christ imputed to the believer for his justification) at key points in the letters of Paul.[10]

9. For elaboration upon and full documentation of the points raised in this and in the following paragraphs, see chap. 3 of Waters, *The Federal Vision and Covenant Theology: A Comparative Analysis* (Phillipsburg, NJ: P&R, 2006).

10. See Peter Leithart, "'Judge Me, O God': Biblical Perspectives on Justification," 203–35 in ed. Steve Wilkins and Duane Garner, *The Federal Vision* (Monroe, LA: Athanasius, 2004).

In so doing, he proposes that the Reformation has illegitimately restricted justification to the legal or forensic sphere. Such a definition of righteousness means that we need to see the Bible's teaching on justification to encompass divine deliverance from the power of sin as well as from the guilt of sin. He therefore proposes that we should broaden our definition of justification to embrace what he terms definitive sanctification. This proponent consequently defines justification in terms of non-forensic, transformational categories. To put it simply, he conflates justification and sanctification. In so doing, his definition of justification cannot sustain the doctrine of *sola fide*.

Another Federal Vision proponent has argued that the Reformers were mistaken to see the apostle Paul's faith/works antithesis as contrasting faith and activity in justification.[11] This antithesis is intended, rather, to contrast faith with specifically Jewish practices as markers of one's inclusion within the covenant community. In so doing, however, this proponent also fails to exclude the believer's obedience from the basis of justification. To say that one is "justified by faith" need not exclude one's believing "faithfulness." Again, this construction of justification by faith cannot sustain the doctrine of *sola fide*.

Federal Vision challenges to *sola fide* have come from yet another quarter: its innovative re-reading of covenant theology. Its claims to the contrary notwithstanding, the Federal Vision compromises and undermines rather than refines and advances historic covenant theology. Historic Reformed covenant theology sees God having made two covenants with men: the covenant of works and the covenant of grace. God entered into a covenant of works with Adam in the Garden of Eden. The condition of that covenant was personal, perfect, and perpetual obedience, manifested in the command to Adam not to eat of the fruit of the tree of knowledge of good and evil. The sanction set forth was death. Adam, representing in that covenant all his posterity descending from him by ordinary generation, sinned, and this posterity sinned in him and fell with him. God has purposed to redeem his elect by the covenant of grace. The Second Adam, the Lord Jesus Christ, represents the elect as their mediator. In behalf of the elect, the Lord Jesus Christ obeys the law perfectly and makes full satisfaction to divine justice. It is this perfect obedience and full satisfaction that are imputed to the believer and received by faith alone for his justification. The covenant of grace is a covenant of *grace* to the elect because it is a covenant of *works* to Jesus Christ.

---

11. See Steve Schlissel, "Justification and the Gentiles," 237–61 in *The Federal Vision*.

Federal Vision proponents question this doctrine at a number of points.[12] Some proponents have criticized the doctrine of the covenant of works. One proponent in particular objects to the "works" principle of the first covenant.[13] This principle, he argues, misconceives and distorts the relational and familial character of this covenant.[14] He also argues that the work of Jesus Christ for the elect should not be understood in terms of *merit*. Consequently, the believer does not receive the merits of Christ for his justification. Jesus' active obedience—his perfect obedience to the law—is not imputed to the believer for his justification, but rather is said to be a precondition for the believer's justification. The believer, in union with Christ, partakes of the verdict pronounced over Jesus at the resurrection. Jesus had to obey the law in order to receive this verdict. The believer, in union with Christ, is said to share in this verdict. He does not, however, have Christ's obedience imputed to him.

Other Federal Vision proponents reason in similar fashion, some affirming this conclusion regarding imputed righteousness more forthrightly than others. None believes that he is setting out to attack the Protestant doctrine of justification. We must nevertheless press the question, what kind of doctrine of justification emerges when one denies the imputation of Christ's merits to the believer? It cannot be the doctrine of the Westminster Standards or of the Scripture.

Federal Vision innovations in the arena of covenant theology cause problems not only for the doctrine of the imputation of Christ's righteousness to the believer for his justification, but also for the doctrine of *sola fide*. One encounters the argument that *merit* should be excised entirely from covenantal thinking. As we have seen, one proponent contends that it is illegitimate to extend this term to Christ's own work on behalf of the elect. But this objection to *merit* extends in another direction as well. Rightly asserting that the believer can in no sense merit favor or acceptance with God, some Federal Vision proponents wrongly create a place for what is said to be the believer's non-meritorious obedience in

---

12. For elaboration upon and full documentation of the points raised in this and in the following paragraphs, see chaps. 2 and 3 of Waters, *The Federal Vision*.

13. See Rich Lusk, "A Response to 'The Biblical Plan of Salvation,'" ed. E. Calvin Beisner, *The Auburn Avenue Theology, Pros and Cons: Debating the Federal Vision* (Fort Lauderdale, FL: Knox Theological Seminary, 2004), 118–48. Compare also Ralph Smith, *Eternal Covenant: How the Trinity Reshapes Covenant Theology* (Moscow, ID: Canon, 2003); James B. Jordan, "Merit Versus Maturity: What Did Jesus Do for Us?" 151–200 in *The Federal Vision*.

14. FV arguments against the covenant of works often illegitimately equate *works* and *merit*. In other words, objecting to the claim that Adam's obedience in the first covenant was to be "meritorious," they therefore dismiss the *works* principle of the first covenant. But such a conclusion does not follow. Many Reformed theologians, firmly committed to the confessional doctrine of the covenant of works, maintain its *works* principle without speaking of the obedience required of Adam in terms of merit.

justification. In other words, provided that the obedience in view is not meritorious but faith-produced, it is thereby said to be acceptable as at least part of the basis of the believer's justification.

This doctrine can have at least two significant consequences. Two Federal Vision proponents speak in such a way as to include one's works as part of the basis of his justification.[15] One Federal Vision proponent will argue that one's faith-produced works may even be conceived as instrumental in justification.[16] If that is the case, then justification is not by faith alone. Justification is by faith *and* works. To say that one's faith-produced works constitute even part of the basis upon which the believer is justified is to deny the doctrine of justification by faith alone.

Conclusions

As different as the New Perspective(s) on Paul and the Federal Vision are, they converge in this respect: they deny the doctrine of *sola fide*: justification by faith alone. Rather than calling men and women to rest on the perfect righteousness of Jesus Christ alone for their justification, the New Perspective on Paul and the Federal Vision give us a modified covenant of works. They tell us "do this (with God's help) and you will live." Unanswered, however, are some crucial questions. How many good works must I produce in order to clear the bar of divine acceptance? How "good" must my good works be? Will certain wicked works disqualify me from my "final justification"—even if I have produced many good works? If so, which are they and where can I find a list of them? Will God lower his standard of justice in order to accommodate my sin-tainted works in justification? If not, how will I ever meet the divine standard of perfection (Matt. 5:48)?

Questions like these plagued adherents of an ancient Judaism that had in many respects departed from the thoroughgoing graciousness of biblical religion. Such questions were discussed among the theologians of the medieval church. Today we encounter them afresh in the New Perspective on Paul and in the Federal Vision. New Perspective proponents not infrequently deride the Reformers' readings of the apostle Paul because they are said to have read the Reformation's critique of late medieval theology into Paul's conflict with ancient Judaism. What such individuals fail to grasp is that the New Perspective on Paul (and the Federal Vision)

---

15. See Rich Lusk, "Faith, Baptism, and Justification" (2003); "The Tenses of Justification" (2003); and Steve Schlissel, "Justification and the Gentiles, in *The Federal Vision*, ed. Steve Wilkins and Duane Garner (Monroe, LA: Athanasius, 2004), 237–61."

16. See Rich Lusk, "Faith, Baptism, and Justification."

are but players in the current act of a drama that has been unfolding for centuries: the conflict between a thoroughly and wholly gracious religion and a partially gracious religion.[17] The difference might seem to consist simply in an adverb (*alone*), but this adverb manifests the chasm that lies between two fundamentally different religions.

What is justification? How is a sinner justified before God? For those who have grasped the Bible's testimony to radical human depravity as *the* human problem, the answer does not fundamentally lie in the realm of who belongs and who does not belong to the people of God. Nor will it nor can it lie in anything within us. The biblical answer lies in the merits of Jesus Christ received by faith alone.

Justification has rightly been termed *articula stantis et cadentis ecclesiae*, the article on which the church stands or falls.[18] The church is facing a threat that strikes at her foundations. I am grateful for the essays that follow in this volume. In them the reader will find a store of material that will both inform him and equip him for a reasoned defense of the doctrines of grace. May God grant that this book will fortify his people to grasp the truth with renewed understanding, and to love with deepened affection the God who has rescued his people from the pit of destruction and has placed their feet firmly upon a rock.

17. That is to say, to compromise *sola fide* is to compromise the graciousness of biblical religion.

18. Cited at John Theodore Mueller, *Christian Dogmatics: A Handbook of Doctrinal Theology for Pastors, Teachers, and Laymen* (St. Louis: Concordia Publishing, 1931), 371.

1

What Did Saint Paul Really Say?

N. T. Wright and the New Perspective(s) on Paul[1]

CORNELIS P. VENEMA

During the last decades of the twentieth century, a quiet revolution occurred in New Testament scholarship, particularly in the study of the writings of the apostle Paul. Though largely unobserved by the proverbial man or woman in the pew, academic study of the apostle Paul has come increasingly to be dominated by an approach that rejected the traditional Protestant consensus regarding Paul's view of the gospel. Long-held convictions regarding Paul's doctrine of justification were dismantled and replaced with a new paradigm, or perspective, on his teaching. Though it remains to be seen how lasting this New Perspective will be, it has so influenced contemporary studies of the apostle that it is perhaps today the consensus view of biblical theologians.[2] What began

1. Some of this chapter is a revision and abridgment of material that was originally published as part of a series of articles in *The Outlook* (Sept. 2002–Oct. 2004; Grand Rapids, MI: Reformed Fellowship), and is used with permission.
2. Cf. D. A. Carson, "Introduction," in *Justification and Variegated Nomism*, vol. 1: *The Complexities of Second Temple Judaism*, ed. D. A. Carson, Peter T. O'Brien, and Mark A. Seifrid (Grand Rapids, MI: Baker Academic, 2001), 1: "This new perspective . . . is now so strong, especially in the world of English-language biblical scholarship, that only a rare major work on Paul does not interact with it, whether primarily by agreement, qualification, or disagreement."

quietly in the academy, moreover, is beginning to seep into the churches. No longer is the New Perspective an exclusively academic point of view. Increasingly this view is gaining adherents and creating controversy within the churches. Since the New Perspective challenges the historic Protestant teaching that justification is the gracious act whereby God declares sinners acceptable to him on the basis of the righteousness of Christ alone, evangelical and Reformed Christians can ill afford to be ignorant of its emphases or influence.

One of the challenges confronting any attempt to address this New Perspective on Paul is that many different views fall under its broad canopy.[3] Advocates of a new approach to Paul's understanding of the gospel represent a wide spectrum of opinion, and, even among recognized proponents of the New Perspective, there are substantial differences. In order to avoid some of the difficulty this poses for a summary of the New Perspective, the approach in this chapter will be to focus upon the position of one of its principal exponents and architects, N. T. Wright. In addition to being a gifted New Testament scholar and prolific author, N. T. Wright has proven to be a persuasive proponent of the New Perspective beyond the boundaries of the academy. Though Wright, who serves as the Bishop of Durham of the Church of England, prefers not to be identified with some monochrome development known as the New Perspective, he believes that a return to the older Reformation view of Paul's teaching on justification would be to turn back the clock.[4]

Like many authors who are identified, to a greater or lesser extent, with the New Perspective on Paul, Wright maintains that we need to take a "fresh" look at the biblical and especially Pauline texts without the encumbrance of the traditional formulations and confessional (especially polemical) positions of the sixteenth-century Reformation. In this way, the contemporary church will honor the Reformation's emphasis upon *sola Scriptura*, while avoiding a slavish adherence to a reading of the apostle Paul that has been largely discredited by more recent historical and biblical scholarship. Wright is a natural choice for our purpose in this chapter

3. The language *New Perspective on Paul* was coined by James D. G. Dunn in an early article on the subject. See Dunn, "The New Perspective on Paul," in *Jesus, Paul and the Law: Studies in Mark and Galatians* (Louisville, KY: Westminster John Knox Press, 1990), 183–214. Proponents and opponents of a newer way of interpreting Paul have noted that we should more accurately speak of New *Perspectives* on Paul. See e.g., N. T. Wright, "New Perspectives on Paul," http://home.hiwaay.net/~kbush/Wright_New_Perspectives.pdf; and Guy Prentiss Waters, *Justification and the New Perspectives on Paul: A Review and Response* (Phillipsburg, NJ: P&R, 2004).
4. "A Reformation & Revival Journal Interview with N. T. Wright: Part One," *Reformation & Revival Journal* 11/1 (Winter, 2002): 117–39. The language "turning back the clock" is Wright's (128).

for another reason. Not only has he popularized the New Perspective for a general audience, but he also views himself as an evangelical whose commitment to the great tenets of Christian orthodoxy is unswerving. Though admitting that he no longer views things in the black-and-white terms he once did, Wright insists that he remains a "deeply orthodox theologian" who wants to present a fresh reading of the gospel to the (post)modern world.

In order to accomplish the purpose of this chapter, which is to provide a summary of Wright's New Perspective on the apostle Paul and his doctrine of justification, I will begin with a general sketch of his position. Though I will not be able to provide anything like a complete assessment of Wright's position, I will also offer a preliminary evaluation of some of its key features.[5] Other chapters in this volume will consider in greater detail some of the exegetical claims of the New Perspective and N. T. Wright; my aim here will be to accomplish two limited goals. First, I will attempt to present a clear statement of Wright's interpretation of Paul's doctrine of justification. And second, I will seek to encourage contemporary evangelical and Reformed Christians to view critically the claims of authors of the New Perspective. My thesis will be that the older perspective on Paul's doctrine of justification ultimately provides a more satisfying and comprehensive interpretation of the gospel than the newer perspective of writers like Wright.

Wright and the New Perspective[6]

To understand Wright's view of the apostle Paul's understanding of the gospel, it is necessary to begin with two figures who have contributed sig-

5. Among the growing number of introductions to and evaluations of the New Perspective, the following studies are particularly useful: Douglas Moo, "Paul and the Law in the Last Ten Years," *Scottish Journal of Theology* 40 (1986): 287–307; Frank Thielman, *Paul & the Law: A Contextual Approach.* (Downers Grove, IL: InterVarsity, 1994), 9–47; Thomas R. Schreiner, *The Law and Its Fulfillment: A Pauline Theology of the Law* (Grand Rapids, MI: Baker, 1993), 13–31; Stephen Westerholm, *Israel's Law and the Church's Faith: Paul and His Recent Interpreters* (Grand Rapids, MI: Eerdmans, 1988); idem, *Perspectives Old and New on Paul: The "Lutheran" Paul and His Critics* (Grand Rapids, MI: Eerdmans, 2004), 101–49, 178–200; D. A. Carson, Peter T. O'Brien, and Mark A. Seifrid, *Justification and Variegated Nomism,* 2 vols. (Grand Rapids, MI: Baker Academic, 2001, 2004); Waters, *Justification and the New Perspectives on Paul*; and Seyoon Kim, *Paul and the New Perspective: Second Thoughts on the Origin of Paul's Gospel* (Grand Rapids, MI: Eerdmans, 2000).
6. Wright has written a number of substantial volumes in New Testament studies and in the contemporary "third quest" for the historical Jesus: *The Climax of the Covenant: Christ and the Law in Pauline Theology* (Minneapolis: Fortress Press, 1991); *The New Testament and the People of God* (Minneapolis: Fortress Press, 1992); *Christian Origins and the Question of God,* 3 vols. (Minneapolis: Fortress Press, 1992, 1996, 2003); *Who Was Jesus?* (Grand Rapids,

nificantly to his thinking. The first of these figures, E. P. Sanders, is widely known for his historical study of Second Temple Judaism. The second of these figures, James D. G. Dunn, is a New Testament colleague who has argued that Paul formulated his doctrine of justification in opposition to Jewish *exclusivism* rather than *legalism*, as was assumed by the older perspective on the apostle Paul. Wright's reinterpretation of the apostle Paul's doctrine of justification builds in large measure upon the insights of Sanders and Dunn. Despite Wright's reluctance to identify himself with anything as monolithic as the New Perspective on Paul, he proceeds from the assumption that the writings of Sanders, Dunn, and other advocates of a new approach require a fresh reading of Paul. The contributions of Sanders and Dunn to a new view of Judaism and the historical context for reading the New Testament and the writings of the apostle Paul have irrevocably altered the landscape of biblical studies. Consequently, any simple return to the past, particularly to the debates and positions of the sixteenth-century Reformation, would be an irresponsible path for contemporary New Testament studies.

E. P. Sanders's View of Second Temple Judaism

Even though there are a number of forerunners who made significant contributions to the emergence of a New Perspective on Paul,[7] the most

---

MI: Eerdmans, 1992). Among Wright's works that most directly represent his understanding of Paul and the doctrine of justification are the following: *What Saint Paul Really Said: Was Paul of Tarsus the Real Founder of Christianity?* (Grand Rapids, MI: Eerdmans, 1997); "New Perspectives on Paul," http://home.hiwaay.net/~kbush/Wright_New_Perspectives.pdf; "The Paul of History and the Apostle of Faith," *Tyndale Bulletin* 29 (1978): 61–88; "The Law in Romans 2," in *Paul and the Mosaic Law*, ed. James D. G. Dunn (Grand Rapids, MI: Eerdmans, 1996), 131–50; "The Shape of Justification," http://www.angelfire.com/mi2/paulpage/Shape.html; *The Letter to the Romans*, vol. 10 of *The New Interpreter's Bible* (Nashville, TN: Abingdon Press, 2002); *Paul for Everyone: Romans Part 1, Chapters 1–8* (Louisville, KY: Westminster John Knox Press, 2004); and "New Perspectives on Paul," in *Justification in Perspective: Historical Developments and Contemporary Challenges,* ed. Bruce L. McCormack (Edinburgh: T. & T. Clark, 2006), 243–64. Wright has a recent volume on Paul, *Paul: Fresh Perspectives* (Fortress, 2005), which does not add anything substantially new to his previous comments on Paul's doctrine of justification.

7. One of these figures whose work is of special significance is W. D. Davies. Davies' study, *Paul and Rabbinic Judaism: Some Rabbinic Elements in Pauline Theology,* 4th ed. (Philadelphia: Fortress Press, 1980), anticipates some features of Sanders's work, especially the claim that Paul was thoroughly shaped by his background within Rabbinic Judaism of the first century of the Christian era. Sanders acknowledges that Davies was, in this respect, a "transitional figure" in New Testament studies. For Sanders's assessment of Davies' contribution, see his *Paul and Palestinian Judaism: A Comparison of Patterns of Religion* (London: SCM, 1977), 7–12. For helpful surveys of the background to the New Perspective in New Testament and Pauline studies, see Westerholm, *Perspectives Old and New on Paul: The "Lutheran" Paul and His Critics*

influential and pivotal figure is undoubtedly E. P. Sanders. Sanders's 1977 volume, *Paul and Palestinian Judaism,* is now generally regarded as a classic presentation of the view of Second Temple Judaism that is basic to the New Perspective.[8] Sanders's stated purpose in his classic study was to compare the pattern of religion evident in Paul's writings with the pattern of religion in Jewish literature during the period between 200 BC and AD 200. By a "pattern of religion" Sanders means the way a religion understands how a person "gets in" and "stays in" the community of God's people.[9]

Traditional accounts of the differences between religions, particularly the differences between Judaism and Christianity, focused upon the distinctive essence or core beliefs of these religions. In doing so, Judaism was often simplistically described as a "legalistic" religion, which emphasizes obedience to the law as the basis for inclusion among God's people, and Christianity was described as a "gracious" religion, which emphasizes God's free initiative in calling his people into communion with himself.

In the first part of his study, Sanders provides a comprehensive survey of Jewish literature during the two centuries before and after the coming of Christ. On the basis of this survey, Sanders maintains that Second Temple Judaism exhibits a pattern of religion best described as *covenantal nomism.* Sanders defines *covenantal nomism* as follows:

> The "pattern" or "structure" of covenantal nomism is this: (1) God has chosen Israel and (2) given the law. The law implies both (3) God's promise to maintain the election and (4) the requirement to obey. (5) God rewards obedience and punishes transgression. (6) The law provides for means of atonement, and atonement results in (7) maintenance or re-establishment of the covenantal relationship. (8) All those who are maintained in the covenant by obedience, atonement and God's mercy belong to the group which will be saved. An important interpretation of the first and last points is that election and ultimately salvation are considered to be by God's mercy rather than human achievement.[10]

Contrary to the traditional Protestant claim that Palestinian Judaism was legalistic, Sanders appeals to evidence in Jewish writings of the Second Temple period to support the view that it was a religion of grace. In the literature of Judaism, God is represented as graciously electing Israel to be his people and mercifully providing a means of atonement and opportunity

---

(Grand Rapids, MI: Eerdmans, 2004), 101–49, 178–200 and Waters, *Justification and the New Perspectives on Paul,* 1–33.

8. Philadelphia: Fortress, 1977.

9. *Paul and Palestinian Judaism,* 17.

10. Ibid., 422.

for repentance in order to deal with their sins. So far as Israel's "getting in" the covenant is concerned, this was not by human achievement but by God's gracious initiative. Obedience to the law was only required as a means of maintaining or "staying in" the covenant.

One of the immediate problems that surfaces, as a result of Sanders's argument for a new view of Judaism, is what to do with the apostle Paul and his polemics against Judaism. If Judaism was not a legalistic religion, what are we to make of Paul's vigorous arguments against claims to find favor with God on the basis of works? Is Paul combating a kind of straw man in his letters (especially in Romans and Galatians), when he combats a righteousness that is by the "works of the law"? Sanders, both in his *Paul and Palestinian Judaism* and in a sequel, *Paul, the Law, and the Jewish People*,[11] answers this question by suggesting that Paul's view of the human plight was a byproduct of his view of salvation. Paul started with Christ as the "solution" to the human predicament and then worked backward to explain the "plight" to which his saving work corresponds.

Though Paul has traditionally been interpreted to teach that the problem of human sinfulness, which is made known and aggravated through the law's demand for perfect obedience, calls for a solution in Christ's person and work, we should recognize that his description of the problem of sin derives from his prior convictions about Christ. Paul, in effect, starts from the basic conviction that Christ is the only Savior of Jews and Gentiles. On the basis of this conviction, he then develops a doctrine of the law and human sinfulness that corresponds to it. According to Sanders, the great problem with Judaism, so far as the apostle Paul was concerned, was not that it was legalistic; Paul's principal objection to Judaism was that it rejected the new reality of God's saving work through Christ. In words that have often been quoted, Sanders concludes: "In short, *this is what Paul finds wrong in Judaism: it is not Christianity*" (emphasis in original).[12]

James D. G. Dunn: A New View of the "Works of the Law"

Next to Sanders, the second figure of importance to Wright's understanding of the apostle Paul's doctrine of justification is James D. G. Dunn.[13] In a 1982 lecture, "The New Perspective on Paul," Dunn acknowl-

---

11. Minneapolis: Fortress Press, 1983.

12. *Paul and Palestinian Judaism*, 552. Cf. Sanders's comment on 497: "It is the Gentile question and the exclusivism of Paul's soteriology which dethrone the law, not a misunderstanding of it or a view predetermined by his background."

13. Among the more important sources for an understanding of Dunn's view are the following: James D. G. Dunn, "The New Perspective on Paul," in *Jesus, Paul and the Law. Studies in*

edged that Sanders's study, *Paul and Palestinian Judaism,* represented a "new pattern" for understanding the apostle Paul. In this lecture, Dunn credited Sanders with breaking the stranglehold of the older Reformation view that had dominated Pauline studies for centuries.[14] The idea that there is a basic antithesis between Judaism, which supposedly taught a doctrine of salvation by meritorious works, and Paul, who taught a doctrine of salvation by faith apart from the works of the law, needs to be set aside once and for all. Judaism was, as Sanders has convincingly demonstrated, a religion of salvation that emphasized God's goodness and generosity toward his people, Israel. The law was given to Israel, not as a means for procuring favor with God, but as a means to confirm the covenant relationship previously established by grace. Dunn fully concurs with Sanders's argument that Judaism's pattern of religion was that of *covenantal nomism.*

In spite of Sanders's groundbreaking insight into the nature of Judaism, Dunn claims that he nonetheless failed to provide a coherent explanation of Paul's relation to Judaism. Though Sanders provided the occasion for a New Perspective on Paul, his own interpretation of Paul's gospel fails to show how Paul's view of the law arises within the context of the Judaism of his day. If the problem with Judaism's understanding of the law was not legalism, which teaches that obedience to the law's requirements is the basis for inclusion among God's covenant people, what was wrong with its teaching? To what error is the apostle Paul responding, when he speaks of a justification that is not according to "works of the law" but according to faith?

If we approach the apostle Paul from the perspective of the new view of Judaism, we will discover, Dunn argues, that Paul was objecting to *Jewish exclusivism* and not legalism. The problem with the use of the law among the Judaizers whom Paul opposed was not their attempt to find favor with God on the basis of their obedience to the law, but their use of the works of the law to exclude Gentiles from membership in the covenant community. The Judaizers were insisting upon certain works of the law that served as boundary markers for inclusion or exclusion from the number of God's people. The law functioned in their thinking

---

Mark and Galatians (Louisville: Westminster/John Knox Press, 1970), 183–215; Dunn, "Paul and 'covenantal nomism,'" in *The Partings of the Ways Between Christianity and Judaism and Their Significance for the Character of Christianity* (Philadelphia: Trinity Press International, 1991), 117–139; Dunn, "Works of the Law and the Curse of the Law (Galatians 3.10–14)," *New Testament Studies* 31 (1985): 523–42; Dunn, *The Theology of Paul the Apostle* (Grand Rapids, MI: Eerdmans, 1998), 334–89; Dunn, *Word Biblical Commentary,* vol. 38a: *Romans 1–8,* and vol. 38b: *Romans 9–16* (Dallas: Word Books, 1988); and Dunn, "Yet Once More—'The Works of the Law': A Response," *Journal for the Study of the New Testament* 46 (1992): 99–117.

14. "The New Perspective on Paul," 184.

and practice as a means of identifying who properly belongs to the community of faith. It was this *social* use of the law as a means of excluding
Gentiles that receives Paul's rebuke, not an alleged appeal to the law as
a means of self-justification. According to Dunn, Paul's real objection to
the Judaizers' appeal to works of the law is clearly disclosed in passages
like Galatians 2:15–16 and Galatians 3:10–14. In these passages, Paul was
not opposing an allegedly legalistic teaching that obedience to the law of
God in general is the basis for finding favor with God. Rather, Paul was
opposing the idea that the *works of the law*, that is, those observances
that particularly distinguish Jews from Gentiles, are necessary badges of
covenant membership. What Paul objects to are those works of the law that
served as ritual markers of identity to separate Jews from Gentiles.[15]

The "Gospel" According to Wright

In his interpretation of Paul's understanding of justification, Wright
proceeds from the conviction that Sanders and Dunn have undermined
two essential features of the older Reformation view. First, whereas the
Reformation perspective assumed that Paul articulated the doctrine of
justification in opposition to Jewish legalism, Sanders's study of Second
Temple Judaism has demonstrated compellingly that no such legalism was
prevalent at the time of the writing of Paul's epistles. The assumption,
which played such an important, even decisive, role in the Reformation
understanding of the apostle Paul—that the Judaizers taught salvation on
the basis of works righteousness—is largely a fiction. Sanders and others
have conclusively demonstrated that Judaism emphasized the grace of God
as the basis for his covenant with Israel. The role of works in Judaism
was merely one of "maintaining" the covenant relationship and not one
of establishing the basis for "entrance into" fellowship with God. Whatever the apostle Paul's problems with Judaism were, they could not be
directed to legalism, since we know that no such legalism was advocated
by Judaism in Paul's day.

Wright's endorsement of Sanders's new view of Judaism and its importance for understanding Paul's gospel is unmistakable: "the tradition of
Pauline interpretation has manufactured a false Paul by manufacturing
a false Judaism for him to oppose."[16] Indeed, the Reformation's understanding of the gospel of free justification amounts to what Wright terms
"the retrojection of the Protestant-Catholic debate into ancient history,
with Judaism taking the role of Catholicism and Christianity the role of

15. "The New Perspective on Paul," 200.
16. "The Paul of History and the Apostle of Faith," *Tyndale Bulletin* (1978): 78.

Lutheranism."[17] Because the Reformation misunderstood the problem to which Paul was actually responding, it failed to grasp the real meaning of Paul's teaching on justification by faith.

Second, in addition to his agreement with Sanders's general description of Judaism as a non-legalistic religion, Wright also makes sympathetic use of Dunn's interpretation of Paul's dispute with the Judaizers and their understanding of the works of the law. The problem with the Judaizers' appeal to the works of the law was not its legalism, Wright insists, but its *perverted nationalism*. The Pauline expression, *the works of the law*, does not refer to a legalistic claim regarding how sinners can find favor with God by obeying the law, but to the nationalistic Jewish claim that God's covenant promise extends only to the Jews. The works of the law are what Dunn calls *boundary markers*, those acts of conformity to the law that served to distinguish the Jewish community from the Gentiles:

> If we ask how it is that Israel has missed her vocation, Paul's answer is that she is guilty not of 'legalism' or 'works-righteousness' but of what I call 'national righteousness,' the belief that fleshly Jewish descent guarantees membership of God's true covenant people. . . . Within this 'national righteousness', the law functions not as a legalist's ladder but as a charter of national privilege, so that, for the Jew, possession of the law is three parts of salvation: and circumcision functions not as a ritualist's outward show but as a badge of national privilege.[18]

The problem Paul confronted in his dispute with the Judaizers was a *boasting* in national privilege and an unwillingness to acknowledge that the covenant promise extends to Gentile as well as Jew.[19] The Reformation claim, therefore, that Paul was opposing legalism when he articulated his doctrine of justification misses the mark rather widely. Consequently, the Reformation's reading of Paul transposes his understanding into a radically different key when it treats the Judaizers as prototypes of a Roman Catholic doctrine of justification by (grace plus) works.

Before directly considering Wright's interpretation of Paul's doctrine of justification, it should be noted that he regards the doctrine of justification to be a subordinate theme in Paul's proclamation of the gospel. Though it is often assumed that the gospel is a "system of how people get saved," Wright insists that this seriously misrepresents the real meaning of the gospel.[20] The gospel does not answer the question of the guilty

17. "The Paul of History," 80.
18. Ibid., 65. See *Romans*, 139, 148–49.
19. *What Saint Paul Really Said: Was Paul of Tarsus the Real Founder of Christianity?* 128–29. Cf. N. T. Wright, "The Law in Romans 2," 139–43.
20. Ibid., 45.

sinner, how can I find favor with God? (cf., e.g., Luther), but rather it
answers the question, who is Lord? One of the unfortunate features of the
Reformation and much evangelical thinking is that it reduces the gospel
to "a message about 'how one gets saved,' in an individual and ahistorical sense."[21] In this kind of thinking, the focus of attention, so far as the
gospel is concerned, is upon "something that in older theology would be
called an *ordo salutis,* an order of salvation."[22]

According to Wright, this kind of an approach can only distort Paul's
gospel and fails to do justice to the broader historical background and
significance of Christ's saving work. All of the focus in this approach to
the gospel is narrowly fixed upon the issue of the individual's relationship with God, and not upon the reach of God's world-transforming
power proclaimed in the gospel concerning Jesus Christ. Because of this
inappropriate focus upon the salvation of individual sinners, the older
Reformation tradition was bound to exaggerate the importance of the
doctrine of justification. Even were the Reformation's understanding of
justification correct, it tends to focus upon what is only a subordinate
theme in Paul's proclamation of the gospel.

If the gospel according to Wright is not primarily about how people
get saved, then what is its primary focus? Wright answers this question
by insisting that the basic message of the gospel focuses upon *the lordship of Jesus Christ*:

> Paul's new vocation involved him not so much in the enjoyment and propa-
> gation of a new religious experience, as in the announcement of what he
> saw as a public fact: that the crucified Jesus of Nazareth had been raised
> from the dead by Israel's God; that he had thereby been vindicated as Israel's
> Messiah; that, surprising though it might seem, he was therefore the Lord
> of the whole world.[23]

Through the cross and resurrection of Jesus Christ, the one true God,
who is the creator of the world, has won a "liberating victory . . . over all
the enslaving powers that have usurped his authority."[24] Though Wright
does not often spell out concretely what he means by *the lordship of Jesus
Christ,* he does offer the following summary description:

> Paul discovered, at the heart of his missionary practice, that when he an-
> nounced the lordship of Jesus Christ, the sovereignty of King Jesus, the very

21. Ibid., 60.
22. Ibid., 40–41. See also *Romans,* 403.
23. *What Saint Paul Really Said,* 40.
24. Ibid., 47. See also *The Climax of the Covenant,* 21–26; and *The New Testament and
the People of God,* 244–79.

announcement was the means by which the living God reached out with love and changed the hearts and lives of men and women, forming them into a community of love across traditional barriers, liberating them from paganism which had held them captive, enabling them to become, for the first time, the truly human beings they were meant to be.[25]

The great theme of the gospel is this message of Jesus' lordship and its life- and world-transforming significance. This, rather than the salvation of individual sinners, is the primary interest of Paul's preaching.

If the gospel is not about how people get saved, but the proclamation that Jesus is Lord, this has implications for our understanding of what Paul means by justification. This doctrine, though an essential, albeit subordinate, theme in Paul's preaching, does not address the issue of how guilty sinners can find favor with God. This would be to assume that Paul's gospel focuses upon the salvation of the individual rather than upon the lordship of Jesus Christ and the consequences of that lordship for the realization of God's covenant promises to Israel. When we view the gospel in terms of the lordship of Jesus Christ, the proper meaning and place of the doctrine of justification becomes apparent. "Let us," says Wright, "be quite clear. 'The gospel' is the announcement of Jesus' lordship, which works with power to bring people into the family of Abraham, now redefined around Jesus Christ and characterized solely by faith in him. 'Justification' is the doctrine which insists that all those who have this faith belong as full members of this family, on this basis and no other."[26]

In order to understand the full meaning of this summary statement of the doctrine of justification, we need to consider briefly several distinct aspects of Wright's position. Chief among these are: (1) his interpretation of the phrase "the righteousness of God" as the basis for the justification of God's people; (2) the precise meaning of the language "to justify"; (3) the role of faith as a "badge" of covenant membership; (4) the past, present, and future tenses of justification; and (5) the relation between Christ's cross and resurrection and the church's justification.

The Righteousness of God

In Wright's discussion of the language of *the righteousness of God*, he begins by noting that this expression would have been readily understood by readers of the Septuagint, the Greek translation of the Old Testament.

25. *What Saint Paul Really Said*, 61.
26. Ibid., 133.

In the Septuagint, *the righteousness of God* refers commonly to "God's own faithfulness to his promises, to the covenant."[27]

> God's 'righteousness', especially in Isaiah 40–55, is that aspect of God's character because of which he saves Israel, despite Israel's perversity and lostness. God has made promises; Israel can trust those promises. God's righteousness is thus cognate with his trustworthiness on the one hand, and Israel's salvation on the other. And at the heart of that picture in Isaiah there stands, of course, the strange figure of the suffering servant through whom God's righteous purpose is finally accomplished.[28]

The righteousness of God does not refer to God's moral character, on account of which he punishes the unrighteous and rewards the righteous. This common medieval idea of God's "distributive justice" is little more than a "Latin irrelevance."[29] Rather, the righteousness of God is his covenantal faithfulness in action. When God acts to fulfill his promises to Israel, he demonstrates or reveals his faithfulness as One who will accomplish his saving purposes on her behalf. This covenant faithfulness refers both to a "moral quality" in God (God is righteous, that is, faithful) and to an "active power which goes out, in expression of that faithfulness, to do what the covenant always promised."[30]

Though the righteousness of God is primarily to be identified with God's covenantal faithfulness in action, Wright does acknowledge that this language, in its Old Testament and Jewish context, makes use of a legal or forensic (courtroom) metaphor. The language of the righteousness of God derives from the Jewish idea of the law court in which three parties are present: the judge, the plaintiff, and the defendant. In the law court, each of these parties has a distinct role to play: the judge is called upon to decide the issue and to do so in a proper manner, that is, justly and impartially; the plaintiff is obliged to prosecute the case and bring an accusation against the defendant; and the defendant is required to answer the accusation and seek to be acquitted. In the functioning of this law court, what matters finally is not the moral uprightness or virtue of the plaintiff or the defendant, but the verdict of the judge. When the judge decides for or against either the plaintiff or the defendant, we may say

27. Ibid., 96. For an extended treatment of the Wright's understanding of the theme of the "righteousness of God" in Romans, see *Romans*, 397–405.

28. *What Saint Paul Really Said*, 96.

29. Ibid., 103.

30. Ibid. For this reason, Wright regards the traditional grammatical debate whether the genitive in "righteousness *of* God" is "possessive" or "subjective" to be beside the point. The righteousness of God is both God's being righteous (possessive) and God's acts of righteousness (subjective). God's covenant faithfulness expresses itself in deeds performed to fulfill his covenant promises.

that they have a status of *being righteous* so far as the court's judgment is concerned. Within the framework of the court's pronouncements, the verdict of "righteous" means that the court has decided in the defendant's favor.

The *righteous* person, therefore, is not the person who is morally upright, but the person in whose favor the court has decided. So far as the judgment of the court goes, *the righteous* are those whom the court vindicates or acquits, *the unrighteous* are those whom the court finds against or condemns. In these respects, the language of *the righteousness of God* and of *justification* is thoroughly legal or forensic in nature.

Even though Wright affirms the forensic nature of this language in a way that is reminiscent of the reformational view of justification, he maintains that the Reformation's idea of the imputing or imparting of God's righteousness to believers makes no sense:

> If we use the language of the law court, it makes no sense whatever to say that the judge imputes, imparts, bequeaths, conveys or otherwise transfers his righteousness to either the plaintiff or the defendant. Righteousness is not an object, a substance or a gas which can be passed across the courtroom.[31]

Students of the Reformation are well aware that one of the key Pauline phrases for a proper understanding of justification is the phrase, "the righteousness of God" (cf. Rom. 1:16–17; 3:21–26). Following Luther's "discovery" that the righteousness of God is not so much the demand of God's law as the gift of his grace in Christ, the Reformers taught that we are justified by the free gift of God's righteousness in Christ, which is granted and imputed to believers. In this understanding, the righteousness of God is revealed through Christ, who, by his obedience to the law and substitutionary endurance of the law's penalty, is the believer's righteousness before God. Those who receive the free gift of God's righteousness in Christ by faith stand acquitted and accepted before God. In Wright's interpretation, the "righteousness of God," which refers to God's faithfulness to the promises he made to Israel, cannot be granted or imputed to believers. Nothing like an act of imputation is required for God to declare in favor of his people.

What It Is "To Be Justified"

Within the context of this understanding of God's righteousness as his covenant faithfulness in action, we can properly understand the idea of

31. Ibid., 99.

justification. Justification is not basically about how guilty sinners, who are incapable of finding favor with God by their works of obedience to the law, can be made acceptable to God, but about *who belongs to the number of God's covenant people.* The primary location of Paul's doctrine of justification, Wright insists, is not soteriology (how are sinners saved?) but ecclesiology (who belongs to the covenant family?). When Paul's treatment of justification is read within the context of Judaism's historic understanding of the covenant, we discover that "[j]ustification in this setting . . . is not a matter of *how someone enters the community of the true people of God,* but of *how you tell who belongs to that community*" (emphasis added).[32] In a comprehensive statement of his view, Wright maintains that justification language functions to describe who belongs to the covenant people:

> "Justification" in the first century was not about how someone might establish a relationship with God. It was about God's eschatological definition, both future and present, of who was, in fact, a member of his people. In Sanders' terms, it was not so much about "getting in," or indeed about "staying in," as about "how you could tell who was in." In standard Christian theological language, it wasn't so much about soteriology as about ecclesiology; not so much about salvation as about the church.[33]

When God reveals his righteousness in the death and resurrection of Jesus Christ, he demonstrates his covenant faithfulness by securing the inclusion of all members of the covenant community, namely, those who are baptized into Christ and are marked by the "badge" of covenant membership, which is faith. Justification, therefore, refers to the inclusion of all believers in the covenant community, whether Jews or Gentiles, who believe in Jesus Christ.

According to Wright, Paul's doctrine of justification does not answer the "timeless" problem of how sinners can find acceptance with God but explains how you can tell who belongs to "the community of the true people of God." When the language of justification is interpreted in terms of its Old Testament and Jewish background, we will recognize that it is covenantal language. Justification does not describe how someone gains entrance into the community of God's people but *who is a member of*

32. Ibid., 119.
33. Ibid., 120. See also *Romans,* 465, 473, 481. Cf. a similar comment on Paul's argument in Galatians: "Despite a long tradition to the contrary, the problem Paul addresses in Galatians is not the question of how precisely someone becomes a Christian, or attains to a relationship with God. . . . On anyone's reading, but especially within its first-century context, it has to do quite obviously with the question of how you define the people of God: are they to be defined by the badges of Jewish race, or in some other way?" (*What Saint Paul Really Said,* 122). Cf. Wright, "Curse and Covenant: Galatians 3.10–14," in *The Climax of the Covenant,* 137–56.

the community now and in the future. In Paul's Jewish context, Wright maintains,

> "Justification by works" has nothing to do with individual Jews attempting a kind of proto-Pelagian pulling themselves up by their moral bootstraps, and everything to do with definition of the true Israel in advance of the final eschatological showdown. Justification in this setting, then, is not a matter of *how someone enters the community of the true people of God,* but of *how you tell who belongs to that community,* not least in the period of time before the eschatological event itself, when the matter will become public knowledge.[34]

Faith: The Badge of Covenant Membership

Because justification focuses upon God's declaration regarding *membership* in the covenant community, Wright interprets Paul's insistence that justification is by faith and not by works in a manner that is quite similar to Dunn's approach. The "boasting" of the Judaizers was not a boasting born of self-righteousness, but a kind of misplaced nationalistic pride or exclusivism. The "works of the law" were those requirements of the law that served to distinguish Jews from Gentiles, and to exclude Gentiles thereby from membership in the covenant community. However, now that Christ has come to realize the covenant promise of God to Abraham, faith in Christ is the *only badge* of membership in God's worldwide family, which is composed of Jews and Gentiles alike. Paul's insistence that justification is by faith expresses his conviction that with the coming of Christ, God is "now extending his salvation to all, irrespective of race." "Justification . . . is the doctrine which insists that all who share faith in Christ belong at the same table, no matter what their racial differences, as together they wait for the final creation."[35]

One of the surprising and provocative implications of this understanding of justification, according to Wright, is that it radically undermines the usual polemics between Protestants and Catholics. Whereas many Protestants have historically argued that justification is a church-dividing doctrine, precisely the opposite is the case—Paul's doctrine of justification demands an inclusive view of membership in the one family of God:

> Many Christians, both in the Reformation and in the counter-Reformation traditions, have done themselves and the church a great disservice by treating the doctrine of 'justification' as central to their debates, and by supposing

34. *What Saint Paul Really Said,* 119 (emphasis Wright's). Cf. *Romans,* 497.
35. Ibid., 122.

that it describes that system by which people attain salvation. They have turned the doctrine into its opposite. Justification declares that all who be-lieve in Jesus Christ belong at the same table, no matter what their cultural or racial differences.[36]

Protestants who insist upon a certain formulation of the doctrine of jus-tification as a precondition to church fellowship, accordingly, are guilty of turning the doctrine on its head. Rather than serving its proper pur-pose to join together as members of one family all who believe in Christ (faith being the only badge of covenant membership), the doctrine of justification is turned into the teaching of justification "by believing in justification by faith."[37]

Justification: Past, Present, and Future

One feature of the doctrine of justification that receives special emphasis in Wright's understanding is its nature as an eschatological vindication of God's people. When God justifies or acknowledges those who are members of his covenant community, he does so in anticipation of their "final justification" or vindication at the last judgment. Justification occurs in three tenses or stages—past, present, and future. The justification of God's covenant community in the present is founded upon "God's past accomplishment in Christ, and anticipates the future verdict."[38]

In the *past* event of Christ's cross and resurrection, God has already accomplished in history what he will do at the end of history. Jesus, who died as the "representative Messiah of Israel," was vindicated or justified by God in his resurrection from the dead. This event, Christ's resurrection, represents God's justification of Jesus as the Son of God, the Messiah, through whom the covenant promise to Abraham ("in your seed all the families of the earth will be blessed") is to be fulfilled. Because that prom-ise comes through the crucified and risen Christ, it cannot come through the law (cf. Rom. 8:3). This past event of Christ's justification becomes a *present* reality through faith. All those who believe in Jesus as Messiah and Lord are justified, that is, acknowledged by God to be members of the one great family of faith composed of Jew and Gentile alike. Because the

36. Ibid., 158–59.

37. "The Shape of Justification," http://www.angelfire.com/mi2/paulpage/Shape.html, 3. This article is Wright's response to Paul Barnett's critical evaluation of his understanding of justification. Barnett is an Anglican bishop from the diocese of Sydney in Australia. Cf. "Tom Wright and The New Perspective," http:///www.anglicanmediasydney.asn.au/pwb/ntwright_per-spective.htm.

38. "The Shape of Justification," 2.

present reality of justification focuses upon membership in the covenant community—justification being, as we noted earlier, a matter of ecclesiology and not of soteriology—baptism into Christ is the event that effects this justification: "The event in the present which corresponds to Jesus' death and resurrection in the past, and the resurrection of all believers in the future, is baptism into Christ."[39]

Though justification has a past and present dimension, its principal focus lies in the future. At the final judgment or "justification," God will declare in favor of his people, the covenant community promised to Abraham. In this final justification, God's vindication of his people will even include a "justification by works." Commenting on Romans 2:13 ("It is not the hearers of the law who are righteous before God, but the doers of the law who will be justified"), Wright insists that "those who will be vindicated on the last day are those in whose hearts and lives God will have written his law, his Torah."[40] The works of the law that justification excludes are those badges of Jewish identity that served to exclude Gentiles. Justification does not exclude, however, those works of the law that are equivalent to the obedience of faith by the working of the Spirit.

Justification and the Work of Christ

One final feature of Wright's view of justification that remains rather undeveloped is his understanding of the work of Christ. Wright speaks of Christ's cross as a representative death and of his resurrection as his vindication by God. But Wright does not provide a complete account of Christ's work of atonement and an explanation of how this work relates to the justification of believers.

One point that emerges clearly in Wright's limited treatment of this subject is that he has little sympathy for the historic view that Christ's cross involved his suffering the penalty and curse of the law on behalf of sinners in general. In an extended treatment of Galatians 3:10–14, for example, Wright insists that its language "is designed for a particular task within a particular argument, not for an abstract systematised statement."[41] Galatians 3 is not about Christ suffering the curse of the law in the place of his people, all of whom have violated the law and are therefore liable to its curse. Paul is not talking about a general work of Christ that

39. Ibid.
40. *What Saint Paul Really Said*, 126–27. Cf. *Romans*, 440: "Justification, at the last, will be on the basis of performance, not possession."
41. *The Climax of the Covenant*, 138.

benefits sinful Jews and Gentiles alike. The traditional reading of this passage, which takes it to refer to Christ's substitutionary atonement for all sinners, is, in Wright's view, "nonsense."[42] If this passage is read in its first-century Jewish context and within the setting of God's covenant promise to Israel, it will become evident that Paul is talking about the curse of the exile that Israel is experiencing as a people. Wright maintains that "in the cross of Jesus, the Messiah, the curse of exile itself reached its height and was dealt with once and for all, so that the blessing of covenant renewal might flow out the side, as God always intended."[43]

Wright's reading of Galatians 3 is characteristic of his treatment of the subject of Christ's atoning work generally. Though it is evident that he does not agree with the older, Reformation understanding of Christ's saving work, what he is prepared to offer as an alternative remains rather obscure. Christ's death and resurrection are representative of Israel's exile and restoration. They are the means whereby the promise of the covenant is now extended to the whole worldwide family of God. However, since Wright maintains that Paul's doctrine of justification is not primarily addressed to the problem of human sinfulness and guilt, his understanding of the work of Christ likewise puts little emphasis upon the kinds of themes that historically formed an essential part of the doctrine of Christ's atoning work.[44]

Though Wright employs a range of biblical terminology to describe Christ's redemptive work, his emphasis upon the assertion of Christ's lordship suggests that his view has more affinity with what historians of doctrine term the "classic" or "victory over the powers" conception than the penal satisfaction emphasis of the Reformation. The language of Scripture regarding Christ's saving work is rich and diverse. However, since Wright insists that the problem to which justification provides an answer is the identification of those who belong to the covenant, he does not articulate the doctrine of the atonement along the lines of classic Protestant theology.

A Critical Assessment of Wright's New Perspective

Now that we have summarized some of the key features of Wright's position, I wish to offer a preliminary answer to the unavoidable ques-

42. Ibid., 150. Wright's claim that Paul (and Second Temple Judaism) viewed Israel to be in exile at the time of Christ's ministry is pivotal to his interpretation, though it remains controversial.

43. Ibid., 141.

44. For a discussion of the way Wright treats the work of Christ as "representative" in Romans 5:12–21, see my recent article, "N. T. Wright on Romans 5:12–21 and Justification: A Case Study in Exegesis, Theological Method, and the 'New Perspective on Paul,'" *Mid-America Journal of Theology* 16 (2005): 29–82, esp. 67–72.

tion: has Wright offered a more biblical alternative to the Reformation understanding of justification? In my judgment, he has not done so. Despite the contemporary influence of newer perspectives on the teaching of the apostle Paul, I am convinced that the older Reformation perspective more faithfully and comprehensively represents the Scriptures' teaching. There are several substantial problems in the perspective Wright advocates. These problems belie the far-reaching claims that Wright makes for his view and illustrate why the Reformation's reading of the apostle Paul remains a more satisfying and coherent one.

The Irony of Sanders's View of Second Temple Judaism

Many contemporary authors advocate a new approach to our understanding of Paul's gospel, and they do so from the conviction that E. P. Sanders's study of Judaism requires a revolution in Pauline studies. N. T. Wright well expresses this consensus when he asserts that E. P. Sanders "dominates the landscape [of Pauline studies], and, until a major refutation of his central thesis is produced, honesty compels one to do business with him. I do not myself believe such a refutation can or will be offered; serious modifications are required, but I regard the basic point as established."[45]

The irony of Sanders's view of Second Temple Judaism, however, is that it does not so much discredit as lend credence to the older Reformation view of Paul. Even though Sanders has mustered a considerable body of evidence to establish that the pattern of religion in Second Temple Judaism was covenantal nomism, there is a remarkable "begging of the question" that characterizes his claims and those of many advocates of the New Perspective. The begging of the question that I have in mind is, "Isn't what Sanders calls *covenantal nomism* formally similar to what historians of Christian doctrine term *semi-Pelagianism?*"

Sanders and other New Perspective authors are fond of arguing that Second Temple Judaism exhibits no substantial traces of Pelagianism, the idea that God's people find favor with him on the basis of their own moral efforts. Sanders's case for this conclusion is, admittedly, a strong one.[46] Whatever the diversity of teaching and practice within the various branches of Second Temple Judaism, few, if any, practiced a religion that was the equivalent of a kind of "pulling oneself up to God by one's moral

45. *What Saint Paul Really Said*, 20.
46. The essays in the two volumes, *Justification and Variegated Nomism*, ed. D. A. Carson, Peter T. O'Brien, and Mark A. Seifrid, remain among the best sources for becoming acquainted with the contemporary discussion of Sanders's thesis.

bootstraps."[47] However, the obvious weakness of Wright's insistence that this requires a new view of Paul's teaching on justification is that he (and other New Perspective writers) does not seriously consider whether covenantal nomism could accommodate a form of religious teaching that regards acceptance with God to be based upon grace *plus good works*.[48]

When the sixteenth-century Reformers opposed the doctrine of justification in the medieval Roman Catholic Church, they did not oppose (let alone claim to oppose) it because it was Pelagian, as writers of the New Perspective insinuate. The Reformers, including Luther and Calvin, objected to the teaching that sinners are justified by God *partly* on the basis of his grace in Christ and *partly* on the basis of their willing cooperation with this grace, which includes good works that increase the believer's justification and merit further grace. What prompted the Reformation was the conviction that the Roman Catholic Church taught that God's grace in Christ was not a sufficient basis for the believer's acceptance into and continuance within the favor of God. The parallel, therefore, that the Reformers drew between the teachings of the Catholic Church and the Judaizing heresy opposed by the apostle Paul was that they both wanted to make human works subsequent to the initiative of God's grace a partial basis for justification in the present and the future.[49] Sanders's study of Second Temple Judaism seems only to confirm the Reformation's claim that such a parallel obtains.

The "Works of the Law" in Paul

If the first pillar of Wright's case for a New Perspective on Paul's doctrine of justification is shaky, the second is equally so. Even though Wright and other New Perspective authors have properly emphasized the particular occasion for Paul's polemic with the Judaizers, he has not demonstrated that Paul's use of the language of "works" or "works of the law" refers primarily, if not exclusively, to those boundary markers that distinguished Jews from Gentiles. A historically contextualized reading of Paul's epistles

47. This language is Wright's (*What Saint Paul Really Said*, 119).

48. Cf. Moisés Silva, "The Law and Christianity: Dunn's New Synthesis," *Westminster Theological Journal* 53 (1991): 348: "Sanders (along with biblical scholars more generally) has an inadequate understanding of historical Christian theology, and his view of the Reformational concern with legalism does not get to the heart of the question."

49. Cf. D. A. Carson, *Justification and Variegated Nomism*, 544: "Nevertheless, covenantal nomism as a category is not really an alternative to merit theology, and therefore is no response to it. . . . By putting over against merit theology not grace but covenant theology, Sanders has managed to have a structure that preserves grace in the 'getting in' while preserving works (and frequently some form or other of merit theology) in the 'staying in.'" See Seyoon Kim, *Paul and the New Perspective: Second Thoughts on the Origin of Paul's Gospel*, 65.

does not require the conclusion that Wright reaches, namely, that Paul's doctrine of justification was addressed principally to Jewish exclusivism or failure to recognize the inclusion of the Gentiles as heirs to the promise to Abraham. Paul certainly emphasizes that faith in Jesus Christ is the only way to become a recipient of the covenant promise to Abraham. But in the course of his epistles, Paul's teaching regarding the law and the works of the law expresses precisely the themes that were integral to the older perspective of the Reformation. For example, Paul does not restrict the reach of works or the works of the law to those provisions in the Mosaic Law that distinguish Jews from Gentiles. By these terms he means to refer to all that the law requires in the way of obedience (e.g., Gal. 3:10–14; 5:2–4; 6:13; Rom. 2:6; 3:20, 28; 4:2–4; 9:32).[50] The requirements of the law extend beyond those provisions that distinguish the covenant community as a corporate reality; they also include all of the moral demands of the law.

Furthermore, Paul clearly rejects the way of works, not simply because it excludes Gentiles, but also because no one, whether Jew or Gentile, is able to do perfectly what the law requires and thereby obtain acceptance with God (e.g., Gal. 3:10; 5:3; Rom. 3:19–20; 5:20; 7:5–12). The "boast" of his opponents, which Wright and other New Perspective authors view as a racial or ethnic boast, includes the claim that their obedience to the law (in whatever particular) commends them before God and above those who do not have the law (Rom. 3:27–4:8; 9:30–10:8; Phil. 3:2–11).[51] Whatever insights Wright provides regarding the occasion for Paul's teaching about justification, therefore, have not demonstrated that the Reformation's view of Paul's teaching on the law was in error. Critical elements of Paul's teaching about the law are either downplayed or left largely unacknowledged in Wright's view.

50. For a more extended defense of this claim than that provided in our discussion, see Douglas J. Moo, "'Law,' 'Works of the Law,' and Legalism in Paul," 90–99; Charles E. B. Cranfield, "'The Works of the Law' in the Epistle to the Romans," *Journal for the Study of the New Testament* 43 (1991): 89–101; and Moisés Silva, "Faith Versus Works of Law in Galatians," in *Justification and Variegated Nomism*, 2:17–48. For instances of a similar, general use of the language of "works" in Paul's epistles, see 2 Cor. 11:5; Col. 1:21; Gal. 5:19. For instances of this usage in passages that are not universally acknowledged as authentically Pauline, see Eph. 2:9–10; 5:11; 1 Tim. 2:10; 5:10, 25; 6:18; 2 Tim. 1:9; 4:14; Titus 1:16; 2:7, 14; 3:5, 8, 14. Even if we were to grant the view that these latter texts are not Pauline (which we do not), they minimally suggest that an author influenced by Paul took him to exclude all boasting in any works whatever in the matter of salvation (Eph. 2:9).

51. Cf. Simon J. Gathercole, *Where Is Boasting?* (Grand Rapids, MI: Eerdmans, 2002). Based upon his study of the motif of "boasting" in Second Temple Judaism and the argument of Romans 1–5, Gathercole concludes that the boast was not only made in relation to others (Gentiles) but also *in relation to God* before whom the faithful Jew expected to be vindicated/justified for his adherence to the law.

The "Righteousness of God" in Paul

Though Wright claims that the "righteousness of God" in Paul refers to the faithfulness of God in fulfilling his covenant promises, this claim does not do justice to Paul's use of this language. This understanding is far too general and imprecise to capture the specific force of this language in Paul's writings. If we say that the "righteousness of God" is his faithfulness to his covenant promise, we still need to ask, how does that faithfulness come to expression? And what exactly does the terminology of "righteousness" tell us about the way God's faithfulness is demonstrated?

Study of the use of this language in Paul's epistles will show that it calls attention to the *judicial* context for God's action in securing the acquittal and vindication of his covenant people, and bringing judgment and condemnation upon his enemies.[52] Consistent with Old Testament usage, the righteousness of God is revealed when God, as judge and king, acts justly in acquitting the righteous and condemning the wicked. This is apparent in the book of Romans, which is a particularly important source for understanding Paul's use of the expression, "the righteousness of God." Though similar expressions are used in his other epistles, this epistle is the only one to use the expression on several occasions (Rom. 1:17; 3:5, 21–22, 25–26; 10:3—eight times in all). Through the response of faith, believers come to benefit from the saving power of the gospel of Jesus Christ, which reveals the righteousness of God. These passages indicate that righteousness is something that God grants to believers and that it restores believers to favor with him. In Romans 5:17, for example, the "righteousness" that acquits believers of condemnation and death is God's "gift" to them (cf. Phil. 3:9). Similarly, in Romans 10:3–6, Paul draws a close parallel between the "righteousness of God" and the "righteousness based on faith" (Rom. 3:21–26; 10:3). Paul's use of the language of the "righteousness of God," therefore, seems to warrant the Reformation view.

Against the background of the Old Testament idea of God's righteousness, the apostle Paul is affirming that the gospel of Jesus Christ reveals God's judicial action in securing the righteous status of his people before him. What is remarkable about the gospel of God's righteousness in Christ is that God has, in the person and work of his Son, entered into

---

52. For brief summaries of the debate regarding this language that largely uphold the Reformation view, see Mark A. Seifrid, "Righteousness Language in the Hebrew Scriptures and Early Judaism," in *Justification and Variegated Nomism*, 1:415–42; Peter O'Brien, "Was Paul a Covenantal Nomist?" in *Justification and Covenantal Nomism*, 2:274–76; Henri Blocher, "Justification and the Ungodly (*Sola Fide*)," in *Justification in Variegated Nomism*, 2:473–8; and Douglas J. Moo, *The Epistle to the Romans* NICNT (Grand Rapids, MI: Eerdmans, 1996), 63–90.

judgment on behalf of *the ungodly* (Rom. 4:5). All who receive the free gift of right standing with God on the basis of the work of Christ are beneficiaries of God's righteousness. They are freed from condemnation and accepted by God, the judge. God's righteousness reveals his covenant faithfulness to secure his people's salvation, to be sure. But it especially reveals God's powerful intervention in his own court to grant a righteous status to believers on the basis of the work of Christ on their behalf.

The Nature of Justification

Though Wright and other writers of the New Perspective insist that justification identifies those whom God acknowledges as his covenant people, this view of the language of justification is inadequate. No doubt justification finds its meaning within the context of God's relationship with those whom he acknowledges as his covenant people. But this does not yet tell us why this language is especially appropriate to describe what God does when he acknowledges people as members of his covenant family.

Perhaps the most serious problem with a simple identification of the language of "justification" with the idea of "belonging to the covenant people" is that it fails to do justice to the biblical context for Paul's discussion of justification. If we consider only the context for the discussion of justification in Romans 1–5, we discover that justification answers to the problem of human sin and guilt before the judgment seat of God. Though there is an undoubtedly ecclesiological dimension to the language of justification (Who belongs to the covenant family? Are Gentiles as well as Jews included?), the principal issue is quite emphatically of a *soteriological* and *theological* nature. The question raised by Paul's argument in Romans 1–5 goes far deeper than who belongs to the covenant people of God. The question is, how can guilty sinners, who have culpably broken the law of God and are subject to condemnation, be received into favor with a righteous God whose wrath is being poured out upon all the ungodliness and unrighteousness of men? Wright's insistence that justification addresses primarily the question of whether Gentiles are also included within the covenant family of God misses the main point of Paul's doctrine. That point, as the Reformers rightly understood, was about the gracious provision in Christ for the justification of all sinners. Since no one can possibly be included within the covenant family of God on the basis of the works of the law, God has demonstrated his righteousness by providing a Savior whose obedience and propitiatory death are the basis for being received into his favor.

In the setting of the argument of Romans, therefore, justification language refers to God's act of granting believers a status of favor and righteousness on account of the work of Christ. Justification is all about the forgiveness of sins and the granting of a new status of righteousness in Christ to otherwise guilty, condemnable sinners. Paul's teaching about justification is not simply about *who is a member of the covenant*, but it goes to the deeper issue of *who has a right to stand before God, despite his sin and unworthiness*. Justification is about God as the One who justifies the ungodly. And it is about nothing if not the *salvation* of guilty sinners. Only within the framework of these basic theological and soteriological issues does the obvious ecclesiological issue (are Gentiles also included in God's family?) have its place.[53]

Substitution, Imputation, and Faith

One of the more troubling features of the New Perspective is its explanation of the connection between the justification of believers and Christ's saving work, which includes the elements of substitutionary obedience and satisfaction for sin. In the Reformation perspective on Paul, there is a close and intimate connection between Christ's obedience, cross and resurrection, and the benefit of free justification that derives from the union of believers with him. Christ's objective work on behalf of believers, his death for their sins, and his resurrection for their justification (Rom. 4:25), constitutes the basis for the verdict that justification declares. Because Christ, though without sin, bore the sins of his people upon the cross and was declared righteous before God in his resurrection, believers enjoy through union with Christ a new status of acceptance with God.

The weakness of the newer perspective of Wright becomes apparent in the way he views the themes of faith and imputation in relation to union with Christ. In the older Reformation view, justification involves a transaction in which Christ assumes the sin and guilt of his people in order that they might become the righteousness of God in him (2 Cor. 5:17; Rom. 8:1). The verdict of free justification stems from God's granting and imputing the righteousness of Christ to believers. Faith is the instrument by which the free gift of God's righteousness in Christ is received (Rom. 1:17; Rom. 3:22, 28; 5:1; 9:30, 32; Phil. 3:9). In the newer perspective of Wright, this emphasis upon faith as an instrument that receives the imputed righteousness of Christ is rejected. Faith in Christ is not a means

53. One way to test the New Perspective's claims regarding the meaning of the language of *the righteousness of God* and *justification* is to try to paraphrase Paul's uses of this language by substituting terms like *covenant faithfulness* or *covenant membership*. Though the substitution might seem plausible in a few instances, it generally makes little sense. On this point, see Charles Hill, "N. T. Wright on Justification," *IIIM Magazine Online* 3/22 (May 28–June 3, 2001): 1–8.

to receive an imputed righteousness; rather, faith is merely the badge that distinguishes those who belong to God's covenant family in Christ from those who do not.

The problem with this view is not only that it fails to do justice to the instrumental role of faith, but it also fails to account adequately for the substitutionary nature of Christ's atoning work and the way believers benefit from that work through faith. In the perspective of the Reformation, there is a deep and necessary correlation between the themes of substitution and imputation. Since Christ's life, death, and resurrection occurred by God's design for or in the place of his people, all that he accomplished counts as theirs so far as God is concerned (imputation). Christ's work on their behalf and for their benefit is reckoned to the account of believers, since it is just as though they had performed it (substitution).[54] When believers are united to Christ through faith, they come to participate in all the benefits of his saving work. Faith is the "empty hand" by which believers acknowledge and receive all that Christ has accomplished for them. To say that God grants and imputes the righteousness of Christ to believers is, accordingly, to acknowledge what is required by the doctrines of Christ's substitutionary atonement and the believer's union with Christ through faith.

Final Justification on the Basis of Works?

One uncertain feature of Wright's newer perspective is the question of justification and a final judgment based on works. According to Wright, the final judgment is on the basis of works and represents a kind of final chapter in the believer's justification. Unlike the Reformation perspective, which distinguishes between justification by grace alone apart from works and a final judgment according to works but not on the basis of works, this concept of a final justification suggests that the present membership of believers in the covenant family of God is suspended upon a yet future

54. Carson, "Atonement in Romans 3:21–26," 134n.53, makes an apt observation regarding the connection between substitution and imputation: "Part of the contemporary (and frequently sterile) debate over whether or not Paul teaches 'imputation,' it seems to me, turns on a failure to recognize distinct domains of discourse. Strictly speaking, Paul never uses the verb λογίζομαι to say, explicitly, that Christ's righteousness is imputed to the sinner or that the sinner's righteousness is imputed to Christ. So if one remains in the domain of narrow exegesis, one can say that Paul does not explicitly teach 'imputation,' except to say slightly different things (e.g., that Abraham's faith was 'imputed' to him for righteousness). But if one extends the discussion into the domain of constructive theology, and observes that *the Pauline texts themselves* (despite the critics' contentions) teach penal substitution, then 'imputation' is merely another way of saying much the same thing."

justification.[55] Whereas believers enjoy a present justification in union with Christ, they face the prospect of a future justification where the verdict depends upon the quality of their whole life of faith. Though it would not be correct to say that this idea of a future justification is a common or consensus opinion of writers of the New Perspective, it is clearly present in Wright's understanding of Paul. Considering Sanders's view of the way God's people "maintain" their covenant status, this idea of a final justification is a troubling but not altogether unexpected feature of Wright's view.

An unqualified affirmation of a future, yet-to-be-determined justification based upon works would surely compromise in the most radical way Paul's teaching that there is now no condemnation for those who are in Christ Jesus. The Reformation's handling of this question does justice both to Paul's teaching of justification by grace alone and a final judgment according to works. In the Reformation view, free justification and the sanctification of believers in union with Christ are inseparable though distinct benefits of the gospel. The carelessness with which Wright and other writers of the New Perspective speak of a final justification on the basis of works threatens a central point of Paul's gospel, namely, that the acceptance and standing of believers before God rests upon the work of Christ alone.

Conclusion

N. T. Wright, like other authors who argue today for a New Perspective on the teaching of the apostle Paul, is not bashful in claiming that the Reformation misunderstood Paul and misrepresented his doctrine of justification. This is a remarkable claim and one that has obvious and far-reaching implications for the contemporary testimony of the evangelical and Reformed churches. If Luther, Calvin, and the confessions of the churches of the Reformation significantly misread the apostle Paul, then their spiritual heirs need to return to the Scriptures for a fresh and new understanding of the gospel.

---

55. Some authors of the New Perspective appeal to Romans 2:13 in support of the idea of a yet-future justification ("For it is not the hearers of the law who are righteous before God, but the doers of the law who will be justified.") The reformational reading of this text takes it as a kind of "hypothesis contrary to fact." Since no one is, strictly speaking, a *doer of the law*, no one is justified by the law. Or it is taken as a statement of fact, namely, that all whom God justifies he also sanctifies; in this sense, no one is justified without obeying the law by the working of the Spirit of sanctification. However, among writers of the New Perspective, this text is interpreted differently. In their view, Paul is positively affirming that, in the final judgment, only those who do what the law requires will be justified/vindicated. Cf. Wright, *Romans*, 440: "Justification, at the last, will be on the basis of performance, not possession [of the law]."

Though I have not provided anything like a sustained defense of the older perspective on Paul and the doctrine of justification, my summary of Wright's position, together with the critical observations outlined above, suggest that the New Perspective ought to be carefully evaluated before it is too quickly embraced. I have noted several significant problems with the New Perspective, problems which suggest that the older perspective of the Reformation may deserve more respect and adherence than advocates of the New Perspective would grant it. My assessment of the New Perspective suggests that it is neither as new as its proponents claim, nor as capable of providing a more satisfying interpretation of Paul as promised.

In my judgment the older perspective of the Reformation will ultimately prove to represent more faithfully what the apostle Paul boldly terms "my gospel" (Rom. 2:16). In one of the well-known summaries of that gospel, Paul speaks in language that the Reformation perspective reflects well: "For while we were still weak, at the right time Christ died for the ungodly. For one will scarcely die for a righteous person—though perhaps for a good person one would dare even to die—but God shows his love for us in that while we were still sinners, Christ died for us" (Rom. 5:6–8). The Reformation, which understood this passage and many others to teach free acceptance with God for believing sinners on the basis of the work of Christ alone, rightly interpreted Paul's teaching on justification. It also rightly understood that justification, so far as it addresses the basic religious question of our standing before God, is the "main hinge" of the Christian religion (Calvin). This gospel of free justification speaks compellingly in every age, in the twenty-first century as much as in the sixteenth. It is also the kind of gospel that invites believers—Jews and Gentiles alike—to the same table, where their boast is in the same Lord and Christ, beside whom there is no other. For it speaks of the free and gracious acceptance of all sinners who put their trust in Christ and share in his righteousness.

2

Observations on N. T. Wright's Biblical Theology

With Special Consideration of "Faithfulness of God"

T. DAVID GORDON

While I have favorably reviewed some of N. T. Wright's work,[1] my opinion about his more-recent work, especially his popular work, *What Saint Paul Really Said: Was Paul of Tarsus the Real Founder of Christianity?* is less favorable[2] (though I continue to find his writings utterly lucid, and profoundly stimulating). Specifically, the following three concerns about Wright's perspective strike me as particularly problematic for understanding Paul's thought.

1) Wright understands the New Testament primarily as a fulfillment of the promises made to *Abraham*, not as a fulfillment of the redemptive pledge imbedded in the *Adamic* curse.

1. *Climax of the Covenant* for the Westminster Theological Journal (56, no. 1: 197–201).
2. N. T. Wright, *What Saint Paul Really Said: Was Paul of Tarsus the Real Founder of Christianity?* (Grand Rapids, MI: Eerdmans, 1997).

When we ask how it was that Jesus' cruel death was the decisive victory over the powers, sin and death included, Paul at once replies: because it was the fulfillment of God's promise that through Abraham and his seed he would undo the evil in the world.

If (conversely) he rose again from the dead, it meant he had indeed dealt with sin on the cross—in other words, that God had achieved at last what he had promised to Abraham and the prophets.[3]

This explains why some associate the New Perspective with the Auburn theology—neither explicates its biblical theology with reference to the Adamic administration. Wright employs a good deal of Adamic christology (especially in *Climax of the Covenant*), but he does not employ the Adamic covenant administration with the same vigor. Thus, especially in his perceiving the phrase "righteousness of God" in Romans 1:17 as God's *faithfulness* to his covenant rather than to his uprightness or *justice* as a judge, the influence and *tendenz* becomes clear: God is a promise-keeper, not an upright judge.

Much of the present debate in some circles[4] is not merely, or primarily, about the relation of faith and works in justification, though it has ramifications for that discussion. The present debate is about whether we can properly handle the doctrine of justification apart from juridical categories, apart from God's right judgment of his creation in terms of its obedience or disobedience to his rule. This question drives us back to the Adamic administration, with the reality of obedience or disobedience, and God's judgment. All promise theology, if it can be called that, is Abrahamic and post-Adamic. It construes God's work in terms of making and keeping promises. Thus, Wright's overall biblical theology (pertaining to Paul, anyway) emphasizes the "seed of Abraham" at the expense of the "seed of the woman," and this failure to relate the Abrahamic story *back* to the Adamic story renders his view of Paul incomplete at best and erroneous at worst.

2) Wright's *Christus Victor* language of defeat of enemies does not mention God's wrath as a serious threat that has been deflected by the death and resurrection of Christ:

The cross is for Paul the symbol, as it was the means, of the liberating victory of the one true God, the creator of the world, over all the enslaving powers that have usurped his authority. . . . For this reason I suggest that

---

3. Ibid., 48–50; hereafter quoted in text of this chapter.
4. Regarding not only N. T. Wright, but also the so-called New Perspective on Paul, the views of Norman Shepherd, and the views of the so-called Auburn theology.

we give priority—a priority among equals, perhaps, but still a priority—to those Pauline expressions of the crucifixion of Jesus which describe it as the decisive victory over the 'principalities and powers.' Nothing in the many other expressions of the meaning of the cross is lost if we put this in the centre. . . . The death of Jesus had the effect of liberating both Jew and Gentile from the enslaving force of the 'elements of the world' (Gal. 4:1–11). And, towering over almost everything else, the death of Jesus, seen as the culmination of his great act of obedience, is the means whereby the reign of sin and death is replaced with the reign of grace and righteousness (Rom. 5:12–21). 'The gospel' is indeed the announcement of a royal victory. (47)

At the heart of Paul's gospel there stands the claim that the death of Jesus the king has defeated evil at is very heart. (52)

The word 'grace' is a shorthand way of speaking about God himself, the God who loves totally and unconditionally, whose love overflows in self-giving in creation, in redemption, in rooting out evil and sin and death from his world, in bringing to life that which was dead. (61)

Here again, the absence of the Adamic administration creates the same problem mentioned before. The enemies and powers defeated by Christ do not (for Wright) include God's own wrath or judgment. Though Wright had stimulating thoughts on propitiation in *Climax of the Covenant* (and I don't believe he denies the concept), he does not appear to have wrestled with the fact that death, our last enemy, is itself, for Paul, the result of "one man's disobedience" and its penal (itself necessarily judicial) consequences. Thus, when he explains Paul's narrative theology, and the cross and resurrection as the center of that narrative, he is entirely right, but when he explains precisely what Christ therein triumphed *over*, the wrath of God is not among the panoply.

3) Wright misunderstands "righteousness of God" in Romans by removing it from its forensic/juridical context there.

> That is why, in the great sweeping argument of the letter to the Romans, Paul's exposition of God's faithfulness to his covenant (in technical language, his 'righteousness'), is explained in terms of the fulfillment of the promises to Abraham (3:21–4:25), and then explored in terms of the undoing of Adam's sin (5:12–21) and ultimately of the liberation of the whole creation (8:17–25). (48)

One must surely object here to the designation of "righteousness" as *technical* language for "God's faithfulness to his covenant." The δικ-group in Paul's day was far from technical. Indeed, if it *was* technical, Wright's point would surely be wrong, for this lexical stock plainly has forensic overtones elsewhere. The only possibility Wright has to construct it as "faithfulness" is, therefore, to argue that it is not technical (i.e., that it does not always mean *righteousness* or *justice*), that it is a fluid lexical stock with a broad range (i.e., not technical) in Paul's thought. The most Wright (or others) could assert is that in addition to denoting *righteousness* or *justice*, the δικ-group in Paul sometimes has another usage, which is to denote something like *faithfulness*. Even then, of course, Wright would necessarily accept the burden of demonstrating that, in any given context, *faithfulness* is the preferred denotation because of various contextual considerations. But in examining Paul's usage in Romans, one comes to just the opposite conclusion because the contextual evidence is so consistently juridical. Let us examine that evidence.

Why "Righteousness of God" Must Be Understood Judicially/ Forensically in Romans 1–3

It has been fairly common, since Ernst Käsemann, to understand the phrase "righteousness of God" in Romans 1:17 (and elsewhere) as referring to God's covenant faithfulness.[5] N. T. Wright renews and perpetuates this interpretive tradition. What follows are counterarguments to this thesis, arguments that question understanding δικαιοσύνη θεοῦ in Romans 1:17 as denoting God's faithfulness. Before listing those counterarguments, I wish to explain briefly why there appears to be an element of truth in the observation that in the Sinai covenant there is a particular kind of relationship between righteousness and covenant faithfulness.

The Element of Truth in the Observation

There are a number of Septuagint texts in which the δικ-group denotes an appeal to God to rescue his covenant people, to vindicate them, on the basis of his righteousness. "Righteous are you, O LORD, when I complain to you; yet I would plead my case before you. Why does the way of the wicked prosper?" (Jer. 12:1). Yet even here, there is a covenantal *context* that makes the matter clearer. The very terms of the Sinai covenant were those of fairly severe justice: six tribes stood on Mt. Gerizim for the blessing and six on Mt. Ebal for the curses, and the terms of the covenant were conditioned upon the obedience of the people of Israel:

5. Cf. the respective articles by Elizabeth and Paul J. Achtemeier on righteousness in the Old and New Covenants in *IDB*.

> If you obey the commandments of the LORD your God that I command you today, by loving the LORD your God, by walking in his ways, and by keeping his commandments and his statutes and his rules, then you shall live and multiply, and the LORD your God will bless you in the land that you are entering to take possession of it. (Deut. 30:16)

Therefore, it is not at all surprising that members of that covenant-administration may rightly appeal to their own national righteousness (especially as personified in the king) or God's righteousness (as rewarder of obedience) as the basis of appealing for God's help.

> The LORD judges the peoples; judge me, O LORD, according to my righteousness [κρῖνόν με κύριε κατὰ τὴν δικαιοσύνην μου] and according to the integrity that is in me. (Ps. 7:8)

> The LORD rewarded me according to my righteousness [καὶ ἀνταποδώσει μοι κύριος κατὰ τὴν δικαιοσύνην μου] according to the cleanness of my hands he recompensed me. (Ps. 18:20)

> Therefore the LORD has recompensed me according to my righteousness [καὶ ἀνταποδώσει μοι κύριος κατὰ τὴν δικαιοσύνην μου] according to the cleanness of my hands in his sight. (Ps. 18:24)

This is because, in terms of the Sinai covenant-administration, Yahweh has committed himself to blessing the Israelites if they are obedient.

> The LORD rewards every man for his righteousness and his faithfulness [καὶ κύριος ἐπιστρέψει ἑκάστῳ τὰς δικαιοσύνας αὐτοῦ καὶ τὴν πίστιν αὐτοῦ] for the LORD gave you into my hand today, and I would not put forth my hand against the LORD's anointed. (1 Sam. 26:23)

> The LORD rewarded me according to my righteousness [καὶ ἀνταπέδωκέν μοι κύριος κατὰ τὴν δικαιοσύνην μου] according to the cleanness of my hands he recompensed me. (2 Sam. 22:21)

Therefore, there is certainly an element of truth within that Sinai covenant-administration in saying that God's *righteousness* is associated with his faithfulness to his part of the covenant administration. The question, however, is more precise and lexical: Is this relationship between righteousness and covenant-faithfulness in the Sinai administration due to the reality that δικαιοσύνη *means faithfulness*, or is it due to the fact that the covenant-administration itself obliged Yahweh, by his own pledge, to reward the righteous? It is certainly true that for the Israelites, their own national "righteousness" reflected their faithfulness to the terms of that covenant-administration, and it is also true that Yahweh proved himself to be *righteous* when he upheld his pledge to bless them for their obedience. But this is not because the lexical stock *itself* denotes this; it is because the particular covenant-administration pledges rewards for righteous behavior.

Further, even if I am entirely wrong about this, and if there are indeed places where the δικ-group denotes a concept such as covenant faithfulness, in and of itself this would not prove that it always denotes such a concept or that it denotes it exclusively. Surely the many passages that use the language in expressly judicial contexts prove that the semantic range is broader than *faithfulness*. Thus, some further argument would be necessary in any given context, such as that of Romans 1–3, to prove that it denoted *faithfulness* there.

Having said this, however, note that there still remain a significant number of counter-arguments to the thesis that "righteousness of God" in Romans 1:17 (and similar texts) denotes God's covenant faithfulness. Much of this discussion hinges upon making careful distinctions between words and concepts; no one disputes that God is faithful, or that he discloses his faithfulness in each of the respective covenant-administrations he has instituted. Conceptually, there is no dispute about this. The question is: does the expression "righteousness of God" in Romans 1:17 denote this concept rather than some other?

I will reiterate what has commonly been stated about the δικ-group: that its predominant usage is to denote God's *justice*—his unwavering commitment to judge his creation uprightly—without compromise, favoritism, or inequity. Luke observed Paul's usage in this manner when he recorded Paul's encounter at Mars Hill: "Therefore he has established a day in which he is about to judge [μέλλει κρίνειν] the inhabited world in righteousness [ἐν δικαιοσύνη]" (Acts 17:31). This reflects the Septuagint usage where the same sentiment is so frequently recorded in the same language (Ps. 9:9; 96:13; 98:9). It also reflects its common usage in secular Greek. When Socrates, for instance, rejects Meletus's arguments that the laws improve the Athenian youth and insists that Meletus tell us what *people* improve the youth, Meletus answers, "the judges," which is a translation of οἱ δικασταί [6] In secular Greek of the period, this is also why a δικανικό is a lawyer, a δική can be a trial, and δικάζω can mean to decide, to judge, or give judgment (cf. Liddell and Scott, ad loc).

There are four specific reasons why the δικ-group in Romans should be understood forensically, as references to God's judicial righteousness:

---

6. Plato, "Apology XII" in *Apology of Socrates and Cato*, ed. Louis Dyer (Los Angeles: Demetrius and Victor, 1973), 63.

1) The *concept* of God's faithfulness to his covenants (and to his covenant people) is indeed affirmed within Romans 1–3; but Paul uses other Greek words to denote it.

> Then what advantage has the Jew? Or what is the value of circumcision? Much in every way. To begin with, the Jews were entrusted with the oracles of God. What if some were unfaithful [εἰ ἠπίστησάν τινε]? Does their faithlessness [ἡ ἀπιστία αὐτῶν] nullify the faithfulness of God [τὴν πίστιν τοῦ θεοῦ]? (Rom. 3:1)

Note that Paul manifestly indicates an awareness of faithfulness and unfaithfulness to the Sinai covenant-administration, whether the unfaithfulness of Israel or the faithfulness of God. But he does not use the δικ-language to denote this concept—he employs πιστ-language. In my estimation, this evidence alone is sufficient to challenge the notion that in the verses prior to this, Paul has used *different* language (δικ-language) to denote this concept—not because people cannot employ terms flexibly or synonymously, but because it would have obfuscated the logical and rhetorical power of his argument to have done so in this context. His reasoning is fairly tight in these chapters, and there would be no reason for him to risk his readers' losing the train of his thought by shifting his vocabulary at this point.

Far more likely, as we shall see below, is the possibility that Paul uses the δικ-group here to refer to righteousness in its moral/ethical (and consequently juridical) sense: as a reference to God's inflexible commitment to the integrity of his own holy and upright character, which then becomes the basis and criterion of the judgment he exercises over the creature made in his image.

2) The pervasive and enduring concern in Romans 1:18–3:26 is the forensic/juridical reality of the judgment of God. The language of the judgment and wrath of God pervades the entirety of this section of Romans. Here, at least, the issue is *not* whether God will be faithful to his covenant; here the issue is whether he will judge the earth in righteousness. What is revealed is the fulfillment of the psalmist's hope: "for he comes to judge the earth. He will judge the world with righteousness, and the peoples with equity [δικαιοσύνη]" (Ps. 98:9). Note some of the references to God's judgment in this passage:

> For the wrath of God is revealed from heaven against all ungodliness and unrighteousness of men, who by their unrighteousness suppress the truth. (1:18)

Therefore God gave them up [παρέδωκεν] in the lusts of their hearts to impurity. (1:24)

For this reason God gave them up [παρέδωκεν] to dishonorable passions. (1:26)

And since they did not see fit to acknowledge God, God gave them up [παρέδωκεν] to a debased mind to do what ought not to be done. (1:28)

Therefore you have no excuse, O man, every one of you who judges. For in passing judgment on another you condemn yourself, because you, the judge, practice the very same things. We know that the judgment of God rightly falls on those who do such things. (2:1–2)

Do you suppose, O man—you who judge those who do such things and yet do them yourself—that you will escape the judgment of God? (2:3)

But because of your hard and impenitent heart you are storing up wrath for yourself on the day of wrath when God's righteous judgment will be revealed. (2:5)

He will render to each one according to his works: to those who by patience in well-doing seek for glory and honor and immortality, he will give eternal life; but for those who are self-seeking and do not obey the truth, but obey unrighteousness, there will be wrath and fury. (2:6–8)

For all who have sinned without the law will also perish without the law, and all who have sinned under the law will be judged by the law. (2:12)

On that day when, according to my gospel, God judges the secrets of men by Christ Jesus. (2:16)

What then? Are we Jews any better off? No, not at all. For we have already charged that all, both Jews and Greeks, are under sin. (3:9)

Contextually, even if we concede that the δικ-group is fairly flexible, denoting somewhat different things in different semantic contexts, the context of Romans 1:16–3:26 is profoundly juridical. Its language and imagery are that of the great tribunal of God, in which he will render to each according to his deeds (2:6). In such a context, the δικ-group presumptively has its ordinary juridical meaning: God will judge the earth in righteousness (ἐν δικαιοσύνῃ).

3) Romans 1:18 serves as the initial explication (continuing through chap. 11) of the thesis stated in Romans 1:16–17.

The revelation of the "righteousness of God" in Romans 1:17 is explained by the revelation of the "wrath of God" in verses 18 and following. The γὰρ that connects verse 18 back to verse 17 can be dismissed only at great peril, especially since the conjunction conjoins the identical verb (ἀποκαλύπτεται) repeated in each verse. God's righteousness is revealed when his judicial *wrath* is revealed, even in the inexplicably mysterious transaction whereby the righteous Son of God bears that wrath as a substitute to propitiate it. One might say, if verse 17 mentions that God has revealed his righteousness, verse 18 and following disclose *how* he has revealed it. He has displayed his *righteousness* by displaying his *wrath*—inflexibly, justly, impartially—upon all who do evil, whether Jew or Greek. The gospel reveals God's righteousness because only by the substitution of Christ can God be both "just and justifier." Any justifying apart from substitution and propitiation questions whether God is truly just. But when the sin-bearer bears that wrath, God's justice is established beyond question.

In this particular context, God's righteousness is revealed because God will judge with perfect impartiality all men, Jews or Greeks, according to what each has done. His righteousness here is the righteousness of a judge, who with unmitigated impartiality (2:11) renders a verdict of guilt upon those who do evil. And the wrath of God, as the evidence and consequence of his inflexible justice, is only mitigated for anyone, Jew or Gentile, through the propitiation of that wrath by Jesus Christ the righteous (3:25). God is righteous (of unimpeachable moral integrity) because he judges the earth with equity, rewarding equally the upright Jew or Gentile (2:7), and expressing wrath equally upon unjust Jew or Gentile (2:8). This inflexible righteousness is revealed historically when even the Son of God quakes and falls beneath that wrath as sin-bearer. Not only will the Jew not escape the wrath of God; even God's Son, if he covenants to redeem the elect, will not escape this wrath. This wrath, poured out upon the propitiatory sin-bearer, reveals the pervasive, comprehensive justice and righteousness of God.

4) Elsewhere in Romans 1:16–4:6, the δικ-group is incontestably forensic. Again, the issue is the semantic use of "righteousness of God" in Romans 1:17, and the resolution is determined, in some measure, by the use of the lexical stock in the context at hand. Therefore, if the use of this lexical stock is prevailingly (if not exclusively) juridical in the context, we must take the expression in 1:17 the same way:

The wrath of God is revealed from heaven against all ungodliness and unrighteousness [ἀδικίαν] of men. (1:18)

They were filled with all manner of unrighteousness [ἀδικία]. (1:29)

Though they know God's decree [τὸ δικαίωμα τοῦ θεοῦ; AV judgment of God] that those who practice such things deserve to die, they not only do them but give approval to those who practice them. (1:32)

You treasure up for yourself wrath in the day of wrath and of revelation of the just judgment [δικαιοκρισίας] of God. (2:5)

. . . And who are persuaded of unrighteousness [πειθομένοις δὲ τῇ ἀδικίᾳ]. (2:8)

[For] the doers of the law will be justified [δικαιωθήσονται]. (2:13 NKJV)

But if our unrighteousness [ἡ ἀδικία ἡμῶν] serves to show the righteousness of God [θεοῦ δικαιοσύνην], what shall we say? That God is unrighteous [ἄδικος] to inflict wrath on us? (3:5)

Their condemnation is just [ἔνδικόν]. (3:8)

. . . as it is written: "None is righteous, no, not one [Οὐκ ἔστιν δίκαιος οὐδὲ εἷ]." (3:10)

Now we know that whatever the law says it speaks to those who are under the law, so that every mouth may be stopped, and the whole world may be held accountable [ὑπόδικος] to God. (3:19)

For by works of the law no human being will be justified [οὐ δικαιωθήσεται] in his sight. (3:20)

But now the righteousness of God [δικαιοσύνη θεοῦ] has been manifested apart from law, although the Law and the Prophets bear witness to it—the righteousness of God [δικαιοσύνη δὲ θεοῦ] through faith in Jesus Christ for all who believe. For there is no distinction: for all have sinned and fall short of the glory of God, and are justified [δικαιούμενοι] by his grace. (3:21–24)

Note the special difficulty posed by this text. The language of God's δικαιοσύνη being manifested surely recalls a similar statement in 1:17. And yet is it at all likely that the noun twice-repeated here has a fundamentally different denotation from the verbal form in the context (δικαιούμενοι)? Is it not far more likely that God's *justice* is manifested when he *justifies* by grace? This holds true also for the following verses:

Whom God put forward as a propitiation by his blood, to be received by faith. This was to show God's righteousness [τῆς δικαιοσύνης αὐτοῦ], because in his divine forbearance he had passed over former sins. It was to show his righteousness at the present time, so that he might be just and the justifier [εἰς τὸ εἶναι αὐτὸν δίκαιον καὶ δικαιοῦντα] of the one who has faith in Jesus. (3:25–26)

Here again, the notion that δικαιοσύνη means "God's faithfulness" requires us either to translate nonsensically ("that he himself is faithful and that he renders faithful") or to translate the same lexical stock differently within the same sentence:

For we hold that one is justified [δικαιοῦσθαι] by faith apart from works of the law. Or is God the God of Jews only? Is he not the God of Gentiles also? Yes, of Gentiles also, since God is one. He will justify [δικαιώσει] the circumcised by faith and the uncircumcised through faith. (3:28–30)

For if Abraham was justified by works [ἐξ ἔργων ἐδικαιώθη], he has something to boast about. (4:2)

For what does the Scripture say? "Abraham believed God, and it was counted to him as righteousness [καὶ ἐλογίσθη αὐτῷ εἰς δικαιοσύνην]." (4:3)

To the one who does not work but trusts him who justifies the ungodly, his faith is counted as righteousness [ἐπὶ τὸν δικαιοῦντα τὸν ἀσεβῆ λογίζεται ἡ πίστις αὐτοῦ εἰς δικαιοσύνην]. (4:5)

David also speaks of the blessing of the one to whom God counts righteousness [λογίζεται δικαιοσύνην] apart from works. (4:6)

Note here again Wright's fundamental lexicographical failure: He takes the one otherwise potentially ambiguous expression (θεοῦ δικαιοσύνη) and renders it in a manner that is *un*like its unambiguous usage in the very same context. One of the most basic of lexicographical conventions is this: that one may employ a potentially ambiguous term unambiguously if in the context unambiguous uses are also employed. At best, we might concede that in the context of the Sinai covenant-administration, which obliges God by his own commitment to reward the righteous, *righteousness* could plausibly refer to God's faithfulness to maintain his duty to reward the righteous. However, another usage is equally plausible and also consistent with the lexical stock in its context.

To illustrate this basic principle, let us use another example with a different word. Our English word *reformed* is used with some variety. We can use it to designate a person as Augustinian or Calvinist, a former

juvenile delinquent as no longer behaving in a delinquent fashion, a Jew
as being within the liberal Jewish tradition, or a former alcoholic as "on
the wagon." Now suppose someone reads Wright's popular book on
Paul and then utters this sentence: "N. T. Wright is reformed." Is there
any likelihood that this would mean that Wright is no longer painting
graffiti on public buildings, or that he is now a liberal Jew or a recovering alcoholic? Of course not! Contextually, a Christian theologian's
theological writing is being assessed, and not one in a thousand people
would interpret the term in any way other than to designate Wright as
an Augustinian or Calvinist.

Similarly, Paul's use of the δικ-group in the first four chapters of Romans
is incontestably juridical/forensic as he employs the term in his discussion
of God's righteous judgment. In light of the pervasiveness of the forensic/
juridical concern and Paul's repeated employing of the δικ-group in a
juridical manner here, any suggestion that it means *faithfulness* in this
context is simply a repudiation of the importance of immediate context for
making lexical determinations. If Wright is permitted to violate so cardinal
a principle here, then I suppose we are free to use *reformed* to describe
Wright as a no-longer-drunken, no-longer-delinquent liberal Jew.[7]

Additional Observation on Wright's Construal of Justification

Wright appears to exclude the middle in his discussion of Paul's understanding of justification. He argues that in the first century, justification
is *not* about an individual's relationship to God but about membership in
the covenant community. This may be true in and of itself (at least on the
negative side), but I'm not aware of any significant Protestant theologian
who has ever argued that justification was or is about a "relationship
with God" in any ordinary sense. Justification is about how an individual
stands before the judgment seat of God; it is about whether the person will
be declared righteous or unrighteous before the bar of God's judgment.
Adoption may genuinely be, in some senses, about sustaining a filial relation to God, but justification is not about a relationship; justification is
about a judicial standing—guilty or innocent. Note Wright's language:

> "Justification" in the first century was not about how someone might estab-
> lish a relationship with God. It was about God's eschatological definition,
> both future and present, of who was, in fact, a member of his people . . .

7. Just as I was completing these thoughts, John Yenchko called my attention to the very
helpful article, "N. T. Wright on Justification," by Prof. Charles Hill of Reformed Theological
Seminary in Orlando, which can be found at the website www.thirdmill.org. Dr. Hill's thoughts
are very similar to my own, and I refer the reader to them.

> Despite a long tradition to the contrary, the problem Paul addresses in Galatians is not the question of how precisely someone becomes a Christian, or attains a relationship with God.[8]

But where in the history of Protestant thought has anyone argued what Wright here denies? Did Calvin, Turretin, Witsius, Hodge, or Warfield define *justification* as how one attains a relationship with God? Where is the "long tradition" that defines *justification* as "how . . . someone becomes a Christian or attains a relationship with God"? I myself have argued that Protestantism has largely misunderstood the problem at Galatia, so I don't object to Wright's suggestion that the historic Protestant view of the letter is wrong, but it is wrong in a far different way than Wright suggests.

By excluding the middle, by refuting a view that (to my knowledge) no one has ever held, Wright then jumps to another view of justification, its only merit being that it is not the refuted (though never actually propogated) view. The real issue we wish Wright to address is whether *justification* is a term that ordinarily denotes a judicial (not a relational) reality, a forensic standing, or whether it is about defining the people of God. He will have grave difficulty arguing his point, if he ever attempts to do so. Israel was, by God's election, God's people. But through most of her history, she was *not* justified; to the contrary, she was judged to be in violation of God's law and covenant again and again by the prophets, beginning with Moses. Thus, Israel can be and was (at least during the Sinai administration) the *un*justified people of God. This strikes me as virtually irrefutable, yet if Wright's definition is correct (to be justified is to be God's people), this plain, generations-long reality in Israel's life is an impossibility.

---

8. Wright, *What Saint Paul Really Said*, 119–20.

3

A Justification of Imputed Righteousness

RICHARD D. PHILLIPS

For our sake he made him to be sin who knew no sin, so that in him we might become the righteousness of God. −2 CORINTHIANS 5:21

In military strategy there is a situation to avoid as much as possible, namely, a two-front war. For centuries, it was the policy of Germany never to fight a two-front war; forgetting this commitment resulted in two lost wars during the last century. The United States fought on two fronts during World War II and showed that it can be done successfully if one is strong enough. Indeed, it remains the policy of the United States today always to be prepared for two simultaneous wars. Our ability to do so demonstrates the rare strength of our nation.

Reformed theology, as classically understood and traditionally established in our creeds and confessions, finds itself fighting a two-front war today. On the one hand is a resurgent theological assault from our traditional foe, Arminianism. Meanwhile, Reformed theology finds itself locked in battle with a more recent but equally heated foe: higher critical scholarship. In this chapter, I will discuss the fight raging at one key place on the battlefield—the doctrine of Christ's imputed righteousness.

Here, Arminian scholars have launched a renewed attack. Meanwhile, new critical-scholarly paradigms have not only challenged imputation but have enlisted a "fifth column" within the Reformed community that is calling for a reconsideration of, and perhaps the renunciation of, this important doctrine. The purpose of this chapter is to reflect on the attack coming from both fronts and to demonstrate the strength of this doctrine to emerge safe and strong.

The doctrine of imputation concerns our understanding of how Christ saves sinners who believe in him. The Reformed faith teaches that a double imputation occurs via Christ's death on the cross. First, we believe that our sins are imputed—that is, transferred by reckoning—to the crucified Lord Jesus. Our sins are recorded under our names before God and we have to answer for them. But God takes our debt and reckons it to Christ's account. This is imputation. Martyn Lloyd-Jones states, "He died to bear my punishment. That is what killed Him. So my guilt has been imputed to Him and it has been taken away from me and therefore I am freely forgiven."[1]

Evangelicals all affirm the imputation of our sins to Jesus Christ, since we believe that he died for us while he was himself perfectly sinless. If he did not participate in our sins and if our sins were not infused into him, then he could only have received them by imputation. What some deny is that a double imputation takes place in our justification. The Westminster Confession of Faith states that God justifies believers "not by infusing righteousness into them . . . not for anything wrought in them, or done by them . . . nor by imputing faith itself, the act of believing, or any other evangelical obedience to them, as their righteousness; but by imputing the obedience and satisfaction of Christ unto them, they receiving and resting on him and his righteousness, by faith" (XI.1). Lloyd-Jones explains: "Out of my ledger goes my sin, put to His account; then His goodness, His righteousness, His purity are put into my account under my name! . . . God sees me in Him clothed with His righteousness."[2] This is what many deny, both evangelicals who deny any need for a positive righteousness (considering simple forgiveness to exhaust the meaning of justification or finding some other ground for our righteousness) and liberal scholars, who configure salvation in wholly different terms. For the Reformed, however, the necessity of an imputed righteousness from Christ is demanded by the requirements of God's law. In the words of W.G.T. Shedd:

> The law requires present and perfect obedience as well as satisfaction for past disobedience. The law is not completely fulfilled by the endurance

1. D. Martyn Lloyd-Jones, *The Kingdom of God* (Wheaton, IL: Crossway, 1992), 80.
2. Ibid.

of penalty only. It must also be obeyed. Christ both endured the penalty due to man for disobedience, and perfectly obeyed the law for him; so that He was a vicarious substitute in reference to both the precept and the penalty of the law. By his active obedience He obeyed the law, and by his passive obedience He endured the penalty. In this way his vicarious work is complete.[3]

The Arminian Challenge to Imputed Righteousness

Signs of a reduced commitment to the imputation of Christ's righteousness have been surfacing for some time. The first that I noticed was the publication by the Evangelicals and Catholics Together (ECT) project titled "The Gift of Salvation" (1997). This statement of accord by prominent evangelicals and Roman Catholics on the doctrine of justification concluded by denouncing "needlessly divisive disputes." These included not only Marian devotion and purgatory, but also "the language of justification as it relates to imputed and transformative righteousness."[4] I was actively involved in the efforts of the Alliance of Confessing Evangelicals to oppose this statement and remember that of all the doctrines compromised by ECT, we were most dismayed by the giving away of Christ's imputed righteousness as necessary to justification. Most striking, however, was the coolness we discovered among many Reformed academics to the doctrine of Christ's imputed righteousness. I was surprised to find my own commitment to this doctrine dismissed by seminary professors, and I started to hear disdain for the doctrine among educated laypersons.

In the aftermath of ECT, many perceived the need for a clear statement on justification to which a strong consensus of evangelicals could be gained. The result was "The Gospel of Jesus Christ: An Evangelical Celebration" (1999). This statement affirmed that "Christ's saving work included both his life and his death on our behalf," and that "faith in the perfect obedience of Christ by which he fulfilled all the demands of the Law of God in our behalf is essential to the Gospel." The statement also denied "that our salvation was achieved merely or exclusively by the death of Christ without reference to his life of perfect righteousness."[5]

3. William G. T. Shedd, *A History of Christian Doctrine*, 2 vols. (Edinburgh: T & T Clark, 1888 [1865]), 2:341.

4. "The Gift of Salvation," *Christianity Today,* vol. 41, no. 14, Dec. 8, 1997, 34. The list of "needlessly divisive debates" included baptismal regeneration, purgatory, indulgences, Marian devotion, the assistance of saints, "and the possibility of salvation for those who have not been evangelized."

5. "The Gospel of Jesus Christ: An Evangelical Celebration?" *Christianity Today*, vol. 43, no. 7, June 14, 1999, 49, Affirmation/Denial No. 9.

Furthermore, it insisted that "the doctrine of the imputation (reckoning or counting) both of our sins to Christ and of his righteousness to us, whereby our sins are fully forgiven and we are fully accepted, is essential to the biblical Gospel," and it denied that we are justified by any righteousness inherent or infused into us.[6] Pastors and theologians loyal to the classic doctrine of imputation were heartened by this statement, especially since it affirmed Christ's active obedience as well as his passive obedience imputed to us.

However, if we concluded that an actual consensus existed among evangelicals on this doctrine, the bubble was burst with the publication of Robert Gundry's "Why I Didn't Endorse 'The Gospel of Jesus Christ: An Evangelical Celebration?' . . . even though I wasn't asked to" in the influential journal *Books and Culture*. His answer is apparent upfront: his own lost confidence in Christ's imputed righteousness—a loss of confidence he believed is widespread among evangelical academics. Gundry objected that "'Celebration' demand[s] . . . the contribution of Jesus' life as well as death to Christian believers' reconciliation to God and justification by him." He also objected to "repeated and explicitly emphasized statements defining justification in terms of the imputation of Christ's righteousness." Gundry was not denying that Christ had lived a life of perfect righteousness but the insistence that this righteousness is imputed to us through faith for our justification. Gundry argued that the proof texts cited to support imputed righteousness did not demand the contribution of Christ's life in addition to his death. (We will consider some of these texts in the course of this study). Gundry appealed to Genesis 15:6, cited in the New Testament at Romans 4:3 and Galatians 3:6: "[Abraham] believed in the LORD; and he counted it to him for righteousness." He concluded that God accepts faith in the place of works as a basis for righteousness: "Since faith as distinct from works is credited as righteousness, the righteousness of faith is a righteousness that by God's reckoning consists of faith even though faith is not itself a work."[7]

After receiving plenty of critique in response to that article,[8] Gundry further developed his argument against Christ's imputed righteousness. The most full and recent presentation occurs in his chapter, "The Non-imputation of Christ's Righteousness," in the book, *Justification: What's at Stake in the Current Debates?* edited by Mark Husbands and Daniel

6. Ibid., Affirmation/Denial No. 12.

7. "Why I Didn't Endorse 'The Gospel of Jesus Christ: An Evangelical Celebration?' . . . even though I wasn't asked to," *Books & Culture*, vol. 7, no. 1, January–February 2001, 6.

8. See Thomas Oden, "A Calm Answer . . . to a critique of 'The Gospel of Jesus Christ: An Evangelical Celebration,'" *Books & Culture*, vol. 7, no. 2, March–April 2001, and John Piper, *Counted Righteous in Christ* (Wheaton, IL: Crossway, 2002).

J. Treier.[9] Gundry denies that his argument is motivated by a commitment to Arminian theology, but in fact it is the Arminian position that he articulates.[10]

Gundry sets forth a number of arguments against imputed righteousness. He launches an extensive treatment of the Greek word for *logizomai*, which means "to reckon." He accurately points out that in the Reformed view, faith serves as the instrument by which Christ's righteousness is imputed to us. However, he argues from his survey that *logizomai* involves an identification of two things, not one serving as the instrument by which the other is received. His burden is to show that faith should be considered equivalent to righteousness, not the instrument by which righteousness is imputed to us. As before, he directs our attention to the important statement that "[Abraham] believed in the LORD; and he counted it to him for righteousness" (Gen. 15:6). This means, he says, that "what God counts as righteousness consists in faith."[11]

Gundry also argues that Paul correlates faith with "the righteousness of *God*" (emphasis added), not the righteousness of *Christ*. He says, "[God's] righteousness, which is never said to *be* counted or imputed (passive voice), consists in his counting (active voice) of our faith as righteousness while at the same time maintaining his moral character. . . . Christ enters the picture as the object of faith, whose obediently righteous act of propitiation made it right for God to count faith as righteousness" (emphasis in original).[12] Further, Gundry points out that Paul never spells out the imputation of Christ's righteousness in so many words, which would be surprising for such a purportedly vital doctrine: "If Paul had meant that the righteousness of Christ replaces our sins, we would expect him to have said so. . . . But he did not."[13]

For these reasons, Gundry not only objects to the doctrine of Christ's imputed righteousness being made an evangelical essential, but he also objects to the doctrine as accurately reflecting the Bible's teaching.

In response to Gundry's rejection of imputation, D. A. Carson published another chapter in the same book, titled, "The Vindication of Imputation." Carson makes a wealth of valuable points to which I will refer at various times in this chapter. First, he points out that while our theology

9. Mark Husbands and Daniel J. Treier, eds., *Justification: What's at Stake in the Current Debates* (Downers Grove, IL: InterVarsity, 2004).

10. For a cogent and detailed discussion of the Arminian understanding of the relationship between faith and justification, see Charles Hodge, *Systematic Theology*, 3 vols. (Grand Rapids, MI: Eerdmans, 1993), 3:167–70.

11. Robert H. Gundry, "The Nonimputation of Christ's Righteousness," in *Justification: What's at Stake in the Current Debates*, 25.

12. Ibid., 36, 39.

13. Ibid., 42.

must always arise from the teaching of Scripture, the language of theology and the language of Scripture will not always be the same. For instance, while systematic theology rightly distinguishes between justification and sanctification, the biblical writers do not always employ the corresponding Greek terms—*dikaiosune* and *hagios*—in ways that consistently match up with the theological categories. When Paul said the Corinthians were "sanctified" in his first letter to that church, he meant that they were set apart by God in a way that corresponds to the doctrine of justification; what Paul goes on to say in that letter shows that, theologically speaking, they were not very sanctified at all. Carson therefore asks, "Even if we agree that there is no Pauline passage that *explicitly* says, in so many words, that the righteousness of Christ is imputed to his people, is there biblical evidence to substantiate the view that the substance of this thought is conveyed?"[14] Carson argues that there is, as will I in the course of this study.

What about Gundry's survey of *logizomai*, which purportedly proves that when the Bible reckons one thing as another, it has identification and not imputation in view? This is an example, in my view, of both the strength and the weakness of so-called biblical theology today: Gundry rigorously examines the usage of a particular phrase, but the conclusions he draws are not at all to the point when it comes to the theological doctrine at hand. The reason for this is that the passages from which Reformed theology deduces the doctrine of imputed righteousness do not rely upon a particular use of *logizomai*. In most of the key passages I will cite, *logizomai* is not used at all; this shows that Paul does not rely on a particular verb in teaching this doctrine but rather on the ideas that he conveys.

A passage that supports imputation, and in which *logizomai* figures strongly, is Romans 4:4–5. This is a particularly valuable text in assessing Gundry's denial of imputed righteousness, because (a) it is held by the Reformed as a strong support for imputation, and (b) it involves Paul's own exposition of Gundry's key proof-text, Genesis 15:6: "[Abraham] believed the LORD, and he counted it to him as righteousness." Carson therefore treats this passage with care. First, he points out that, contrary to Gundry's claims, ancient Jewish exegetes were united in teaching that this verse presents faith as a meritorious work. This is established by Paul himself in Romans 9:30–10:4. In light of this, Paul's reason for citing Genesis 15:6 is to make the point that the Jews were wrong to think that Abraham merited righteousness by means of believing. Paul reasons,

14. D. A. Carson, "The Vindication of Imputation: On Fields of Discourse and Semantic Fields," in *Justification: What's at Stake in the Current Debates*, 50.

"Now to the one who works, his wages are not counted [*logizetai*], as a gift but as his due. And to the one who does not work but trusts him who justifies the ungodly, his faith is counted [*logizetai*] as righteousness" (Rom. 4:4–5).

Paul is contrasting two approaches to righteousness. The one is secured by works and the other by faith. The one is based on merit ("his due") and the other on grace ("as a gift"). So far, Gundry might agree since he asserts that Abraham's righteousness "consists of faith even though faith is not itself a work."[15] But Carson answers, "Merely to assert, however, that faith of such equivalent value is not itself a work would not have impressed readers familiar with the Jewish background, where the precise counter-claim was standard fare."[16]

Most significant is Paul's contrast between something that is earned, so that it is credited to the person "as his due," versus something that is received by faith, which is credited "as a gift." In other words, Paul says that Abraham received righteousness not because of something he did but because of God's gracious gift. Carson explains: "Romans 4:4 establishes that there is a crediting, an imputing, that is nothing more than getting your desert; there is also a crediting, an imputing, that means something is credited to your account that you do *not* deserve." This means that "when faith is imputed to Abraham as righteousness, it is *unmerited*, it is all of grace, because it is nothing more than believing God and his gracious promise."[17] Paul's whole argument here is that while Abraham's believing is correlated to his being credited with righteousness, this is not because he did something that earned it.

Whatever nuance is placed upon it, what Paul denies is the unavoidable implication of the Arminian view of Genesis 15:6. There are two choices. The Reformed view looks upon faith as the instrument by which Christ's righteousness was imputed to Abraham as a gift of God's grace. The Arminian view looks upon faith as that which Abraham did in the place of works so as to be credited with righteousness. In the Reformed view, the instrumental faith is passive in receiving an imputed righteousness as a gift. In Gundry's Arminian view, faith is active in being identified as equivalent to righteousness, which Abraham thus received as his due. But Paul explicitly states that Abraham's righteousness was by imputation and not "as his due." This shows that imputed righteousness follows Paul's line of reasoning in Romans 4:4–5, whereas Gundry's Arminian view refutes the apostle's logic.

15. Gundry, "Why I Didn't Endorse," 8.
16. Carson, "The Vindication of Imputation," 57.
17. Ibid, 60.

Furthermore, note that in Romans 4:5 Paul adds the statement that faith "trusts him who justifies the ungodly." This can only be a reference to God justifying Abraham. If Abraham was ungodly when he was credited with righteousness, it cannot be because he did something that God considered righteous. If Abraham was faithful at the time he was justified, then this could not be an instance of God "justifying the ungodly." Carson argues, "In Paul's understanding, then, God's imputation of Abraham's faith to Abraham as righteousness *cannot* be grounded in the assumption that that faith is itself intrinsically righteous."[18] If Abraham was "ungodly" at the time of his justification, his must have been what Reformed theology has termed an *alien righteousness*—a righteousness that is not based on Abraham's actual condition or faith, but on the righteousness of another imputed to him. "Thus God credits us with a righteousness we do not have."[19]

This is made even more obvious as we continue to the next series of verses. In Romans 4:6–8, Paul applies the same principle to what David said in Psalm 32:1–2. Paul comments, "Just as David also speaks of the blessing of the one to whom God counts [*logizetai*] righteousness apart from works." Carson highlights the parallel Paul has established between Romans 4:5 and 4:6:

| 4:5 | God | justifies | the ungodly |
| 4:6 | God | credits righteousness | apart from works |

Here, "justifies" (*dikaiounta*) is equated with "crediting righteousness" (*logizetai dikaiosune*), and "ungodliness" is defined as "apart from works." We have already seen that the righteousness that God credits must be an "alien righteousness" because it is granted to persons who are "ungodly." In citing Psalm 32:1–2, Paul further makes clear that these are people who have "lawless deeds" and "sins" (Rom. 4:7–8). Altogether, the apostle teaches that "ungodly" people characterized by "lawless deeds" and "sins" are "justified" in that God "credits righteousness" to them "apart from works." Carson thus concludes, "We perceive that justification of the ungodly *means* the imputation of righteousness."[20]

As if that were not enough, Carson adds the frequency with which Paul speaks of faith as the instrument of justification, contrary to Gundry's claim. Quite tellingly, Carson finds his proof in the passage immediately preceding Romans 4:4–5. In Romans 3:28, Paul writes, "One is justified by faith [*pistei*] apart from the works of the law." Here, faith is the

18. Ibid.
19. Ibid., 61.
20. Ibid., 63.

agent by which justification takes place. In Romans 3:30, Paul adds, "He will justify the circumcised by faith [ek pisteos] and the uncircumcised through faith [dia tas pisteos]." Carson explains that these expressions "presuppose faith as the means of appropriating the gift, not that which is reckoned as the gift."[21] We should remember that it is immediately after assigning this instrumental quality to faith that Paul exposits Gundry's proof-text, Genesis 15:6. This persuasively argues that Abraham's faith was not received by God as a form of righteousness, but his faith was the instrument by which he received an alien righteousness, namely, the righteousness of Christ imputed to him through faith.

This study shows that in Romans 4:3–5, where Paul exposits Genesis 15:6—Gundry's key text for the Arminian view—the apostle not only does not refute the doctrine of imputation but instead demands it. In this way, faith safeguards the principle of salvation by grace, as Paul explains in Romans 4:16: "That is why it depends on faith, in order that the promise may rest on grace." It is faith in the God "who gives life to the dead and calls into existence the things that do not exist" (Rom. 4:17). All this shows that faith justifies not because of the character of faith but because of the character of the God in whom we believe. Relating this to imputed righteousness, Carson concludes: "Paul detects a pattern of God doing the unthinkable, the transforming, the reversing," just as God did in the resurrection of Jesus from the dead.[22] Thus we observe that in the key text by which Gundry seeks to deny the doctrine of imputation, imputation is instead justified as the only position consistent with the apostle's teaching.

The New Perspective Challenge to Imputation

Gundry's denial of imputation may gain traction in the broader evangelical community due to the widespread influence of Arminianism, but it is not likely to make strong inroads among the Reformed. However, there is another denial of imputed righteousness that is making a significant impact in Reformed circles, though it arises from the world of liberal critical scholarship. I refer to the New Perspective on Paul and most particularly to the widely admired writings of the Anglican bishop and scholar, N. T. Wright.

Wright's work is voluminous and his treatment of Paul involves numerous complex strands. However, by his own reckoning, Wright's approach to the book of Romans centers on one key consideration: his

21. Ibid., 65.
22. Ibid., 67.

understanding of Paul's phrase "the righteousness of God." The student of historical theology will immediately realize the connection between this phrase and the doctrine of imputed righteousness. After all, this was the expression that haunted the tortured mind of Martin Luther until he had his evangelical conversion. Luther read Paul's statement that in the gospel "the righteousness of God is revealed" (Rom. 1:17), and he trembled with fear. For Luther, "the righteousness of God" meant God's terrible, avenging justice against all sin. Night and day, Luther pondered the fact that Paul joins "the righteousness of God" with faith in Romans 1:17. He stared at Paul's conclusion: "The righteous shall live by faith." What could this possibly mean? Luther describes the solution that led to his conversion: "Then I grasped that the justice of God is that righteousness by which through grace and sheer mercy God justifies us through faith. Thereupon I felt myself to be reborn and to have gone through open doors into paradise. . . . This passage of Paul became to me a gate to heaven."[23] In the expression "the righteousness of God" as revealed in the gospel, Luther had been set free from anguish by his discovery of the righteousness that God gives to those who believe, namely, the imputed righteousness of Christ.

Like Luther, N. T. Wright develops his understanding of Paul's gospel from the same expression. This is where the similarities end, however, for Wright explicitly denies Luther's understanding of the "righteousness of God." Instead, following the earlier theologian Ernst Käsemann, Wright understands the expression to refer to "the creator god's own righteousness, not 'a righteousness which comes from/avails with god.'" Wright sets forth the expression he consistently uses to express Paul's point: "This divine righteousness always was, and remained throughout the relevant Jewish literature, the *covenant faithfulness* of God."[24] God is just in his actions, Wright of course admits, but God's righteousness consists primarily of faithfulness to his covenant promises and obligations.

This understanding provides an assessment of Paul's argument in the book of Romans that is strikingly at odds with the classic Reformed view. According to Wright, Romans is not about how sinners are personally justified with the holy God. Rather, he says, the pressing need that prompted Paul to write Romans had to do with the tension between Jews and Gentiles in the Roman church. The letter's primary purpose was ecumenical, not soteriological. Paul's strategy was to show that in

---

23. Roland Bainton, *Here I Stand: A Life of Martin Luther* (New York: Penguin, 1955), 49–50.

24. N. T. Wright, "Romans and the Theology of Paul" (Originally published in *Pauline Theology, Volume III*, ed. David M. Hay and E. Elizabeth Johnson [Minneapolis: Fortress Press, 1995], 30–67), http://www/ntwrightpage.com/Wright_Romans_Theology_Paul.pdf.

the death and resurrection of Christ, God had shown his faithfulness to the covenant so that, despite the failure of Israel, evil would be reversed for both Jews and Gentiles.[25]

Under this view, Romans 1:18–2:24 involves an exposé of Gentile paganism, combined with the lamentable failure of Israel to serve as the faithful covenant people through whom God would overthrow evil. In a significant passage, Wright explains where this leads:

> Israel was *entrusted* with the oracles of the creator god (3:2); that is, it was to be the messenger through whom the creator's saving purpose would be carried to the whole world. What is the covenant god to do about the failure of his covenant people (3:2) to be faithful, on their part, to this covenant? Somehow, this god must be faithful nonetheless. . . . This means, logically, that there must somehow, after all, be an Israel that is faithful to the covenant, so that through this Israel the creator/covenant god can deal with the evil of the world, and with its consequences (i.e., wrath, as in 1:18 ff). What is provided in 3:21–31 is just such a solution. . . . The covenant faithfulness of the creator of the world is revealed *through the faithfulness of Jesus*, the Messiah, for the benefit of all, Jew and Gentile alike, who believe[26] [emphasis in original].

Here, we have the second of Wright's key definitions. Whereas the *English Standard Version* of Romans 3:22 speaks of "the righteousness of God through faith in Jesus Christ," Wright sees "the covenant-faithfulness of god through the faithfulness of Jesus Christ." Wright explains, "The central emphasis of this passage, I suggest, lies not on the human faith/faithfulness, which, in the place of works-of-Torah, becomes the badge of covenant membership, but on the faithfulness of the Messiah, Jesus, as the means through which the covenant faithfulness of the creator is enacted."[27]

This directly impacts the doctrine of imputation, since "the righteousness of God" is no longer considered a righteousness that humans receive from God through faith. Since Paul's concern is the equal status of Jews and Gentiles in Christ, justification is about one's membership in God's covenant. Paul's concern is not that we should be individually declared righteous but that we should be incorporated into God's covenant people, that is, those who are "in the right" with God. The issue is not one's moral standing but one's covenantal relationship with God and the community of his faithful people. In Wright's words, justification "wasn't so much

25. Wright, "Romans and the Theology of Paul," 4.
26. Ibid., 7
27. Ibid.

about soteriology as about ecclesiology; not so much about salvation as about the church."[28]

Against this backdrop, Wright takes direct aim at the doctrine of imputed righteousness. Again, let me quote him directly:

> God does indeed "reckon righteousness" to those who believe. But this is not, for Paul, the righteousness either of God or of Christ. . . . This is not God's own righteousness, or Christ's own righteousness, that is reckoned to God's redeemed people, but rather the fresh status of "covenant member," and/or "justified sinner," which is accredited to those who are in Christ, who have heard the gospel and responded with "the obedience of faith."[29]

We should acknowledge that Wright does see a righteous status being applied to those who have faith in Christ. For this reason, it is often argued that Wright does not deny imputed righteousness. Clearly, however, Wright pointedly refutes and denies that Christ's righteousness is imputed to believers. For him, faith is not the instrument by which righteousness is imputed. Instead, faith is a badge of covenant membership. Faith is not *how* sinners receive righteousness; rather, faith is *what* identifies a person as belonging to that covenant community that is "in the right" with God. In Wright's words, "Faith is the badge of covenant membership, not something someone 'performs' as a kind of initiation test."[30]

When Wright turns to the context of the courtroom, as demanded by the biblical language for "righteousness," he again dismisses imputation: "In the Hebrew lawcourt the judge does not give, bestow, impute or impart *his own 'righteousness'* to the defendant." His point is that a judge's righteousness is simply his fairness and impartiality in deciding a case, a category without relevance to the other parties in court. He adds, "'Righteousness' is not a quality or substance that can thus be passed or transferred from the judge to the defendant. The righteousness of the judge is the judge's own character, status, and activity, demonstrated in doing these various things." In contrast, for defendants to be declared righteous is simply "the status they possess when the court has found in their favor. Nothing more, nothing less." By analogy, divine righteousness and human righteousness fall into two completely different categories, even though both are described by the same word.[31]

28. N. T. Wright, *What Saint Paul Really Said* (Grand Rapids, MI: Eerdmans, 1997), 119.

29. N. T. Wright, *New Perspectives on Paul*, 10th Edinburgh Dogmatics Conference, Rutherford House, Edinburgh.

30. Wright, *What Saint Paul Really Said*, 125.

31. Wright, "Romans and the Theology of Paul," 7.

Before assessing Wright's position, we should examine how this approach plays out when applied to one of the texts that is classically regarded as a proof of imputed righteousness—2 Corinthians 5:21: "For our sake [God] made him to be sin who knew no sin, so that in him we might become the righteousness of God."

In a paper focused on this verse, Wright characteristically begins with the statement "the righteousness of God." Again, he assumes the phrase to be "a clear Pauline technical term meaning 'the covenant-faithfulness of [Israel's] God.'"[32] It is significant that Wright calls it "a technical term" because this means that he does not consider it necessary to consult the local context in order to ascertain the meaning of "the righteousness of God." It is therefore not surprising that his exegesis of this important verse will yield a result that is friendly to his pre-conceived formulation.

Wright offers three objections to the classical view of this verse that sees Paul as speaking of "what Luther called a 'wondrous exchange' . . . in which Christ takes our sin and we his 'righteousness'"[33]—that is, the imputation of Christ's righteousness. The first reason is that "Paul never actually says this anywhere else." Second, "Here it is God's righteousness, not Christ's that 'we' apparently 'become.'" Third, the statement as such would make no sense in the flow of Paul's argument in this portion of 2 Corinthians. According to Wright, the "we" of verse 21 is Paul and his apostolic associates, not Paul and his readers. By sharing in the sufferings of Christ as his ambassadors, they have become embodiments of "the covenant faithfulness of God." Wright says, "The 'righteousness of God' in this verse is not a human status in virtue of which the one who has 'become' it stands 'righteous' before God, as in Lutheran soteriology. It is the covenant faithfulness of the one true God, now active through the paradoxical Christ-shaped ministry of Paul, reaching out with the offer of reconciliation to all who hear his bold preaching."[34]

It is obvious that the place to begin a critique of Wright's approach to Paul's theology is with his understanding of "the righteousness of God" as "God's covenant-faithfulness." First, it is not obvious why this should be considered a "technical term." The only explanation Wright provides is that this is common in extrabiblical writings of the time. But every word has a semantic range whereby its meaning is shaped by the local context, so the burden is on anyone who claims a "technical" status for a particular expression. Additionally, the argument that Paul's use of a

---

32. N. T. Wright, "On Becoming the Righteousness of God: 2 Corinthians 5:21" (Originally published in *Pauline Theology, Volume II*, ed. D. M. Hay [Fortress Press, Minneapolis, 1993], 200–208), http://www.ntwrightpage.com/Wright_Becoming_Righteous.pdf.

33. Ibid.

34. Ibid., 5.

genitive preposition to link righteousness and God shows a possessive relationship—so that it must be the righteousness that God possesses—is not valid, because the genitive preposition does not fix a particular relationship. A genitive establishes a mere relationship: it may be that of possession; it may be either objective or subjective; and it may have to do with location or some other point of reference. Wright's monolithic approach to the vital phrase "the righteousness of God" eradicates the influence of context on semantic range and assumes a fixed understanding of the genitive as possessive, in both cases without needed warrant. Moreover, returning to the book of Romans, we find that this approach is not justified by the various verses in which the expression is found.

Consider Romans 1:17 again: "For in it [the gospel] the righteousness of God is revealed from faith for faith, as it is written, 'The righteous shall live by faith.'" Unless we approach this verse with a preconceived notion of "the righteousness of God," we might notice that it is joined to an Old Testament citation (Hab. 2:4), in which the believers are described as "the righteous." It is at least possible, then, that "the righteousness of God" is that righteousness bestowed by God on those who believe. Another example is Romans 3:22, where Paul writes of "the righteousness of God through faith in Jesus Christ for all who believe." Unless one's metanarrative approach has already ruled out the option, the local context would suggest that this righteousness is bestowed on believers.

A significant example is Romans 10:3, which says of the Jews, "For, being ignorant of the righteousness that comes from God, and seeking to establish their own, they did not submit to God's righteousness." Here, "the righteousness that comes from God," which clearly has reference to a righteous standing the Jews were seeking, is equated with "the righteousness of God." These examples, among others, suggest that Wright's assumption that "righteousness of God" serves as a technical term for "God's covenant faithfulness" ought to be questioned.

One way to gauge the semantic range of a given term is to consult a lexicon, which will show all the ways a word is used. Regarding the word "righteousness," we may ransack all the lexicons in the world and find no reference having to do with a covenant relationship, the very meaning upon which Wright hangs his whole understanding of Paul's theology. In the standard scholarly Greek lexicon by Bauer, Arndt, and Gingrich (BAG), the listing for the various *dikaioo* words (*righteousness*) takes up four pages.[35] But in those pages is found not a single reference related to "covenant faithfulness."

35. Walter Bauer, William F. Arndt, and F. Wilbur Gingrich, *A Greek-English Lexicon of the New Testament and Other Early Christian Literature* (Chicago: University of Chicago, 1979), 195–98.

This is confirmed by Mark A. Seifrid in two studies related to the biblical (specifically Old Testament) usage of *righteousness*. He found that "The language of 'righteousness' appears with remarkable frequency in association with the vocabulary of 'ruling and judging.'" Moreover, *righteousness* consistently pertains to the maintenance and restoration of a norm or standard of performance, so that righteousness "cannot be reduced to the idea of a proper relation, as often has been done in recent interpretation."[36] An example of righteousness being wrongly viewed as a relational category would be Wright's reading of it as "covenant faithfulness." Instead, Seifrid concludes, "The biblical usage of 'righteousness' is essentially forensic in orientation."[37] This is the very thing we find in the book of Romans, if we do not begin with Wright's preconceived idea. The problem with which Paul begins is not God's need to demonstrate his covenant faithfulness, but that "the wrath of God is revealed from heaven against all ungodliness and unrighteousness of men" (Rom. 1:18).

In another study, Seifrid explored further, showing that in the Old Testament the Hebrew words for "covenant" [*berith*] and "righteousness" [*zedeq*], even though they occur with great frequency, are almost never found in close proximity. To be sure, covenant-keeping is one kind of righteousness, so that faithfulness and righteousness are occasionally connected. But it is mistaken to fundamentally equate the two ideas.[38] An example of "covenant-faithfulness" and "righteousness" appearing in proximity is illuminating. Psalm 98:2–3 says,

> The LORD has made known his salvation;
>> he has revealed his righteousness in the sight of the nations.
> He has remembered his steadfast love and faithfulness
>> to the house of Israel.
> All the ends of the earth have seen the salvation of God.

Here, "The LORD has made known his salvation" is parallel to "he has revealed his righteousness," much as Paul puts it in Romans 1:17. The psalmist then speaks of God's covenant love and faithfulness. But there is a difference. God's righteousness is "revealed"—that is, God the Judge upholds what is right and true. But he "remembers" his covenant faithfulness, which corresponds not to a righteous norm but to his loving attitude toward the people who have received his promises.

---

36. Mark A. Seifrid, *Christ Our Righteousness: Paul's Theology of Justificaton* (Downers Grove, IL: InterVarsity, 2000), 40–41.

37. Ibid., 43.

38. Mark A. Seifrid, "Righteousness Language in the Hebrew Scriptures and Early Judaism," in *Justification and Variegated Nomism*, Vol. 1, *The Complexities of Second Temple Judaism*, ed. D.A. Carson, Peter T. O'Brien, and Mark A. Seifrid (Grand Rapids, MI: Baker, 2001), 424.

"Righteousness" and "faithfulness" are not the same thing, and they do not function in the same way. Carson concludes from Seifrid's study, "Righteousness language is commonly found in parallel with terms for rightness or rectitude over against evil." This is consistently found in the Old Testament and "the attempt to link 'being righteous' with 'being in the covenant' or with Israel's 'covenant status' does not fare much better in Qumran and rabbinic literature."[39]

In light of this critique, we find that Guy Waters's sharp summation is not unjustified. N. T. Wright's definition of *the righteousness of God* as *God's covenant faithfulness* "is the imposition of a foreign biblical-theological model upon the text of Paul. A sounder and more textually faithful method of proceeding is to examine each instance of 'righteousness' where it occurs and to allow the context to define this term for us."[40] By clearing away N. T. Wright's imposed grid, we may proceed to examine the biblical evidence that has caused classical Reformed theology to affirm vigorously the imputed righteousness of Christ.

Before concluding, there are two more observations that should be made regarding Wright's teaching. The first has directly to do with his denial of imputation. Wright rules out the idea of imputation in a courtroom setting because "'righteousness' is not a quality or substance that can thus be passed or transferred from the judge to the defendant." But this objection relies on a category mistake. The doctrine of imputation does not look upon righteousness as a "quality" or "substance" that is passed. Douglas Wilson explains, "It is like saying that he hates 'all vegetables—whether peppers, carrots, beans, peas, or beef jerky.' The way Wright states this, it would appear that he is correcting the notion that imputation is some sort of substantive transfer like an impartation or infusion, when every definition of imputation I have ever heard in my life denies any such equation."[41] Wilson is right, because, contrary to Wright's position, righteousness is a status that is imputed. Wright's argument, if valid, would speak equally against the doctrine of adoption; he might say, "We cannot be adopted into God's family, because sonship is not a substance or quality that can be passed to another." But adoption does not involve the passing of anything; it involves a new way of looking upon someone. So it is with the imputation of righteousness.

39. Carson, 51.

40. Guy Prentiss Waters, *Justification and the New Perspectives on Paul* (Phillipsburg, NJ: P&R, 2004), 180. Wright's view that "faith in Christ" should instead refer to "the faithfulness of Christ" has fared little better under scrutiny. See a thorough refutation by Moisés Silva, "Faith Versus Works of Law in Galatians," in *Justification and Variegated Nomism*, vol. 2, *The Paradoxes of Paul*, ed. D. A. Carson, Peter T. O'Brien, and Mark A. Seifrid (Grand Rapids, MI: Baker, 2004), 217–48.

41. Douglas Wilson, posted on *Blog and Mablog* internet site, www.dougwils.com.

A further observation deals with the implication of Wright's New Perspective. Carson and Waters, among others, warn that the whole complex of Wright's redefinitions—the redefinition of "righteousness" from legal judgment to covenant faithfulness, the redefinition of justification from a soteriological to an ecclesiological doctrine, and the rejection of imputed righteousness for a covenant membership status—moves our attention one step further from the atoning death of God's Son upon the cross. However unintended this may be and however fervent Wright and others may be in their devotion to and teaching of the crucified and risen Lord, their ecumenical and covenant-centered perspective contrasts with Paul's in that to him, "the act or declaration of justification [is] grounded squarely and solely on Jesus' sacrificial and redemptive death."[42]

If my great need is to be numbered among the righteous community of God, then the covenant suffices. But if my great need is to be cleansed of sin, forgiven of guilt, and accounted righteous by God's perfect standards, then nothing but the blood of Christ himself will do. As Robert Gundry writes, "If righteousness were covenantal apart from God's moral character, no need would arise for Christ to be made sin for us, to become a curse for us, to shed his blood as a propitiation of God's wrath against our unrighteousness—a wrath that derives from the righteousness of God as a moral attribute."[43]

Christ's Imputed Righteousness: Biblical Affirmations

In his critique of 2 Corinthians 5:21, N. T. Wright argued against imputed righteousness not only on the basis of his focus on "covenant faithfulness," but also on the basis that Paul nowhere else teaches imputed righteousness and that wherever righteousness is in view for our salvation it is God's righteousness and not Christ's. Let us conclude our study by examining some texts from which Reformed theology has classically derived imputed righteousness and consider its relationship to Christ.

Among the texts I find most persuasive in teaching imputed righteousness is Genesis 3:21. Adam and Eve had fallen into sin and under God's subsequent curse. God had said that disobedience to his command would receive the penalty of death (Gen. 2:17). Adam and Eve would die, being barred from the tree of life and thus kept from living forever (Gen. 3:22). But at the same time God announced his gracious purpose to achieve their salvation, and to each of the players in the drama of the fall, God spoke of a Savior who would achieve that salvation. In Genesis

42. Waters, *Justification*, 175.
43. Gundry "Why I Didn't Endorse," 35.

3:15 he warned the serpent of a seed from the woman who would crush his head. But in Genesis 3:21, God proclaimed Christ to Adam and Eve in a different and wholly wonderful way: "The LORD God made for Adam and for his wife garments of skins and clothed them." We remember that sin had contaminated the first couple's nakedness with shame, so God covered their sin and guilt with the skins of an innocent substitute. Here was a spotless creature who had not participated in our first parents' sin but who nonetheless paid sin's penalty of death.

Adam and Eve, not participating in the sacrifice's righteousness, nonetheless are clothed by it so as to stand justified before God. George Whitefield elaborates:

> What were the coats that God made to put on our first parents, but types of the application of the merits of righteousness of Jesus Christ to believers' hearts? We are told, that those coats were made of skins of beasts; and, as beasts were not then food for men, we may fairly infer, that those beasts were slain in sacrifice, in commemoration of the great sacrifice, Jesus Christ, thereafter to be offered. And the skins of the beasts thus slain, being put on Adam and Eve, they were hereby taught how their nakedness was to be covered with the righteousness of the Lamb of God.[44]

What a testimony this bears—not merely to the truth of this doctrine, but to its central place in the salvation that God offers to us—that God responded with a typological enacting of Christ's imputed righteousness as his first redemptive act of grace toward fallen mankind.

Another bold depiction of this doctrine in the Old Testament is found in the vision of Zechariah 3. Joshua the high priest, representing all of Israel in their return from punishment in the exile, stood before the Lord in filthy clothes. At his side was Satan accusing him of his guilt. The Lord rebuked the devil, reminding Satan of the Lord's saving grace in Joshua's life. Then we read, "Now Joshua was standing before the angel clothed with filthy garments. And the angel said to those who were standing before him, 'Remove the filthy garments from him.' And to him he said, 'Behold, I have taken your iniquity away from you, and I will clothe you with pure vestments'" (Zech. 3:3–4). What a glorious depiction that is of what the Lord Jesus offers to us by his cross: he takes our sins onto himself and places his own righteousness onto us.

A third passage comes from Jesus' parable of the wedding feast. The king sent his servants out to bring the people in for the feast of his son's wedding. But after they were gathered "he saw there a man who had no wedding garment. . . . The king said to his attendants, 'Bind him hand

---

44. George Whitefield, *Select Sermons of George Whitefield* (Edinburgh: Banner of Truth, 1958), 117.

and foot and cast him into the outer darkness. In that place there will be weeping and gnashing of teeth'" (Matt. 22:11–13). This refutes those who teach that we need only be forgiven to enter into heaven; we have no need of any positive garment of righteousness. But John Owen was right to say:

> It is not enough to say that we are not guilty. We must also be perfectly righteous. The law must be fulfilled by perfect obedience if we would enter into eternal life. And this is found only in Jesus (Rom. 5:10). His death reconciled us to God. Now we are saved by his life. The perfect actual obedience that Christ rendered on earth is that righteousness by which we are saved. His righteousness is imputed to me so that I am counted as having perfectly obeyed the law myself. This must be my righteousness if I would be found in Christ, not having my own righteousness which is of the law, but the righteousness which is of God by faith (Phil. 3:9).[45]

Many of the texts that so clearly teach imputed righteousness came from the pen of the apostle Paul. We have already considered Romans 4:5–6, in which the expression "God justifies the ungodly" is paralleled with the matching statement, "God counts righteousness apart from works."

We also saw N. T. Wright's refutation of imputed righteousness in 2 Corinthians 5:21. But, returning to that important verse, we find ample reason to reconsider. In verse 19, Paul states that "in Christ God was reconciling the world to himself, not counting their trespasses against them, and entrusting to us the message of reconciliation." In other words, God acted to save sinners by the death of his Son and through the apostolic preaching of the gospel. In verse 20, Paul continues, "Therefore, we are ambassadors for Christ, God making his appeal through us. We implore you on behalf of Christ, be reconciled to God." Then, in verse 21, Paul offers the substance of his gospel message of what God has done to make our reconciliation possible: "For our sake [God] made him to be sin who knew no sin, so that in him we might become the righteousness of God."

Verse 21 presents a parallel structure. Paul says that God "made him to be sin who knew no sin." Obviously it was our sin that the otherwise sinless Christ bore. When Paul says that Christ was "made sin" he cannot mean that Jesus *became* personally a sinner. Instead, Jesus received our sins *by imputation*. Our sins were not *infused* into Christ, nor did he receive them by *participation*. In Paul's construction, however, Christ was "made sin"; we in the same manner "might become the righteousness of God"—namely, by imputation. The guilt of our sin was imputed to Christ so that he could bear it on the cross. Likewise, his righteousness

45. John Owen: *Communion with God* (Edinburgh: Banner of Truth, 1991), 94–95.

was imputed, or credited, to us, so that we might enter into the blessing of eternal life.

Wright argues, however, that this speaks of "the righteousness of God," not the righteousness of Christ. But notice that all this is "in Christ." Paul had said, "in Christ God was reconciling the world to himself" (2 Cor. 5:19). Just as only God the Son could suffer humiliation and death upon the cross—not God the Father—so also only the Son was born into this world under the law to fulfill it for us. Yes, it was God's righteousness—"in Christ."

Another vital passage is Romans 5:12–21, which we will consider only briefly. Here, Paul compares and contrasts Adam and Christ as our covenant heads. Through Adam's fall "sin came into the world through one man, and death through sin." Indeed, so fully are we identified with our first father and covenant representative that when he sinned, we sinned in him: "death spread to all men because all sinned" (Rom. 5:12). Adam was "a type of the one who was to come" (Rom. 5:14), since both were federal representatives for their people. But Christ is different from Adam because of his perfect obedience and the salvation it brings. Paul writes, "Therefore, as one trespass led to condemnation for all men, so one act of righteousness leads to justification and life for all men. For as by the one man's disobedience the many were made sinners, so by the one man's obedience the many will be made righteous" (Rom. 5:18–19).

A couple of observations are important. First, notice the structure of justification as Paul presents it here. In verse 18 he establishes the progression: "righteousness leads to justification and life." This is the way of salvation found all through the Bible. If we want to enjoy salvation life, with all the fullness that speaks of, then we must be justified. But in order to be justified, we must possess righteousness. Verse 19 completes the progression by adding, "by the one man's obedience the many will be made righteous." Now we insert *obedience* at the beginning of the progression. Working backwards, life requires justification, which relies upon perfect righteousness, and that in turn is based on obedience to God's commands. The forward progression is: obedience, then righteousness, justification, and life.

Second, observe that our problem in Adam is that we have not obeyed—either federally via Adam or personally in our own lives. Therefore, we do not possess righteousness, so that we will be not justified but condemned. Instead of life, we partake of death. The good news is the saving work of Christ: "By the one man's obedience the many will be made righteous." Does this mean we need a moral change or a spiritual transformation, so that we will become righteous? No, for our corrupt Adamic natures are incapable of that kind of reform and our prior sins cry out for condemnation. But Paul writes not that we should be *transformed* into righteous persons but "appointed" or "established" righteous [Greek, *katastath-esontai*] (Rom. 5:19). It is a legal term and a synonym for "imputed."

This, then, is Paul's way for us to enter into eternal life: Where we have disobeyed, Christ has obeyed perfectly; where we are unrighteous, his righteousness is imputed to us; so clothed, we are justified before God, and being justified we enter into life. Now we have the clean garments of which the angel spoke to the high priest Joshua in Zechariah 3, and of which the exalted Lord Jesus spoke in the last chapter of the Bible: "Blessed are those who wash their robes, so that they may have the right to the tree of life and that they may enter the city by the gates" (Rev. 22:14).

Another text we may rightly claim for imputed righteousness is 1 Corinthians 1:30: "He is the source of your life in Christ Jesus, whom God made our wisdom and our righteousness and sanctification and redemption." N. T. Wright dismisses this text as a support for imputation since, he argues, if righteousness is imputed then all the rest would have to be imputed: wisdom, sanctification, and redemption. But there is no reason for such a claim; Paul is spelling out in shorthand the categories in which Christ is our all in all. We receive each appropriately for their category: sanctification by Christ's life in us and redemption by his death on the cross. But just note what Paul says here: God has made Christ to be our righteousness. As we know from the other passages, the ungodly are justified by faith in Christ alone, and his perfect righteousness becomes ours through imputation.

Last, let us consider Paul's great statement in Philippians 3:9. Paul begins the chapter by recalling all the fleshly forms of righteousness he once trusted but now counts as rubbish: circumcision, ethnicity, tribal membership, Jewishness, and legalistic self-righteousness. But he now counts all those things as loss "because of the surpassing worth of knowing Christ Jesus my Lord" (Phil. 3:8). Even if it means suffering, what Paul now wants is to "gain Christ and be found in him, not having a righteousness of my own that comes from the law, but that which comes through faith in Christ, the righteousness from God that depends on faith" (Phil. 3:9). There can be no question that Paul is talking about a righteousness that involves a moral standing for himself. Here, too, it is explicitly said to be a righteousness "from God" (*ek theou*) by the instrumentality of faith (*epi te pistei*).

Thy Blood and Righteousness

I noted earlier the difficulty of fighting a two-front war. You can succeed on one hand, but failure on the other destroys you. This is the sinner's plight before God. We have two requirements necessary for entering into the blessings of eternal life, neither of which we have the ability to fulfill. On the one hand is our need to deal with the problem of our sins. What can we do to remove the black stain of our well-earned guilt before God? On the other hand, the holy God requires a perfect righteousness we have not attained and do not possess. How can ungodly people like us gain the righteousness without which we must be cast into outer darkness? The answer is that given in the title of the great hymn of Count Zinzendorf: "Jesus, Thy Blood and Righteousness." These are resources equal to my need. What can wash away my sin? The blood of Jesus can do it, can make me "pure as snow" (Isa. 1:18). But what robe shall I wear in God's presence? John Murray answers, "The righteousness of Christ is the righteousness of his perfect obedience, a righteousness undefiled and undefilable, a righteousness which not only warrants the justification of the ungodly but one that necessarily elicits and constrains such justification. God cannot but accept into his favour those who are invested with the righteousness of his own Son."[46]

Indeed, the glory of imputed righteousness is not merely that it overcomes the threat that I have looked upon with mortal horror, namely, the perfect righteousness of the divine Judge. The glory of this scriptural truth is not mainly that it permits me to escape this praiseworthy office of God and his glorious attributes of perfect holiness, justice, and truth. Instead, the glory of imputed righteousness is that it provides the grounds by which the Judge in his perfect justice acclaims me righteous and embraces me to his heart. Clothed in the perfect righteousness of the Lord Jesus Christ I no longer fear God's justice but I rejoice in it, for it now demands that I be entered into life with all the blessings of heaven. God "shows his righteousness" in my justification; he is "just and the justifier of the one who has faith in Jesus" (Rom. 3:26).

My situation in Christ is now that so gloriously depicted in Hebrews 12. Once I faced the mountain of God's just condemnation with the dread the Israelites felt at the foot of Mount Sinai. There was "a blazing fire and darkness and gloom and a tempest," all directed against me in my sin. But now in Christ—washed clean of sin and clothed in his perfect righteousness—the writer of Hebrews says of me: "You have come to Mount Zion and to the city of the living God, the heavenly Jerusalem, and to innumerable angels in festal gathering, and to the assembly of the firstborn who are enrolled in heaven, and to God, the judge of all" (Heb. 12:22–23).

---

46. John Murray, *Redemption Accomplished and Applied* (Grand Rapids, MI: Eerdmans, 1955), 124.

Notice that it is to God in his justice that I come with joy—for clothed in Christ's imputed righteousness, his justice no longer condemns me but demands my justification. I am saved by grace; yes, that is how I was forgiven and granted this perfect righteousness I did not achieve. But now I am saved into the arms of perfect justice, which demands that I be granted everything that is due to Jesus Christ himself, even an inheritance in eternal and glorious life. Among the activities the Bible ascribes to this life in the presence of the glory of God is the singing of praise with joy. And if we comprehend now what God has done for us in Christ—making him who knew no sin to be sin for us, so that in him we might become the righteousness of God—then we will not wait to start singing:

> Jesus, thy blood and righteousness,
> My beauty are, my glorious dress;
> 'Midst flaming worlds in these arrayed,
> With joy shall I lift up my head.

The doctrine of Christ's imputed righteousness should be upheld because of its biblical affirmations. It should be treasured by believers because of the assurance it gives of an entrance into God's glory that is held upon by the joined demands of the mercy and the justice of God. But there is another consideration, for which this great doctrine must be demanded with great zeal and defended at great cost, namely, the honor and glory of the Lord Jesus Christ. To this end, let me repeat the words of John Piper:

> Alongside the pastoral preciousness of the doctrine of the imputed righteousness of Christ is the great truth that this doctrine bestows on Jesus Christ the fullest honor that he deserves. Not only should he be honored as the one who died to pardon us, and not only should he be honored as the one who sovereignly works faith and obedience in us, but he should also be honored as the one who provided a perfect righteousness for us as the ground of our full acceptance and endorsement by God. I pray that the "newer" ways of understanding justification, which deny the reality of the imputation of divine righteousness to sinners by faith alone, will not flourish, and that the fullest glory of Christ and the fullest pastoral help for souls will not be diminished.[47]

This, it turns out, is the very line of thinking to which the apostle Paul was himself directed by thoughts of the righteousness that comes from Christ. In Philippians 3, he specifically repudiated anything in and of himself that might stand for righteousness before God, including his

---

47. John Piper, *Counted Righteous in Christ* (Wheaton, IL: Crossway, 2002), 125.

faith as something that itself merited its own righteousness, and certainly his status as a covenant member, of which faith was a badge of honor. Instead, Paul says, "Whatever gain I had, I counted as loss for the sake of Christ." Instead of any righteousness of his own, Paul clings only to "the righteousness from God that depends on faith" in Christ (Phil. 3:8–9). Having said that Christ is "our righteousness" (1 Cor. 1:30), Paul hastens to the application that should most animate our heart: "Let the one who boasts, boast in the Lord" (1 Cor. 1:31). Therefore, let us defend and promote this great doctrine of Christ's imputed righteousness. And let us go on to follow the example of Esther in putting on this royal robe, approaching our "royal spouse." Even more, we can kneel before him in adoration, drawing near with confidence to worship God and to pray.

4

The Foundational Term
for Christian Salvation

Imputation

C. FITZSIMONS ALLISON

The crucial importance of this word *imputation* is too often obscured by the various English words used to translate the Greek term *logidzomai*: impute, reckon, treat as, esteem, and think. Imputation is, in fact, *word* made verb, *logos* in its verb form. The classical Anglican affirmation of this imputation, as the "formal cause" of our justification, is indubitably clear in the Articles (# XI),[1] in Homilies,[2] and in Richard Hooker's claim that "The grand question, which hangeth yet in the controversy between us and the Church of Rome, is about the matter of justifying righteousness."[3] His short, timeless summary of soteriology is unmatched:

1. Articles of Religion "as established by the bishops, the clergy, and the laity of the Protestant Episcopal Church in the United States of America, in convention, on the twelfth day of September, in the year of our Lord, 1801," *The Book of Common Prayer* (Church Hymnal Corp: NJ, 1979), 867.
2. *The Book of Homilies* issued under Edward VI in 1547. A "Second Book" was issued under Elizabeth I in 1563.
3. "A Learned Discourse on Justification," *Of the Laws of Ecclesiastical Polity*, Everyman Edition, 17.

The righteousness, wherewith we shall be clothed in the world to come, is both perfect and inherent. That whereby here we are justified is perfect, but not inherent. That whereby we are sanctified, inherent, but not perfect. [4]

The Council of Trent is in explicit difference, holding that the righteousness by which we are justified is inherent, infused, perfect, and ours.[5] Justification was indeed the "grand question" between the Anglican settlement and post-Tridentine Roman Catholicism. For classical Anglicanism the righteousness of justification was the imputation of Christ's righteousness to the sinner. It was seen as a virtual *communicatio idiomatum* (exchange of properties) between sinful humans and the sinless Lord. No other righteousness but Christ's could make it possible for sinners to be one with the justice of God. "For our sake he made him to be sin who knew no sin, so that in him we might become the righteousness of God" (2 Cor. 5:21).

This was the teaching of Thomas Cranmer, Richard Hooker, George Herbert, John Donne, Lancelot Andrewes, John Davenant, and Classical Anglicanism into the middle of the seventeenth century.[6] Unfortunately the adherence to or even the knowledge of this Anglican view is being largely lost.

An example of the loss of classical Anglican teaching on this subject is found in the indispensable *Oxford Dictionary of the Christian Church*, edited by F. L. Cross. In its first edition (1958) *imputation* was described in the following way:

In theology the ascription to a person by deliberate substitution of the righteousness or guilt of another. The idea plays an important part in the Lutheran doctrine of Justification by Faith, which asserts that a man is formally justified by the imputation of the obedience and righteousness of Christ without becoming possessed of any personal righteousness of his own. By a legal fiction God is thus held to regard the sinner's deeds as covered by the imputation of the sanctity of Christ. This doctrine seeks support in certain passages of St. Paul (notably Romans 3.21–30, 5.1f; Gal. 3.21f), and also from St. Augustine. It is opposed both to the traditional Catholic teaching, according to which the merits of Christ are not imputed but imparted to men and produce a real change from the state of sin to the state of grace, and to the doctrine of Liberal theologians to the effect that our highest vocation consists in the following of Christ who is our supreme example.[7]

4. Ibid., 16.
5. Council of Trent, Sessions 5 and 6.
6. C. F. Allison, *The Rise of Moralism* (Vancouver: Regent College Publishing, 2003).
7. *The Oxford Dictionary of the Christian Church*, ed. F. L. Cross (London: Oxford University Press, 1958), 683–84.

The inexcusable misrepresentation of imputation, which claimed that neither the Lutheran nor Anglican teaching cared about good works or personal righteousness in the regenerate, is no longer found even in Roman Catholic scholarship. Both Lutherans and Anglicans taught that there was beginning righteousness in the justified, but before God such righteousness was like filthy rags. The emotive language ("This doctrine seeks support in certain passages of St. Paul") was eliminated in subsequent editions, but not the outrageously erroneous reference to Romans 3:21–30 and 5:1ff, where imputation (*logidzomai*) does not appear at all but does so eleven times in the twenty-five verses of chapter 4. This mistake went uncorrected for forty years. The current article refreshingly reads as follows:

> [I]mputation . . . A central aspect of classical Protestant theologies of justification, according to which the righteousness of Christ is imputed or reckoned to the believer, despite being extrinsic to his person, in order that he may be justified on its basis. This is contrasted with the teaching of the Council of Trent, that the believer is justified on the basis of an imparted or infused righteousness, intrinsic to his person. Acc. to classical Protestant theology, the justification of the believer on account of the "alien righteous of Christ" is followed immediately by a process of renewal and growth in personal righteousness. Support for this doctrine is found in certain passages of St. Paul (notably Rom. 4; Gal. 3:21 f).[8]

The original article does however serve a purpose in acknowledging a third way to look at justification by liberal theologians who depend on human justification by following the example of Christ. This latter position with its Pelagian, Adoptionist, Socinian soteriology has been the banana peel on the cliff of Unitarianism within Anglican history in spite of the Anglican communion's uncompromising Augustinian Prayer Books.

Until recently it seemed that there were only these three alternatives: (1) We are justified by the imputation of Christ's righteousness; (2) We are justified by the infusion of inherent righteousness (Trent); and (3) We are justified by following Christ's example. Professor John Macquarrie, however, from an apparently panentheism perspective has vehemently objected to imputation, for it "involves us in untenable theories of the atonement."[9] Also, Bishop N. T. Wright's jettisoning of imputation seems to follow, not the Tridentine alternative, but a new confidence in human nature, *Coram Deo* (before the face of God), that needs no imputation of righteousness found only in Christ.

8. *The Oxford Dictionary of the Christian Church*, ed. F. L. Cross; 3rd edition, ed. E. A. Livingstone (London: Oxford University Press, 1997), 824.

9. *Principles of Christian Theology* (New York: Scribners, 1966), 304.

A report was made to the Episcopal House of Bishops in 1982 by the Anglican/Roman Catholic International Commission entitled "The Final Report."[10] A question was raised as to why it was called "The Final Report" when there had been no discussion of justification—that which Richard Hooker called the "grand question" between the Anglican and Roman Catholic churches. The answer given by the head of the Episcopal Church's delegation to the ARCIC deliberations was: "There have never been any differences between Anglicans and Roman Catholics on the matter of justification."[11] A list of some twenty Anglican theologians who had treated this "grand question" during the last four hundred years was given to that bishop in private. Reference should also be made to Article XI of the Thirty-nine Articles: "We are accounted (imputed) righteous before God," as well as such commentaries on the Articles as those by W. H. Griffith Thomas, T. P. Boultbee, and William Beveridge.[12]

The denial of imputation and the amnesia regarding this crucial question on the part of ecclesiastical leadership on the highest level was also demonstrated in 1987 in *Salvation and the Church: An Agreed Statement by the Second Anglican-Roman Catholic International Commission*. This "agreed statement" (ratified by neither of the Communions) astonishingly failed to mention that which *both sides* have agreed to be the central issue for four centuries: the formal cause of justification. Paragraph 15 quotes Richard Hooker, but the much more famous quotation from the same source is glaringly omitted. From among a dozen seventeenth-century Anglican divines expressing Hooker's insistence on imputation, the committee chose the only Anglican, William Forbes, who attempted a sympathetic approach to Trent (see paragraph 2 of the above "Agreed Statement"). But on the question of formal cause even Forbes could not accept *unica formalis causa* (the single formal cause) as being the infusion of inherent righteousness and insisted that it must include the remission of sins ("nay by it [remission] principally").

This is precisely the hole in Trent's bucket concerning the formal cause. *Formal cause* merely meant "that which makes a thing to be what it is." Trent claimed that the infusion of inherent righteousness at baptism is a righteousness that is now one's own and is that which makes one justified before God. It is the single formal cause. This claim at the Sixth Session

10. Anglican-Roman Catholic International Commission: *The Final Report* (Cincinnati: Forward Movement, 1982).

11. Oral statement at General Convention, House of Bishops Meeting, New Orleans, September 1982.

12. W. H. Griffith Thomas, *The Principals of Theology*, 7th edition (Philadelphia: Philadelphia Theological Seminary Pub., 1996); T. B. Boultbee, *A Commentary on the Thirty-nine Articles*, 6th edition (London: Longmans, 1882); William Beveridge, "A Discourse upon the Thirty-nine Articles" in *The Theological Works*, Vol. 7 (Oxford: 1844–1848).

of the Council of Trent repudiated the position of a "double formal cause" held by Cardinal Contarini at Ratisbone in 1541, and defeated the position held by Cardinal Seripando and Reginald Pole who could not be persuaded that the righteousness infused at baptism could be, by itself, the adequate righteousness *Coram Deo*. A sympathetic and scholarly treatment of Pole, with his "break-down" and departure from Trent over the question of justification is provided by the Cambridge scholar D. Fenlon. He gives a poignant human dimension to this controversial issue within Roman Catholicism and does a masterful job in describing how the issue had divided non-Protestant Catholics before the Counter Reformation. It was resolved unhappily at Trent.[13]

The difficulty these Catholics found with Trent's single formal cause was that it allowed for nothing in the face of God's justice but our justice, even if ours had been infused and given. Imputation, on the other hand, acknowledged that from the beginning to the end, the Christian before God asks for mercy on the basis of Christ's righteousness.

Imputation is the unanimous testimony of saints on their death beds. None pleads one's own infused righteousness before God but only the mercy of Christ. The seventeenth-century Anglican Lancelot Andrewes said it well:

> But let us once be brought and arraigned *coram Rege justo sedante in solio* [face to face before God seated in His established justice], let us set ourselves there, we shall then see that all our former conceit will vanish straight, and righteousness in that sense [inherent] will not abide the trial.[14]

Modern blindness in ignoring the issue, agreed to on both sides since the sixteenth century concerning the formal cause, obviates any responsible treatment of the issue. Granted that scholastic terms such as *formal cause* are not the current parlance of today, but the simple and clear meaning is anything but difficult to grasp.

Nothing illustrates the crucial and yet abiding historically agreed difference concerning the single formal cause (*unica formalis causa*) than John Henry Newman's *Lectures on Justification* (1838). When the third edition was published in 1874, Newman, as a Roman Catholic obliged to follow Trent, changed nothing but his teaching on formal cause. Like Contarini, Seripando, and Pole before him, Newman was so embarrassed by the necessity to make his work consonant with Trent's *unica formalis causa* that he sought to supplement it with something like "the presence

13. D. Fenlon, *Heresy and Obedience in Tridentine Italy: Cardinal Pole and the Counter Reformation* (London: Cambridge University Press, 1972).

14. Library of Anglo-Catholic Theology, Oxford, 1841–1852, 5:116.

of our Lord in the soul."[15] If the very thing that makes our justification before God what it is were not only our inherent righteousness by which we have been "made righteous," but also the presence of Christ within us, it would be in some measure congruent with Christ's righteousness imputed and would obviate much of the criticism of Trent. It could then be admitted that regenerate Christians were yet sinners. It took Newman six pages in his preface and sixty-one pages in the index to finally acquiesce in Trent's teaching. To cover these sixty-seven pages is to view a tortuous struggle.

If, in some way, the righteousness of Christ is still currently and always the ground of our place before God, we can acknowledge what Trent denied: that sin remains in us all, even in a state of grace. This denial of *simul justus et peccator* is reflected in the article on grace in the *Catholic Encyclopedia*:

> For since sin and grace are diametrically opposed to each other the mere advent of grace is sufficient to drive sin away . . . immediately brings about holiness, kinship with God, and a renovation of spirit . . . and therefore a remission of sin without a simultaneous interior sanctification is theologically impossible. As to the interesting controversy whether the incompatibility of grace and sin rests on merely moral, or physical, or metaphysical contrariety, refer to Pohle ("Lehrbuch der Dogmatik II" 511, sqq., 1909), Scheeben (die Myst. des "Christentums" 543 sqq., Freiburg1898).[16]

The logic deriving from the traditional interpretation of Trent in regard to denying *simul justus et peccator*, or sin in the regenerate, seems to preclude not only any recognition of unconscious sin but also any teaching of corporate or collective guilt.

An article entitled "Collective Responsibility" in the *New Catholic Encyclopedia* deals with this as a legitimate Old Testament phenomenon and teaching, but not one appropriate to the New Testament or to church history. If sin to be sin must have "full knowledge and consent of the will," citizens of a country where torture is practiced have no culpable responsibility so long as they themselves neither perpetrate nor assent to the torture. The *New Catholic Encyclopedia* acknowledges that, throughout the Old Testament, God holds Israel corporately responsible for justice and faithfulness.[17] Is this corporate responsibility

15. John H. Newman, *Lectures on Justification*, 3rd edition (London: Riventons, 1874), x.
16. "Sanctifying Grace" in *The Catholic Encyclopedia*, Vol. 6 (Robert Appleton Co., 1909).
17. *The New Catholic Encyclopedia*, ed. William J. McDonald (Washington, DC: The Catholic University of America, 1981).

not also ascribed under the new covenant? Are not the responsibility and accountability even loftier and more arduous in the new than the old? The old is not abrogated but fulfilled. Does not this claim—that what is true for the Old Testament is not true for the New Testament—border on Marcionism?

For Christians to share responsibility for the Holocaust and other horrors which they as individuals had no part in is, of course, an unbearable burden for one whose state of grace depends upon the absence of any culpability. William Wilberforce owned no slaves and gave no consent of his individual will to the institution of slavery, but his sense of corporate responsibility drove him and others to the abolition of slavery. Surely it can be shown in both Augustine and Bernard that similar responsibilities were on the shoulders of Christians in regard to the Empire, papal schism, or the rescue of the Holy Land. This was, however, a bearable responsibility because such acknowledgement of culpability was not tantamount to the loss of grace. Sin was a much deeper and wider phenomenon in patristic and medieval theology than its post-Tridentine definition in the matter of justification would encompass.

Since 1547 it seems to be assumed that any statements by Thomas Aquinas, Anselm, Bernard, or others concerning unconscious, unknown, non-deliberate, or corporate sin must be understood as venial sin because "full knowledge and consent of the will" is not involved. (Venial sin does not have the "formal nature" of sin according to the Council of Trent. Therefore, venial sins can exist in a regenerate person and do not destroy one's state of grace. Mortal sin, on the other hand, does destroy one's state of grace and requires the sacrament of penance to recover the state of grace.) If it were possible to regard unconscious fault or corporate guilt as sin, it would be virtually impossible, since Trent, to maintain the interpretation that sin and grace are mutually exclusive. Because of the principle of *inhesion*, they cannot, according to Trent, exist together in a state of grace. After Trent, vincible ignorance must be interpreted as a venial sin.

When a regenerate person sins, that person no longer abides in a state of grace and must be restored through the sacrament of penance. In contrast to patristic and medieval Catholicism, after Trent the church taught that sin must involve full knowledge and consent of the will. Thus, there can be no acknowledgement of "unconscious sin," for it would be tantamount to losing one's state of grace.

Ancient pastoral wisdom and contemporary depth psychology testify to the reality that many intractable patterns and compulsions are symptoms of unconscious roots. These need to be exposed and acknowledged in order that the damaging patterns no longer will have damaging sway over a person's actions. Dom Victor White, the English Dominican authority on C. G. Jung, saw this serious limitation in the way Trent was understood:

> This idea of "unconscious sin" is often a difficult one for the moral theologian to grasp. Especially if he has been brought up in the traditions of Reformation Catholicism (after the Council of Trent) he may find it particularly hard to square with his correct notions that mortal sin must be voluntary, performed with full knowledge and consent. But it is a fact that the psyche is much less indulgent to unconscious breaches of its own laws and demands . . . and will revenge itself for their disregard . . .

He continues:

> We know of a young woman who had lived for some time with a married man, fully aware that what she was doing was morally wrong in the eyes of her church and her parents, but with no psycho-pathological symptoms. Her parents came to hear of the liaison, brought strong pressure upon her to break it up, succeeded in doing so, and in bringing her home to the parental roof. At once, obsessive guilt took hold of her, and she became quite incapacitated for life. Her sense of guilt was clearly to be attributed, not to her having lived with her lover, but to her having left him and submitted weakly to parental pressure and allowing herself to accept externally the parents' moral judgment in spite of her own convictions. Whatever the objective standards of right and wrong, she had "sinned psychologically" in an infantile regression to dependence on the parents, in which she felt she had abdicated her adult autonomy and responsibilities.

He appends this valuable observation:

> The exclusive emphasis of later theologians on "full knowledge and consent" can have the unfortunate result of putting a certain premium on unconsciousness, irresponsibility and infantilism.[18]

White must put "unconscious sin" in quotation marks because it seems to conflict with the "correct notions" that, since Trent, mortal sins must have full knowledge and consent. But clearly he feels quite unhappy with this restraint under which spiritual directors and psychiatrists must work to stay in accord with the church's teachings.

The article on "The Psychology of Guilt" in the *New Catholic Encyclopedia* indicates the same direction but with new and even more awkward problems. Although it recognizes unconscious guilt to be a pervasively destructive phenomenon, it seemingly does not relate such

---

18. P. Mairet, ed. *Christian Essays in Psychiatry* (London: Camelot Press, 1956), 165.

guilt to one's salvation and distinguishes it from moral guilt by terming it "material guilt."

> The issue of material guilt has no meaning to it other than its producing a feeling of excessive fear of retaliation in interpersonal relationships about wrongdoing (due to ignorance, misconceptions, immaturity, or to repression, displacement, and substitution), which loses its significance at death since it vanishes then, or before death as one learns from experience. Moral guilt, however, binds one to an accounting for wrongdoing in the relationship with God, to be resolved by His judgment at death; therefore one must consciously seek to do good and avoid evil. Such bipolar terms describing guilt as genuine and irrational, real and unreal, normal and neurotic, true and repressed, theological and psychiatric refer simply to the moral and material and to the conscious and unconscious aspects.[19]

This solution puts a premium on keeping material guilt unconscious while rewarding irrationality, ignorance, "repression, displacement, and substitution." The article insists that unconscious aspects of guilt "must be considered, for they are recognized as disruptive in personality function," but when they are *once realized* they become sin.[20] If true, this would mean all therapy jeopardizes one's state of grace at precisely those points where it successfully brings into consciousness the hitherto unknown roots of one's sins.

It would seem to follow that separating material guilt from moral guilt and claiming that material guilt is neither sinful nor something for which we must account, do exactly what Dom Victor White warns against: they invite repression and endeavor to keep such matters unconscious, where they do not endanger one's soul but merely infect one's psyche. So separating matters of the psyche from matters of the soul has no theological or philological rationale. Bruno Bettelheim has argued somewhat convincingly that translators have made spurious use of Freud to make "scientific" what was essentially humane.[21] Translating the German to read "psyche" instead of "soul" is one such case. It would be a shame for Christians to continue this distortion by making separate arenas for psyche (material guilt) and soul (moral guilt).

Treating material guilt as having "no meaning to it" in relation to our souls' health echoes the seventeenth-century Jesuit teaching concerning sins done in ignorance, which, as Pascal pointed out, puts a premium on ignorance. Surely the traditional recourse to distinguishing between

19. *The Catholic Encyclopedia.*
20. Ibid.
21. Bruno Bettelheim, *Freud and Man's Soul*, ed. P. Mairet (New York: Alfred Knopf, 1983), 73ff.

vincible and invincible ignorance can serve certain practical purposes in avoiding administrative and penal injustices that would punish people for what they were unable to alter. (Invincible ignorance excuses one from sin because it does not involve the will to sin. Vincible ignorance, however, is culpable for it involves neglect to acquire information necessary to avoid sin.) Nevertheless, it falls short of positively approaching those areas of darkness in a person's soul (or psyche?) that need the light of grace for one to grow toward the perfect image that is Christ.

It is necessary to interrupt the argument at this point to insist that in Scripture, in Augustine, and in Bernard, there is ample evidence to regard actual sin in the unconscious as no invariable cause for "condemnation to them that are in Christ Jesus." Unless one can at least consider the possibility that sin can be consonant with a state of grace, any suggestion of unconscious sin or corporate guilt will sound to one nurtured in what Dom Victor White called "post-Reformation moral theology"[22] like the blackest of malign Jansenism.

On the contrary, once one has allowed for the discrepancy between a regenerate person's righteousness and the righteousness that "is to be" and has called this discrepancy *sin* following Augustine's dictum that "what is not of love is of sin," then acknowledging sin in the regenerate is a gracious matter of staking out areas for grace to do its work until we all attain "to the measure of the stature of the fullness of Christ" (Eph. 4:13).

Another example of the importance of embracing ignorant and unconscious actions in soteriology is that of marriage. A woman married to an alcoholic told a conference of clergy what Al Anon (an organization for helping families of alcoholics) had done for her. "It was not until they helped me to see what I was doing that it began to be possible for Jim to stop drinking. By making excuses, by covering up, by doing all those things I thought were a Christian's conscientious responsibility to her husband, I was unwittingly being an enabler, enabling Jim to continue drinking."

To teach her that so long as it remained unconscious or non-deliberate, she shared no complicity in the very complex tragedy of alcoholism, is no kindness to her. Our universal temptation to self-righteousness scarcely needs any nurture to help us believe that we are without responsibility so long as our complicity is unconscious.

The very fact that *hamartia*, Scripture's most prevalent word for *sin*, literally means "missing the mark" indicates that "falling short" characterizes all Christians, even the saints, which their own testimonies verify. It is no kindness in the long run to lower the mark of righteousness in

22. Ibid., 165.

the kingdom of God to the level of the actual righteousness of regenerate people. Another word, *agnoema*, translated *sin* in the New Testament, explicitly means "ignorance of what one ought to have known."

Geoffrey Wainwright is correct when he insists that the "nub of the matter appears to reside in the *simul justus et peccator*."[23] The replacement of "infusion" for "imputation" must lower the definition of sin to a manageable level or none would be in a state of grace. Hence, sin is described in post-Tridentine moral theology as having to have "full knowledge and consent of the will." This definition of sin suggests a level of sinlessness that can be improved upon, resulting in the teaching of supererogation. It lacks acknowledgment of any culpable responsibility of Christians in the face of societal evil. Christian assurance of the Word made verb, *logidzomai* (imputation), even in culpable social responsibilities, enabled Robert Penn Warren to put the matter in a simple paradoxical nut shell: "For the recognition of complicity is the beginning of innocence."[24]

Objections to Reformation teaching regarding justification seem to come from fear of antinomianism. A contemporary example is Robert H. Gundry's essay, "The Nonimputation of Christ's Righteousness."[25] He proposes jettisoning the imputation of Christ's righteousness for the following reasons: (1) the righteousness that is imputed is not called Christ's righteousness in any of the texts; (2) obedience will be more clearly necessary as it does "not shortchange sanctification"; and (3) removing the imputation of Christ's righteousness will go a long way in satisfying Roman Catholic and pietists' objections.[26]

A criticism of Gundry's position by D. A. Carson is found in that same volume.[27] But it would seem to be a simple matter of asking what righteousness is there *Coram Deo* other than Christ's that will provide us the Wedding Garment, the clothing necessary before the justice of God?

Bishop N. T. Wright, another who wishes to give up on imputation, was interviewed in *The Christian Century* and stated that his studies had undermined his earlier views, and that "the big question about justification for Paul was not, 'How do I find a gracious God?' but 'How do Jews and Gentiles who believe in Christ share table fellowship?'"[28] Paul's conversion on the Damascus road was certainly not that he suddenly realized: Now I can eat with the Gentiles! One doesn't have to charge Second Temple Judaism with crude works righteousness nor deny imputation insight in

23. Mark Husbands and Daniel J. Treier, eds., *Justification: What's at Stake in the Current Debates* (Downers Grove, IL: InterVarsity, 2004), 264.

24. *Brother to Dragons*, (New York: Random House, 1953), 214.

25. *Justification: What's at Stake in the Current Debates*, op. cit.

26. Ibid., 44.

27. Ibid., 46–78.

28. *Christian Century*, December 18–31, 2002.

the Old Testament to understand that none of us is worthy *Coram Deo.* The graciousness of God's action in his Son for us is the only basis for our hope. Table fellowship became an issue in consequence of the disclosure of the graciousness of the cross and resurrection. In a culture characterized by the loss of any sense of God's majesty, justice, and transcendence, it should not be surprising that all that is symbolized by the term *Coram Deo* is missing in our consciences.

"For historians, and that includes Christian historians as well, supernaturalism is simply not a live option." These are the words of the noted Van A. Harvey, emeritus professor of religious studies at Stanford University and author of *The Historian and the Believer.*[29] In this climate it is no wonder that even the best (and N. T. Wright is among the best) are tempted to the confidence that something less than Christ's righteousness can be the Word, *logidzomai,* (the verb form of *logos*) of our trust and hope.

The most formidable barrier to appreciation of imputation is the cultural climate in which we live. The historian Carl Becker coined the phrase "climate of opinion" while pointing out that the best historians of all times were guilty of unconsciously reading the assumptions and judgments of their own times onto the ages they studied and recorded. Similarly, theologians are not altogether immune to having their views of Scripture shaped by the climate they breathe. Thus, it is necessary to have a careful and critical look at this climate.

Any responsible diagnosis of contemporary times must conclude that we live in an age bereft of the sense of God's justice, transcendence, and awesomeness. In the presence of God, Moses, Amos, Ezekiel, and Isaiah are thunderstruck and in abject humility so unlike contemporary reflections on God. The very best vehicles for diagnosing the characteristics of an age are those rewritings of some classical work to make it congruent to our times. Such a work is Archibald McLeish's Job story, *J. B.* It ends with the relinquishing of any hope for justice, now or ever:

> *J. B.:* Why did you leave me alone?
> *Sarah:* I loved you. I couldn't help you any more. You wanted justice and there was none—only love.[30]

The well respected and positively reviewed bestselling book, *A History of God,* by Karen Armstrong, ends with a claim not atypical of our climate: "If we are to create a vibrant new faith for the twenty-first century, we should, perhaps, ponder the history of God for some lessons

---

29. *Christian Century,* January 26, 2000, 91.
30. Archibald MacLeish, *J. B.: A Play in Verse* (Boston: Houghton Mifflin, 1956) 151.

and warnings."[31] Another ex-Roman Catholic, Jack Miles, has written a book, *Christ: A Crisis in the Life of God*, in which he claims that Christ died for God's sins, not ours.[32] This book has received a Pulitzer Prize, become a *New York Times* bestseller, and received the John Templeton Prize for Progress in Religion. Nothing better verifies C. S. Lewis's charge in *God in the Dock* that modern man has in his arrogance switched places with God.[33] We are now on the judge's bench, and God is in the dock, the place of the accused. As Reinhold Niebuhr is said to have observed: "In the beginning God created us in his own image and ever since we have attempted to return the compliment."

Christian scholars may not be fans of these conceits but we can scarcely escape altogether the influence, usually unconscious, of this climate in which we live and breathe, a climate bereft of the biblical awe of God's justice and transcendence. We know by careful biblical scholarship that there is no forgiveness of sins except by God (Luke 5:17–25), but we forget this when we assert that sinful man is reconciled to God by something less than the righteousness of Christ imputed to him. Is the radical necessity for divine forgiveness for sins not easier to forget in an age in which we have switched places with the Almighty and most of our lectionaries have removed any biblical hint of God's wrath?

This very absence of any sense of God's justice in our climate results in a concomitant failure to appreciate the exquisite and miraculous mercy which God has shown in his Word, his *Logos*. His wording of us sinners as righteous is no legal fiction but the very means by which he begins to make us righteous. As Don Quixote in *The Man of La Mancha* persists against all worldly reality in calling (wording) Aldonza, the whore, as "my Lady Dulcinea," giving (imputing to) her a dignity and purity she didn't have, astonishingly she begins to become as she is worded, reckoned, regarded (imputed) to be—a gracious person unlike what she had been.[34] It is a wonderfully artistic example of the power of *impute*. God's Word made verb is the Christian imputation (*logidzomai*) that declares us righteous, and in that persistent declaration we have begun to become what "no eye has seen, nor ear heard, nor the heart of man imagined, what God has prepared for those who love him" (1 Cor. 2:9).

E. Brooks Holifield's *A History of Pastoral Care in America: From Salvation to Self-Realization*[35] is an insufficiently appreciated scholarly diagnosis of our theological education. The subtitle discloses a serious

---

31. *A History of God* (New York: Ballentine Books, 1993), 399.
32. Jack Miles, *Christ: A Crisis in the Life of God* (New York: Alfred A. Knopf, 2001).
33. C. S. Lewis, *God in the Dock* (Grand Rapids, MI: Eerdmans, 1970), 240–44.
34. Dale Wasserman, *Man of La Mancha* (New York: Random House, 1965).
35. Nashville, TN: Abingdon, 1983.

secular reduction of the Christian faith that would tend to make not only Christ's *logidzomai* irrelevant but also virtually all of the Nicene Creed. The generations of clergy trained in "self-realization" would naturally teach a gospel in which drowning humans need no savior, just a swimming coach. The strikingly popular slogan "What Would Jesus Do?" is indicative of an age that understands something about Christ as example but nothing about his being a sacrifice for sin. It is an age that cares about self-realization but not salvation. Much theological concern about the "historical Jesus" is at the expense of his messiahship, atoning sacrifice, resurrection, ascension, and his relationship to the Father and the Holy Spirit. It is as if the attempt is being made to reduce the Christian faith to what we can conjecture about the blank space in the creed between the sentence about the Virgin Mary and the sentence about Pontius Pilate. The Christian faith is not about self-realization but about salvation, and that comes only by God's Word made verb, *logidzomai*.

5

Reflections on Auburn Theology

T. DAVID GORDON

Several years ago Knox Theological Seminary, under the leadership of E. Calvin Beisner, hosted a conference to discuss the Auburn theology, in which a number of individuals delivered (and responded to) papers on both sides of the question. This resulted in the publication of *The Auburn Theology Pros and Cons: Debating the Federal Vision*.[1] The essays in that collection were and are helpful in both understanding and assessing the Federal Vision, or Auburn theology. In what follows I attempt to add my own thoughts to those contained in that series of essays without, I trust, repeating what was said there.

The Pros and Cons of Auburn Avenue Theology

I find myself in profound sympathy with the concerns of the Auburn theologians. I share vigorously each of Auburn's stated concerns about the individualist, revivalist/pietist, non-ecclesiastical, non-sacramental nature of so much of the Reformed experience today, as my hapless Gordon-

1. *The Auburn Theology Pros and Cons: Debating the Federal Vision*, ed. E. Calvin Beisner (Ft. Lauderdale, FL: Knox Theological Seminary, 2004).

Conwell and Grove City students will abundantly testify. In this sense, I have profound, vital, energetic, and zealous affinities with the stated concerns of the Auburn theology.

However, I fear that Auburn theology moves in a Romish direction (rather than in historic Protestant direction) for the cure. For this reason, my sympathies are with those critics of Auburn theology who defend (and articulate unambiguously) the historic federal theology with its corollary doctrines of the conditional/probationary nature of the Adamic covenant, the imputation of Christ's righteousness, and the exclusive (*sola*) role of faith as the instrument of our justification. In this sense, I have profound, vital, energetic, and zealous affinities with the theology of the opponents of Auburn theology.

The Nature of Auburn Avenue Theology

Auburn Avenue theology is reactionary. It is like the little girl who had a curl right in the middle of her forehead: When it is good, it is very, very good, but when it is bad it is horrid. Its very strength is its weakness; its keen perception of the errors of individualist, pietist, revivalist, and dispensationalist evangelicalism has driven it to make statements that are nearly as erroneous in the opposite direction. We might even suggest that Pastor Steven Schlissel embodies the best and worst of Auburn theology: a great, bombastic provocateur, who may be temperamentally unsuited to be a theologian. As a Socratic myself, I love those who make us think and am delighted that Pastor Schlissel does the very thing Socrates promoted—question the received tradition. No one does it with greater verve or point than Pastor Schlissel, and I am pleased that the God who gives differing gifts has given us this genuinely unique individual with his distinctive contributions.

Raising a question and answering it are not the same thing, however; and the broad, sweeping, synthetic mind that can perceive patterns that others might not otherwise see is not necessarily the best mind for solving intricate questions of theology. I think Pastor Schlissel has served us well by belling several cats, but I'm not sure he knows what to do after he has belled them. And, in a nutshell, that is how I view Auburn: I "hate the Nicolaitans, which they also hate" (Rev. 2:2), but I have attempted to avoid being reactionary. I dislike dispensationalism, for instance, but don't intend to wear a yarmulke.

Concerns Regarding New Ways of Seeing

Generally, those who think they are working within a new paradigm have a tendency to dismiss counterarguments without engaging them or refuting them. Whether they do so overtly, or merely implicitly (not really permitting the force of the arguments to be registered), there can be a gnostic tendency to believe that "outsiders" just can't appreciate what one is saying. Several of the Auburn contributors appear to have embraced such a belief—that they are working within another paradigm—which outsiders just cannot understand.

Further, those who consider themselves to be working within a different paradigm often fail to recognize that their *own* presuppositions are also culturally conditioned. While intellectual history is a perfectly valid academic discipline, and while it is always appropriate to consider the cultural conditioning of any theological or creedal statement, it is also equally necessary to recognize that a century from now, others will be studying *us* in the same manner. For instance, as I have already mentioned, there are profound evidences that the Auburn theology is American, conditioned by (and largely in reaction to) distinctive features of the American Reformed and evangelical experience. It is animated by its reaction to individualism, pietism, revivalism, and (especially but less self-consciously) dispensationalism. Thus, Auburn theology is not presuppositionally pure (nor could any human movement be so), nor is it merely or even primarily influenced by its ostensible commitment to biblical theology vs. systematic theology.

Indeed, I would suggest that, ironically, Auburn theology is a remarkably twentieth-century, American, evangelical phenomenon; it shares the biblicism that has characterized much of late nineteenth- and early twentieth-century fundamentalist and conservative evangelical thinking. It wishes to "hear the Bible on its own terms," and to do theology ostensibly as it is done in the Bible (a goal of the various pietist predecessors to evangelicalism). These are biblicist mantras, the somewhat naïve chant of those who dismiss all of those earlier, diligent laborers in the church as though they did *not* care to be biblical. Ostensibly, Auburn theologians wish to employ biblical terms as they are employed in the Bible, leaping over nineteen centuries of usage of such language. Even if this were a laudable goal (and I don't necessarily think it is), the confusion that results is enormous: terms that have been traditionally understood (I mean that literally: understood in a particular way by a particular Christian tradition) in one manner are employed in another manner, without explaining that this is being done.[2] This necessarily leads to confusion, so Auburn theologians have no right to complain or whine about being misunderstood when they so frequently use old terms in new ways without explaining to their audience that they are doing so.

2. Cf. the criticism by Calvin Beisner on this point.

For example you can almost employ, as a litmus test, the term *covenant* to determine whether a person is "Auburn" or not. If a person uses the term in the singular, and with the definite article, he is ordinarily an Auburnite. They refer again and again to *the covenant*, as opposed to *a* covenant, *the* covenants, or some *particular* covenant (e.g. the first Noahic covenant, the Abrahamic covenant, the covenant with the Levites to be priests, the covenant with David to build God's house, the Sinai covenant, and the new covenant.). I must say that I never know what they are talking about when they say "the covenant." Do they mean the Sinai covenant, the Abrahamic covenant, the new covenant? Do they mean the Adamic covenant of works (certainly not)? Do they mean the (confessional-but-not-very-biblical) covenant of grace?

Ironically here, they use language that is *neither* confessional/traditional *nor* biblical. The Bible frequently refers to covenants in the plural, or to some *particular* covenant, but never refers to *the* covenant, without an immediate context that delineates the specific covenant being referred to.[3] Why this neologistic reference to some nebulous, unspecified *the* covenant? Because, like their not-too-distant progenitor John Murray, the Auburn theologians are deeply driven by an anti-dispensationalist agenda; and therefore, like their more proximate progenitors, Norman Shephard and Greg Bahnsen, they shy away from using biblical language, either biblically *or* traditionally, in a manner that candidly recognizes the *plurality* of biblical covenants.[4] For all the Auburn approval of a kind of biblicist using of biblical terms in a biblical manner, their oft-repeated but lexically unbiblical "the covenant" is a profound exception to their profession. And for all their professed interest in the biblical narrative, they remove from that narrative one of its most important features—the narrative of a succession of *different* historical covenants that God has made with a variety of *different* parties, for *different* proximate purposes, although with the same distant end (the redemption of sinners in Christ).

Some Auburnites have objected to theology that is informed by Enlightenment rationalism or earlier (medieval?) concern to make contrasts or distinctions. Totally apart from this anachronism of perceiving the fifteenth or sixteenth centuries as influenced by the Enlightenment, Calvin Beisner has additionally (if pointedly) criticized the Auburn objection to logic or careful definitions. If the pairing of contrasts is an extrabiblical tendency of later intellectual traditions, how do we account for the Bible itself making so many such dualistic contrasts as these: light and darkness, folly and wisdom, righteous and unrighteous, wide way and narrow way, good and evil, etc.? The Auburn shotgun assault on (all?) contrasting pairs

3. See my Addendum, 125.
4. I will say more on the Murray-Shepherd-Bahnsen connection below.

probably makes some Auburn theologians themselves nervous, especially since the contrast between being "in the covenant" and "outside of the covenant"[5] is so common in their own language.

Similarly, if making refined distinctions is a bugaboo of a later intellectual heritage, how does this square with John's statement, often referred to in the essays, "They went out *from us*, but they were not *of us*; for if they had been *of us*, they would have continued *with us*" (1 John 2:19, emphasis added). The very fact that commentators and theologians still debate what John may have meant by this, as well as the commonsense recognition that the statement is a little difficult to fathom, suggests that the tendency to make fine intellectual distinctions was not an invention of the medieval era. Indeed the distinction here is so fine that in the first three prepositional phrases, the Greek is actually identical (*ex hemon*). That is, in the original, the subtlety is even greater: "They went out of us, but they were not of us; for if they had been of us, they would have continued with us." This kind of exegetical version of "who's on first?" may not be easy, but it is not a post-biblical invention.

Assurance

Assurance is an important pastoral and theological issue. While I have expended a good amount of my professional life in academia (thirteen years at Gordon-Conwell and six years at Grove City College), I also spent nine years as a pastor and other years as a ruling elder. This pastoral part of me cannot help but join the Auburnites in lamenting the effects of unsacramental pietism (including Puritan pietism) in robbing saints of that appropriate assurance of faith that should be one result of the church's ministry. I also join them in believing that baptism should be of greater importance (especially in our regard for infant children of believers) than it ordinarily is. Indeed, when we buried our first daughter, who died of leukemia, we marked her grave with a stone that had only her full name, the dates of her birth and death, and the date of her baptism. The baptism of infants declares that it is right for both church and family to include children in prayers, instruction, and worship, and to regard them as belonging to Christ until/unless they prove otherwise. Similarly, when I pastored, we observed the Lord's Supper weekly, believing with Calvin that the sacrament should seal the Word preached and offer comfort to saints, confirming their interest in him.

5. Whatever such ambiguous expressions mean; cf. the concerns expressed by Richard Phillips in chapter 7.

Yet even here, I do not believe the sacraments *themselves* are the appropriate source of assurance, or any particular *doctrine* of the sacraments. The appropriate source of Christian assurance is the person, character, and work of Christ, which is explained by the Word of God and sealed by the sacraments. Thus, even in the case of our little Marian Ruth, it was not her baptism itself that gave us comfort before and after her death, but the picture therein of a sin-washing Christ, who suffered the little ones to be brought to him, since of such were the kingdom of heaven. That this Christ permits us to symbolize his saving work in a rite that includes even our infant children is a reflection of his sovereign graciousness—that he can rescue even those who do not yet recognize their need to be rescued. The rite of baptism itself gives me no comfort either for my daughter nor for myself (as I write this I have cancer also, and may join our Marian not only by leaving this life prior to threescore-and-ten, but by leaving it through a similar vehicle); my comfort comes from believing that Christ can save the vilest and most helpless of sinners.

John Murray's Mono-covenantalism

I am staggered by the lack of discussion of John Murray's biblical theology. Many families have a dark secret that they prefer not to talk about: the uncle who gets drunk every Thanksgiving and makes passes at the womenfolk, the eccentric nephew who can't hold a job, etc. Such family secrets are well-known but rarely discussed. The Reformed version of this is John Murray's biblical theology. For all of the discussion of biblical/narrative theology vs. systematic theology in the essays, only Dr. Smith and Rev. Robbins made reference to the particular biblical theology of John Murray, and that only in passing as they (properly) focused on the consequences of Murray's rejection of the covenant of works for the doctrine of imputation. And the Auburnites, whose entire paradigm comes from Murray, appear hesitant to state the matter publicly, with the exception of Pastor Trouwburst.

John Murray despised dispensationalism. We all disagree with it, but few of us with the passion of John Murray. In denominational periodicals of his day, Murray frequently wrote against dispensationalism. Indeed, some of the historic premillenialists who left Westminster Seminary complained that Murray's attack on dispensational premillenialism occasionally made them feel attacked also. In reaction to dispensationalism, Murray proposed in his pamphlet "Covenant of Grace" what he called a *recasting* of covenant theology. Several things should be noted about this proposed recasting.

First, Murray himself had the intellectual candor to say that he considered covenant theology to be sufficiently defective that it needed his proposed "recasting." That is, any notion that Murray's view was/is the prevailing view within the covenant theology tradition is contrary to Murray himself, who did not consider himself to be re*stating* the majority view, but re*casting* the majority view. Murray did not wish to discard the tradition entirely; and that is why he called his view a recasting, which suggests a new way of articulating the view without jettisoning every aspect. Nonetheless, he candidly referred to his own formulations on this point as being *not* the prevailing view within the tradition, but a *recasting* of that tradition's salient features.

Second, what Murray has retained from the tradition is the value of using *covenant* as a significant organizing principle of biblical and systematic theology. It is evident that he considered the commitment to the idea of covenant to be a positive, beneficial aspect of the tradition, one that was to be retained and developed theologically (though, arguably, his definition of *covenant* differed from that of the previous tradition).

Third, what Murray jettisoned was the notion of distinctions of kind between the covenants. Specifically, and most significantly, he rejected the traditional distinction between covenant of works and covenant of grace, wishing to construe all covenantal relations as gracious. He also redefined *covenant* as a relationship, not a contract or treaty (essentially describing covenants in their essence by the *goal* achieved thereby: "I shall be their God, and they will be my people"). Additionally, Murray rejected the notion that there was any distinction of kind between the Abrahamic covenant and the Mosaic covenant, saying that there was not "any reason for construing the Mosaic covenant in terms different from those of the Abrahamic."[6] This has the logical consequence that there is no distinction between the Sinai covenant and the new covenant, as Rich Lusk reminds us: "the Mosaic Law was simply the Gospel in pre-Christian form."[7] This is the kind of overstatement that staggers non-Auburnites (and, one hopes, embarrasses many Auburnites). Much better is the more measured statement of Charles Hodge, who recognized *both* an "evangelical" *and* a "legal" aspect (i.e., not *simply* evangelical) to the Mosaic covenant:

> Besides this evangelical character which unquestionably belongs to the Mosaic covenant, it is presented in two other aspects in the Word of God. First, it was a national covenant with the Hebrew people. In this view the parties were God and the people of Israel; the promise was national security

6. The Covenant of Grace, 20.
7. *The Auburn Theology Pros and Cons: Debating the Federal Vision*, 130. This strikes me as analogous to saying: "Early-1944 Hiroshima was simply a Japanese city in pre-nuclear form."

and prosperity; the condition was the obedience of the people as a nation to the Mosaic Law; and the mediator was Moses. In this aspect it was a legal covenant. It said, "Do this and live."[8]

It is not a mere accident of publishing history that John Murray never wrote anything about the Galatian epistle. His mono-covenantalism could not have made any sense at all of the arguments in chapters 3 and 4 wherein Paul contrasts the Abrahamic and the Sinai covenants and illustrates them at the end with the figure of Sarah and Hagar, saying "these are two covenants" (one more than Murray could comfortably accommodate). We can only be grateful for Murray's silence here, for anything he might have ventured to say about the central part of the Galatian letter, or specifically 3:6–22, could only have contributed substantially to exegetical confusion.

Fourth, Murray (and his followers) implicitly believe that the only *relation* God sustains to people is that of Redeemer (which, by my light, is not a relation but an office). I would argue, by contrast, that God was just as surely Israel's God when He *cursed* the nation as when He *blessed* it. His pledge to be Israel's God, via the terms of the Sinai administration, committed him to curse Israel for disobedience just as much as to bless her for obedience. In being Israel's God, he sustained the relation of covenant suzerain to her; he did not bless or curse any other nation for its covenant fidelity or infidelity. In this sense, he was *not* the God of other nations as he was the God of Israel. Murray's (unargued and unarguable) assumption that "I shall be their God" implies gracious redemption, election, or union with Christ is entirely unmerited (should I say "unwarranted?") by the biblical evidence.

The first generation of those to whom the Sinai covenant was given died in the wilderness, in a situation that they perceived as being worse than their situation in Egypt. Why? Because Yahweh was *not* their God? No, because Yahweh *was* their God (i.e., covenant Lord); and because, as such, he was committed to imposing the sanctions of the Sinai covenant upon them. I suppose one could strain language here, and say that it was "gracious" of Yahweh to impose curse-sanctions upon the Israelites (but not upon the nations); but I certainly would take no comfort in God's grace, if it entailed such.

Taking all four of these recastings together, Murray proposed a biblical theology that was and is effectively mono-covenantal. I don't have time here to demonstrate the grounds on which I consider Murray's recasting to be a retrograde movement within covenant theology. Rather, I would like to indicate that I think his view ought to be given due and serious

8. Charles Hodge, *Systematic Theology* (Grand Rapids, MI: Eerdmans, 1977), 2:375.

consideration because of Murray's stature within the Reformed tradition, and because of his otherwise orthodox views on most matters. For this reason, while I think his view is unbiblical, and therefore confuses our effort to understand the Bible, and while I think he has retained the wrong thing and jettisoned the right thing from the tradition, I think we should discuss his views for a few generations.[9]

So, ironically, I would be willing to recast (or at least refine) the covenant theology also, but I would do so by retaining what Murray rejected and by rejecting what he retained (an ahistorical understanding of *covenant* that tends to confuse it with God's decree). I also think we should always be open-minded about our tradition, and when an individual of Murray's ability and stature suggests a recasting of our tradition, we should consider that challenge seriously for at least a generation or two.

But why don't we consider it fair game to talk about this? Why do we all know that Murray desired to recast the historic covenant theology, but we never publicly acknowledge that he did so? Further, since it is so patently obvious (to me, anyway) that the real distinctive of Auburn theology is not some alleged difference between biblical theology and systematic theology, but the distinction between historic covenant theology and Murray's recasting thereof, why didn't the essays address this matter? What we need is a conference addressing Murray's proposed recasting of covenant theology, with pros and cons weighing in on both sides of the four matters I mentioned above (and others, if I've missed them).

The effect of Murray's mono-covenantalism is a new, implicit hermeneutic that was not formerly part of covenant theology: a presumption of continuity. Since dispensationalism proposed a presumption of discontinuity, and since Murray saw red (rather than the desirable Scottish blue) when he encountered dispensationalism, he implicitly proposed a hermeneutic of continuity, which is an even greater difference with the historic covenant theology than the other specifics I mentioned above. Geerhardus Vos, for instance, expressly described biblical theology as the discipline that studied the Scriptures historically and chronologically, observing always two principles: the organic principle (what we would call *continuity*) and the principle of periodicity (an awkward way of defining what we call *discontinuity*). He also referred to these terms as *continuity* and *multiformity*: "Biblical Theology, rightly defined, is nothing else than

9. I am perfectly happy with retaining the covenant of works, by any label, because it was a historic covenant; what I am less happy with is the language of *covenant of grace*, because this is a genuinely unbiblical use of biblical language: biblically, *covenant* is always a historic arrangement, inaugurated in space and time. Once *covenant* refers to an over-arching divine decree or purpose to redeem the elect in Christ, confusion is sure to follow. Thus, in my opinion, Murray kept what ought to be discarded and discarded what ought to be kept.

the exhibition of the organic progress of supernatural revelation in its
historic continuity and multiformity" (emphasis in original). [10]

This is precisely what one observes in earlier biblical theologies by, e.g.,
Owen or Edwards. Indeed, the first generation of the magisterial Reformers would have undoubtedly emphasized *dis*continuity: their differences
with Rome were precisely over the hierarchical nature of its government
(in the etymologically original sense of the word, to wit, rule by priests),
and the priestly/sacrificial nature of its liturgy. In each case, the Reformers believed that Rome retained too much continuity with the levitical
aspects of the Sinai administration. Later, in debates with Anabaptists and
Libertines, the magisterial Reformers also found it polemically necessary
to discuss continuities between the various biblical covenants.

Throughout the Auburn Avenue essays, one finds several evidences that
Auburnism is essentially an outworking of Murrayism. First, few of the
Auburnites can describe what covenant theology is without reference to
dispensationalism, despite the historical reality that covenant theology was
here for several centuries before dispensationalism appeared.[11] Covenant
theology is not merely or primarily a reaction to dispensationalism, nor
does it need to define itself negatively by what it is *not*. Second, referenc-
ing *the covenant* without explaining *which* covenant one is referring to is
a dead giveaway to Murray's mono-covenantalism. Third, the sometimes
expressed presumption of continuity (noted especially in, e.g., Leithart's
discussion of biblical feasts, and in almost every sentence of Barach's
material) demonstrates the same.

It is thus not at all surprising that Murray's followers confuse:

- works and faith (Norman Shepherd), since the Mosaic covenant was
  not primarily characterized by faith but by works (Gal. 3:12), and,
  presumptively, the Sinai covenant was not different in kind from the
  new covenant;
- the imputation of the obedience of Christ with our own personal
  obedience (Shepherd, et al.), since the basic premise of federal/cov-
  enant theology (the Adamic covenant of life/works/creation) has
  been rejected;
- the Mosaic civil law with the civil laws of other nations (Greg Bahnsen), since again there is a presumption of continuity between theo-
  cratic Israel and other, non-theocratic states;

10. *Redemptive History and Biblical Interpretation*, 15.
11. My own impish way of discerning whether a person really has an understanding of
covenant theology is to see whether he can describe it without reference to dispensationalism.

- the primary Sinai meal (Passover, which was observed by families) with the primary new covenant meal (the Lord's Supper, which is expressly distinguished by Paul *from* family meals), and so paedo-communion, championed by Steven Wilkins, Robert Rayburn, Peter Leithart, et al.

At any rate, pre-Murray covenant theology did *not* employ a hermeneutic of continuity; nor did it employ a hermeneutic of discontinuity. It employed a hermeneutic of covenantal *integrity*. That is, it expected the ordinances, officers, sacraments, and laws of a particular covenant to be well-integrated into that particular covenant, sharing as many differences and similarities as the particular covenant did with other covenants.

Again, I do not wish us to remove advocates of Murray's view from Reformed church courts; in this I deliberately distinguish myself from those whose views are identical to mine, but who feel the Murrayans must go. But I do wish us to be candid about his own candid disagreement with the historic covenant theology, and I wish us to stop regarding Professor Murray's recasting of covenant theology as we do the drunk uncle, as something we cannot discuss openly. And further, I'd like to retain the right, after a generation or two of discussion, to remove Murrayism if we discover that his views are genuinely fatal to consistent federalism.

My current tolerance of his view is due, in no small measure, to the fact that in two of his published works (*The Imputation of Adam's Sin* and the Romans Commentary),[12] Murray defends the historic federal position. Thus, I want to leave open the possibility that his reticence regarding *covenant of works* may be merely semantic (if it is more than this, it may genuinely be that within a generation or two we'll simply find it necessary to declare his views unacceptable). At any rate, I find it utterly remarkable that neither the Auburn theologians nor their detractors discussed Murray's biblical theology and its hermeneutic consequences (with the aforementioned exception of a few paragraphs from Smith, Robbins, and Trouwburst).

Murray's "recasting" of covenant theology *per se* remains unopened to discussion in Reformed circles; yet, in my judgment, his recasting has generated several other important divergences from the historic Reformed tradition: the views of Shepherd and Bahnsen, paedocommunion, and now Auburn theology. Murray himself embraced none of these errors; his knowledge of historic covenant theology prevented him from ever taking his recasting of covenant theology to these particular consequences.

12. John Murray, *The Imputation of Adam's Sin* (Grand Rapids, MI: Eerdmans, 1959); *The Epistle to the Romans*, New International Commentary on the New Testament (Grand Rapids, MI: Eerdmans, 1965).

But his followers have not always had the same orthodox instincts; and, following the lead of his implicit mono-covenantalism, they foster errors that Murray himself would not have approved.

I am especially surprised that the opponents of the alleged federal theologians did not call attention to the following two ironies: the federal theologians deny the historic federal theology (the works/probationary/legal character of the Adamic administration), and they don't appear to have a biblical understanding of what a covenant is or whether the Bible contains more than one. Simply as a matter of intellectual integrity, their view should be called the *Non*-Federal Vision. And when they suggest that we need to do theology from a covenantal perspective, we should demand that they do the same, and candidly acknowledge that the Bible not only *records* a multiplicity of covenants but also *speaks* of them in the plural.

A Media Ecology Observation

I teach an introduction to media ecology at Grove City College, and one of the tentative conclusions I propose is that the revolution in electronic communications in the last thirty years has tended to increase the quantity (speed and frequency), but not necessarily the quality, of human communication. A correlate of this tentative conclusion is that there is a necessary reason for this. The more frequently we communicate, the less time we have to think. In a day with a limited amount of time, every choice to communicate what we currently think is a choice not to think further about the matter before we do.

Looking at the bibliography for these chapters, one cannot help but notice the role of the Internet in contemporary theological discourse. I wonder if this whole affair might have been different if the Auburn theologians, before publishing their views, had taken the time to sit down with distinguished senior theologians in the Reformed tradition (such as, but not limited to, Morton Smith, Douglas Kelly, David Calhoun, Robert Peterson, David Wells, and Richard Gaffin), to see if there were a way to articulate their concerns in a manner more consistent with our confessional heritage. I suspect their valid concerns would have been accommodated, yet without the controversy occasioned by sounding Roman while alleging to be Protestant.

In some of the essays, we find that the more-extreme statements are eventually modified, retracted, or qualified (with the possible exception of the Adamic covenant of works and its correlates, where more work needs to be done). However, the amount of effort it takes to find the qualifications is fairly substantial, and I think, at the end of the day, the

Auburn men must accept responsibility for the controversy that has ensued. Perhaps, in a pre-email, pre-Internet generation, there would have been more private conversation and handwritten (read: slow) communications before the matter went public.

Addendum: The Covenant, the Covenants, a/the (Particular) Covenant

1) *The covenant* is rarely employed in the Bible; indeed Paul never uses the expression. And where it is used, there is almost always an immediate contextual clue as to *which* biblical covenant is being referred to, such as "the covenant of circumcision" (Acts 7:8). In the New Testament, where the greatest amount of confusion could exist (since all biblical covenants are by this time instituted), the (potential) confusion is always obviated by contextual clues.

2) *The covenants* (or its equivalent) is employed to indicate the plurality of Old Testament covenant-administrations. This indicates that the New Testament authors were not only not mono-covenantal in their general orientation, but that they were not even mono-covenantal regarding the Old Testament (see Rom. 9:4, Eph. 2:12, Gal. 4:24).

One of the profoundest, most glaringly self-contradictory aspects of Auburn theology is its professed intent to employ biblical language biblically (rather than through the lens of the dreaded systematic theology), when in the most central language to the discussion (the biblical use of *covenant*), they do not use the term as the Bible uses it; to wit, with a self-conscious recognition of the plurality of biblical covenants.

All of us, Auburn or non-Auburn, would be more helpful if, when we employ the term *covenant*, we would clarify which covenant we are speaking about—whether one of the nine or so biblical covenants, or one of the three covenants within our theological tradition (covenant of works/life/creation, covenant of grace, covenant of redemption, the last of which is regrettably absent from the Westminster standards, but happily *not* absent from the theological tradition). In saying this, I am of course making more than a grammatical statement. I am not suggesting that, linguistically, we must qualify the word *covenant* every time we use it. If, in a given context, it is clear from previous statements which usage we are employing, then we need not be pedantic about it. But we would be clearer if somewhere in our context we explained which of the biblical or traditional usages we are employing.

6

To Obey Is Better Than Sacrifice

A Defense of the Active Obedience of Christ in the Light of Recent Criticism

DAVID VANDRUNEN

One crucial aspect of the Reformation's doctrine of justification is commonly known as the *active obedience of Christ*. This doctrine, in short, teaches that Christ not only endured the punishment of the law on behalf of his people (his passive, or suffering obedience) but also fulfilled all of the positive obligations of the law on their behalf. God requires perfect obedience of all people who would attain eternal life, and Christ has provided what sinners could never provide for themselves. Thus, according to Reformation teaching, justification consists both of the forgiveness of believers' sins, based on Christ's passive obedience, and of the crediting or imputing of Christ's righteousness, his active obedience, to believers.

Although recent criticism of the traditional Reformed doctrine of justification has taken many forms, nearly all critics seem to concur in dismissing the idea of active obedience. This is true of figures associated with the New Perspective on Paul and the Federal Vision. This chapter addresses the idea of active obedience in the light of recent critique of the doctrine. After briefly summarizing the teaching of Reformed theology

and identifying critiques of the doctrine, I will discuss the biblical and
theological basis for Christ's active obedience. There are many technical
exegetical debates that the constraints of space do not allow me to address
here. Nevertheless, the biblical teaching upon which the Reformed tradition has articulated the doctrine of active obedience is clear and worthy
of reaffirmation. I argue that, despite recent claims to the contrary, God
does demand perfect obedience to his law and that Christ has indeed
provided this obedience on behalf of his people.

The Reformed Tradition and Recent Critique

As stated above, the doctrine of Christ's active obedience has vivified
exposition of justification from the earliest days of the Reformed tradition. Even this historical claim has been disputed of late, however. Norman Shepherd, for example, has argued that Casper Olevianus and the
Heidelberg Catechism in the sixteenth century taught that justification
rested only upon the passive obedience but not upon the active obedience of Christ, and that the idea of active obedience was a later addition
to Reformed theology.[1] Space does not allow for a thorough treatment
of the historical development of this doctrine here.[2] Even a brief survey,
however, should show that the idea of active obedience (even if the precise terminology was a later development) was present in early Reformed
theology, enshrined in the Reformed confessions and catechisms, and
embraced by Reformed theologians ever since.

As for Calvin, he writes, after citing Galatians 2:21: "For we hence
infer, that it is from Christ we must seek what the Law would confer on
any one who fulfilled it; or, which is the same thing, that by the grace of
Christ we obtain what God promised in the Law to our works." He adds,
after citing Leviticus 18:5 and Acts 13:38–39: "For if the observance of
the Law is righteousness, who can deny that Christ, by taking this burden
upon himself, and reconciling us to God, as if we were the observers of the
Law, merited favour for us?"[3] At a later point in the *Institutes* he states:
"Thus we simply interpret justification, as the acceptance with which

1. Norman Shepherd, "Justification by Works in Reformed Theology," in *Backbone of the Bible: Covenant in Contemporary Perspective*, ed. P. Andrew Sandlin (Nacogdoches: Covenant Media Press, 2004), 103–20.

2. For a more detailed historical survey, see R. Scott Clark, "Do This and Live: Christ's Active Obedience as the Ground of Justification," in *Covenant, Justification, and Pastoral Ministry: Essays by the Faculty of Westminster Seminary California*, ed. R. Scott Clark (Phillipsburg, NJ: P&R, forthcoming).

3. English translation taken from John Calvin, *Institutes of the Christian Religion*, trans. Henry Beveridge (Grand Rapids, MI: Eerdmans, 1953), 2.17.5.

God receives us into his favour as if we were righteous; and we say that this justification consists in the forgiveness of sins and the imputation of the righteousness of Christ."[4]

The Reformed confessional documents express this teaching. Among sixteenth-century statements, both the Belgic Confession and Heidelberg Catechism provide clear examples. Belgic Confession Article 22 states that justifying faith "embraces Jesus Christ with all His merits, makes Him our own, and does not seek anything besides Him" and later adds that Christ "imputes to us all His merits and as many holy works as He has done for us and in our place." Similarly, the Heidelberg Catechism teaches that God "grants and imputes to me the perfect satisfaction, righteousness and holiness of Christ, as if I had never committed nor had any sin, and had myself accomplished all the obedience which Christ has fulfilled for me" (60). Immediately thereafter it says that we are acceptable to God not on account of the worthiness of our own faith, "but because only the satisfaction, righteousness and holiness of Christ is my righteousness before God" (61).

In the seventeenth century, the Westminster Confession of Faith and Larger and Shorter Catechisms articulate the same doctrine, and in fact explicitly situate it in a covenantal context. The Confession says: "The first covenant made with man was a *covenant of works*, wherein life was promised to Adam; and in him to his posterity, upon condition of perfect and personal obedience" (7.2, emphasis added). The Confession goes on to speak of man making himself "uncapable of life by that covenant" because of the fall into sin and points to Jesus Christ and the covenant of grace as that whereby "life and salvation" may now be obtained (7.3). The Confession elaborates on this saving work of Christ, the Mediator, in chapter 8. Christ "was made under the law, and did perfectly fulfil it" (8.4) and "by his perfect obedience, and sacrifice of himself . . . hath fully satisfied the justice of his Father" (8.5). The reference here to Christ's "perfect obedience" echoes the requirement of Adam's "perfect . . . obedience" (7.2), indicating that Christ fulfilled the terms of the covenant of works.

In its chapter on justification, the Confession speaks of this blessing coming by God's "imputing the obedience and satisfaction of Christ" unto believers" (11.1). It adds that "Christ, by his obedience and death, did fully discharge the debt of all those that are thus justified, and did make a proper, real, and full satisfaction to his Father's justice in their behalf" and that "his obedience and satisfaction" are "accepted in their

---

4. Ibid., 3.11.2. Calvin's comments on Romans 5:19 in his commentary on Romans are also very illuminating on this point.

stead" (11.3). The same teaching also appears in the Westminster Larger Catechism 20, 32, 39, 70–72 and in the Shorter Catechism 12, 33.

The theologians of the Reformed churches provide innumerable examples of the importance of this doctrine. A few can be mentioned. In the seventeenth century, Francis Turretin defined the Reformed view: "Hence it follows . . . that God cannot show favor to, nor justify anyone without a perfect righteousness. For since the judgment of God is according to truth, he cannot pronounce anyone just who is not really just. . . . Therefore he who is destitute of personal righteousness ought to have another's, by which to be justified."[5] Earlier in his *Institutes* Turretin had already explained:

> But the common opinion and the one received in our churches is that the satisfaction of Christ, which is imputed to us for righteousness before God, embraces not only the sufferings which he endured either in his life or at his death, but also the obedience of his whole life, or the just and holy actions by which he perfectly fulfilled the demands of the law in our place. Thus from these two parts, the full and perfect price of our redemption proceeds.[6]

Herman Witsius, also writing in the seventeenth century, affirmed:

> The *obedience* of Christ bears to these *blessings*, not only the relation of *antecedent* to *consequent*, but of *merit* to *reward*: so that his obedience is *the cause*, and *the condition* now fulfilled, by virtue of which he has *a right* to the reward, as several express passages of scripture declare. . . . And the merit of Christ *for himself* is so far from being prejudicial to his merit *for us*, that on the contrary, they are inseparably conjoined. For if he merited for *himself*, in order to be the head of the elect in glory, and to receive gifts for them, he certainly at the same time, merited for *the elect*, in order to their being glorified, and enriched with gifts becoming the mystical body of Christ[7] [emphasis in original].

Among American Presbyterians the testimony remains clear. Charles Hodge, for example, asserted:

> Redemption from bondage to the law includes not only deliverance from its penalty, but also from the obligation to satisfy its demands. This is the fundamental idea of Paul's doctrine of justification. The law demands, and

5. Francis Turretin, *Institutes of Elenctic Theology*, vol. 2, trans. George Musgave Giger, ed. James T. Dennison, Jr. (Phillipsburg, NJ: P&R, 1994), 647 (T.16, q.3).

6. Ibid., 445 (T.14, q.13).

7. Herman Witsius, *The Economy of the Covenants Between God and Man* (Phillipsburg, NJ: P&R, 1990), 1:190–91.

from the nature of God, must demand perfect obedience. It says, Do this and live; and, 'Cursed is every one that continueth not in all things which are written in the book of the law to do them.' . . . The only possible method, according to the Scriptures, by which men can be saved, is that they should be delivered from this obligation of perfect obedience. This, the Apostle teaches, has been effected by Christ.[8]

Later Princeton theologian Geerhardus Vos, responding to challenges to Protestant understandings of Paul's doctrine of justification (which sound remarkably relevant one hundred years later), writes:

The transfer of the fulfillment of the law from the sinner to Christ at one and the same time safeguards the interests of the divine righteousness and absolutely prevents the intrusion of those sinful motives which . . . rendered the plan of works impracticable and irreligious in the apostle's estimation. The earthly life of Christ offers the only instance of the working of the scheme under normal conditions, outside of the original state of rectitude. Christ by His perfect obedience was just before God, and on the ground of His being just received eternal life.[9]

John Murray also defended the doctrine of the active obedience of Christ as part of the ground of justification. Among other examples, he writes:

But it is prejudicial to the grace and nature of justification to construe it merely in terms of remission. This is so to such an extent that the bare notion of remission does not express, nor does it of itself imply, the concept of justification. The latter means not simply that the person is free from guilt but is accepted as righteous; he is declared to be just. In the judicially constitutive and in the declarative sense he is righteous in God's sight. In other words, it is the positive judgment on God's part that gives to justification its specific character.[10]

This positive righteousness he identifies in many places as the imputed obedience of Christ.[11]

8. Charles Hodge, *Systematic Theology* (Grand Rapids, MI: Eerdmans, 1995), 2:517.

9. Geerhardus Vos, "The Alleged Legalism in Paul's Doctrine of Justification," in *Redemptive History and Biblical Interpretation: The Shorter Writings of Geerhardus Vos*, ed. Richard B. Gaffin Jr. (Phillipsburg, NJ: P&R, 1980), 398.

10. *The Collected Writings of John Murray*, vol. 2 (Edinburgh: Banner of Truth, 1977), 218.

11. E.g., see ibid., 212–15; *Redemption Accomplished and Applied* (Grand Rapids, MI: Eerdmans, 1955), 156–58; *The Imputation of Adam's Sin* (Grand Rapids, MI: Eerdmans, 1959), 70; *The Epistle to the Romans* (Grand Rapids, MI: Eerdmans, 1959, 1965), 1:199–206.

Murray's contemporary Louis Berkhof teaches the same doctrine: "If Christ had suffered only the penalty imposed on man, those who shared in the fruits of His work would have been left exactly where Adam was before he fell. Christ merits more for sinners than the forgiveness of sins."[12] And later he claims: "Positively . . . the ground of justification can be found only in the perfect righteousness of Jesus Christ, which is imputed to the sinner in justification."[13]

Despite this overwhelming consensus through nearly five hundred years of Reformed theology, many proponents of the Federal Vision theology, though claiming to be Reformed, have rejected the doctrine of active obedience. James B. Jordan, for example, makes his position clear: "This brings up the matter of Jesus' 'active and passive obedience.' The merit theology sometimes assumes that Jesus actively earned a reward, and passively went to the cross. This notion cannot stand inspection."[14] Shortly thereafter, he raises "the matter of double imputation. That there is a double imputation of our sins to Jesus and His glory to us is certainly beyond question, and I am *not* disagreeing with the general doctrine of imputation, or of double imputation. But merit theology often assumes that Jesus' *earthly* works and merits are somehow given to us, and there is no foundation for this notion." He explains: "It is not Jesus' earthly life and 'works and merits' that are transferred to us, but His glorified and resurrected life in the Spirit that is transferred to us."[15]

Along similar lines, Shepherd denies the active obedience of Christ by equating justification with the forgiveness of sins. In examining several texts in Romans, Shepherd claims:

> Justification is the forgiveness of sins. . . . Paul makes clear that justification is the forgiveness of sin grounded in the righteousness of Jesus Christ. That righteousness is his propitiatory sacrifice offered on the Cross in obedience to the will of his Father in heaven. . . . The death and resurrection of Jesus secure our justification. That is to say, they secure the forgiveness of our sin. . . .We are constituted righteous by God when he justifies us by forgiving our sin. . . . Paul equates justification with the forgiveness of sins. . . . The

12. Louis Berkhof, *Systematic Theology* (Grand Rapids, MI: Eerdmans, 1938; 1993), 380.

13. Ibid., 523.

14. James B. Jordan, "Merit Versus Maturity: What Did Jesus Do for Us?" in *The Federal Vision*, ed. Steve Wilkins and Duane Garner (Monroe, LA: Athanasius Press, 2004), 194. This quotation and the comments that follow in his text seem to indicate that Jordan understands the *passive* in passive obedience in a way different from traditional Reformed use of the term. Jordan takes *passive* not to refer to Christ's suffering, but to his being placid or receptive.

15. Ibid., 194–95.

ground of justification—the basis on which forgiveness is possible—is the suffering and death of our Lord.[16]

Other writers associated with the Federal Vision who reject the doctrine of active obedience include Rich Lusk and P. Andrew Sandlin.[17]

Proponents of the New Perspective on Paul also critique the idea of active obedience. N. T. Wright, for example, dismisses traditional Reformed ideas based upon his understanding of the important Pauline phrase "the righteousness of God." Rather than referring, at least in certain crucial contexts, to the active obedience of Christ that is imputed to believers, Wright identifies "the righteousness of God" with God's covenant faithfulness. In one of his books he writes: "If we use the language of the law court, it makes no sense whatever to say that the judge imputes, imparts, bequeaths, conveys or otherwise transfers his righteousness to either the plaintiff or the defendant. Righteousness is not an object, a substance or a gas which can be passed across the courtroom."[18] Shortly thereafter, Wright explains further: "If and when God does act to vindicate his people, his people will then, metaphorically speaking, have the status of 'righteousness.' . . . *But the righteousness they have will not be God's own righteousness.* That makes no sense at all. God's own righteousness is his covenant faithfulness"[19] (emphasis in original). James D. G. Dunn advocates a similar view of "the righteousness of God."[20]

In light of the affirmations of the Reformed tradition for nearly five hundred years and the recent criticisms of the doctrine, what issues rise to the surface and demand attention? Two matters of central importance are whether God demands perfect obedience as the condition for eschatological life and whether Jesus Christ, in light of this demand, provided this perfect obedience, the "righteousness of God," as the basis for our justification.

16. Norman Shepherd, "Justification by Faith in Pauline Theology," in *Backbone*, 87–89.

17. See Rich Lusk, "A Response to 'The Biblical Plan of Salvation,'" in *The Auburn Avenue Theology, Pros and Cons: Debating the Federal Vision* (Fort Lauderdale, FL: Knox Theological Seminary, 2004), 139–43; P. Andrew Sandlin, "Covenant in Redemptive History: 'Gospel and Law' or 'Trust and Obey,'" in *Backbone*, 69–70.

18. N. T. Wright, *What Saint Paul Really Said* (Grand Rapids, MI: Eerdmans, 1997), 98.

19. Ibid., 99. Wright provides a chart on page 101 that differentiates his own view of "the righteousness of God" from other views, including that of imputed righteousness.

20. See James D. G. Dunn, *The Theology of Paul the Apostle* (Grand Rapids, MI: Eerdmans, 1998), 340–46.

The Requirement of Perfect Obedience

Does God require perfect obedience to his law as a condition for eternal life? In writings cited above, Federal Vision proponents have argued that the doctrine of justification does not depend upon an affirmative answer to this question. In a different academic context, but also relevant to the present discussion, E. P. Sanders, a fountainhead of the New Perspective movement, and New Perspective advocates themselves have claimed that first-century Jewish writers, who influenced Paul, did not believe that the law of God demanded perfect obedience.[21] In the face of such claims, I now address the biblical basis for the idea that God requires perfect obedience to his law and argue that the historical and confessional Reformed position—that God demands perfect and personal obedience—is solidly grounded in Scripture.

The extremely important background to the question of the demand for perfect obedience is the character of the God who demands it. God is just. He will never permit his justice to be compromised. When he judges, he cannot ignore people's works: "I will not acquit [justify] the wicked" (Exod. 23:7) and "the LORD will be no means clear the guilty" (Nah. 1:3). God cannot compromise his justice, for he "is not partial and takes no bribes" (Deut. 10:17). Thus, he demands similar conduct from earthly judges, who must answer to him: "He who justifies the wicked and he who condemns the righteous are both alike an abomination to the LORD" (Prov. 17:15). God is not petty or tyrannical in judging according to works or in requiring obedience from those who would dwell with him forever. Rather, as a righteous judge it is a mark of his justice. "O LORD, who shall sojourn in your tent? Who shall dwell on your holy hill? He who walks blamelessly and does what is right" (Ps. 15:1–2a); "Who shall ascend the hill of the LORD? And who shall stand in his holy place? He who has clean hands and a pure heart" (Ps. 24:3–4a).

The demand for perfect obedience to the law is already evident in the opening chapters of Genesis. As articulated in the Reformed doctrine of the covenant of works, God made man in covenant with him, requiring

---

21. See E. P. Sanders, *Paul and Palestinian Judaism: A Comparison of Patterns of Religion* (Philadelphia: Fortress, 1977), 137, 175–76, 204. Among New Perspective advocates, see Dunn, *The Theology of Paul the Apostle*, 361. Scholars have contested the view of Sanders that the Judaism of Paul's day did not think that the law required perfect obedience. Among Reformed writers, see Guy Prentiss Waters, *Justification and the New Perspective on Paul: A Review and Response* (Phillipsburg, NJ: P&R, 2004), chap. 4; and Bryan D. Estelle, "The Covenant of Works in Moses and Paul," in *Covenant, Justification, and Pastoral Ministry: Essays by the Faculty of Westminster Seminary California*. A thorough treatment appears in A. Andrew Das, *Paul, the Law, and the Covenant* (Peabody, MA: Hendrickson, 2001), chap. 1 and pp. 143–44. Also see Peter Stuhlmacher, *Revisiting Paul's Doctrine of Justification: A Challenge to the New Perspective* (Downers Grove, IL: InterVarsity, 2001), 40–42.

of him perfect obedience and promising him eschatological life if he was obedient during a probationary period. While the present chapter cannot explore every facet of this doctrine, readers may note at least the fact that God put Adam under his law from the beginning and did indeed hold him to the standard of perfect obedience.

The very first words that God speaks to his human creation are commands: "Be fruitful and multiply and fill the earth and subdue it and have dominion over the fish of the sea and over the birds of the heavens and over every living thing that moves on the earth" (Gen. 1:28). God adds a more specific command to this general precept in the next chapter: "And the LORD God commanded the man, saying, 'You may surely eat of every tree of the garden, but of the tree of the knowledge of good and evil you shall not eat, for in the day that you eat of it you shall surely die" (Gen. 2:16–17). This is not simply imperative, but law. The mode of expression in the Hebrew of 2:17—לא תאכל, "you shall not eat"—is legal in character. The same way of speaking occurs in the "you shall not" commands of the Decalogue in Exodus 20: לא תרשצ . . . etc.[22]

The probationary command of Eden anticipates the Mosaic Law; the Mosaic Law is an echo of Eden. Thus, God puts his people under law. This does not compromise the relational or filial elements of the covenant of creation, but clarifies that the relationship is, in part, forensic in nature.[23] Did this law of creation demand perfect obedience of our first parents? The unavoidable conclusion is that it did. In Genesis 2:16–17, God threatens that the violation of just one precept will bring immediate death. The events of Genesis 3 then demonstrate that one sin indeed incurred the promised punishment. The fact that a single sin ushered in the curse means that perfect obedience was the standard (as James 2:10–11 reinforces).

What effect does the fall into sin have upon this obligation of perfect obedience? Scripture teaches throughout its pages that God saves his people from the guilt of their sin by means of sacrificial atonement. First, he instituted sacrifices in the Old Testament. These were shadows that

22. This point is noted in J. V. Fesko, *Last Things First: Genesis 1–3 in the Light of Christology and Eschatology* (Fearn, Scotland: Mentor, forthcoming).

23. On this point, and for a more technical examination of the Hebrew of Genesis 2:16–17 pertaining to the character of the covenant of works, see Bryan D. Estelle, "The Covenant of Works." As Meredith G. Kline has noted, "Manifestly, paternal love and the legal justice of the works principle are not mutually exclusive but entirely compatible. . . . We are obliged by the biblical facts to define works and justice in such a way that we can apply both the legal-commercial and family-paternal models to explicate the same covenants." See *Kingdom Prologue: Genesis Foundations for a Covenantal Worldview* (Overland Park: Two Age, 2000), 110. That the Reformed tradition has not seen a dichotomy generally between the forensic and the filial is made evident, for example, in WCF 11.3, which notes that Christ made satisfaction "to his Father's justice."

could never themselves take away sin but pointed ahead to a greater sacrifice. Then, in the Lord Jesus Christ, he provided the perfect sacrifice that cleansed his people. Without this passive, suffering obedience, we would still be in our sins and condemned to eternal death. But is this passive obedience sufficient? Does the forgiveness of sin itself provide the right to eternal life?

An analogy may help to put this question in proper perspective. Imagine that a father tells his son to do his homework and promises him dessert if he does. The son fails to do his homework and thus receives a suitable punishment. May the son then, on the basis of his punishment, claim his dessert? It seems silly to think so. The son must still do his homework; the punishment for failing a task does not suddenly wipe out the obligation to do the task. The punishment does no more than put the son back in his original position, his past failure now forgotten. The situation with the human race in Adam is similar. Even after the forgiveness of sins in Christ, the commands given to Adam in Genesis 1–2 still remain unaccomplished. When the original promise of life was based upon completing a course of obedience, it seems strange to think that God would proceed to grant eternal life simply on the basis of man being returned to Adam's original state of guiltlessness.

This is not merely a point of logic. Scripture repeatedly reminds sinful people that sacrifice and the forgiveness of sins, though necessary, are not sufficient for one's right standing before God. In his confrontation with Saul, Samuel uttered words that recur many times through subsequent redemptive history: "Has the LORD as great delight in burnt offerings and sacrifices, as in obeying the voice of the LORD? Behold, to obey is better than sacrifice, and to listen than the fat of rams" (1 Sam. 15:22). In the Old Testament, slight variations of this affirmation appear in Psalm 40:6–8, Jeremiah 7:22–23, Hosea 6:6, and Micah 6:6–8. One might argue that God is simply exhorting his people not to offer sacrifices with insincere hearts. God indeed does desire sincere worshipers, and some of these verses may be amenable to such an interpretation.

At least some of these examples, however, speak of something more than this. God desires not simply obedience in the act of sacrifice, but obedience even apart from consideration of sacrifice: "For in the day that I brought them out of the land of Egypt, I did not speak to your fathers or command them concerning burnt offerings and sacrifices. But this command I gave them: 'Obey my voice, and I will be your God, and you shall be my people. And walk in all the way that I command you, that it may be well with you'" (Jer. 7:22–23). Holistic obedience is more basic than sacrifice; sacrifice can never replace it. Similarly, Micah 6:6–8 speaks generally of how a person might dare to present himself before God. Sacrifice by itself falls short; holistic obedience is also required:

> With what shall I come before the LORD, and bow myself before God on high? Shall I come before him with burnt offerings, with calves a year old? Will the LORD be pleased with thousands of rams, with ten thousands of rivers of oil? Shall I give my firstborn for my transgression, the fruit of my body for the sin of my soul? He has told you, O man, what is good; and what does the LORD require of you but to do justice, and to love kindness, and to walk humbly with your God?

Christ's own words confirm this interpretation. Though he appeals to this Old Testament theme on other occasions as well (see Matt. 9:13; 12:7), his conversation with a scribe in Mark 12 is perhaps most significant. Here Jesus affirms the wisdom of the scribe's comment that obedience is much more than all sacrifice. Not only does God desire obedience in the act of sacrifice, but, more fundamentally, he desires wholehearted love of God and neighbor: "to love him with all the heart and with all the understanding and with all the strength, and to love one's neighbor as oneself, is much more than all whole burnt offerings and sacrifices" (v. 33). Sacrifice can never replace the obligation of perfect love. Hence Jesus, when asked by a lawyer what he had to do to inherit eternal life, responded: "'What is written in the Law? How do you read it?' And [the lawyer] answered, 'You shall love the Lord your God with all your heart and with all your soul and with all your strength and with all your mind, and your neighbor as yourself.' And [Jesus] said to him, 'You have answered correctly; do this, and you will live'" (Luke 10:25–28; see also Matt. 19:17–19).

The apostle Paul reminds his readers of the same idea. Not insignificantly, he does so most explicitly in the context of discussions about justification (Gal. 3:10; 5:3; Rom. 2:13). In Galatians 3 Paul sets forth and defends his doctrine of justification generally. In the verses immediately preceding and immediately following 3:10, Paul explains that justification must be by faith. Justification by faith, however, entails that justification is not by works of the law, and this is Paul's particular point in 3:10. Why is justification by works impossible? The answer is not based upon some abstract metaphysical principle that somehow makes justification and works inherently incompatible. No, as Paul goes on to say in 3:12, quoting Leviticus 18:5, "The one who does them shall live by them." Justification would in fact be granted to those who obey the law. Instead, justification by works is impossible precisely because the law demands perfect obedience: "For all who rely on works of the law are under a curse; for it is written, 'Cursed be everyone who does not abide by all things written in the Book of the Law, and do them'" (3:10). As many commentators have pointed out, Paul makes use of an implied premise here; in other words, he assumes a fact that anyone under the influence of his ministry would surely know, namely, that all people are sinners. And thus Paul's reasoning in 3:10 is evident: the law demands perfect obedience; all people are sinners; therefore everyone relying on the law for justification is under a curse.[24]

One further point may be worth noting in connection with Galatians 3:10. Paul, rather than shying away from the idea that the law demands perfect obedience, in fact emphasizes it. In 3:10 Paul quotes Deuteronomy 27:26, which reads according to the Hebrew: "Cursed be anyone who does not confirm the words of this law by doing them." Careful readers of Galatians 3:10 will note that Paul adds something to the words of Moses. Following the Septuagint, the Greek translation of the Old Testament, Paul says not "the words of this law" but "*all* things written in the Book of the Law." Under the inspiration of the Spirit, Paul modifies the Hebrew text in a way that highlights that those who are under the law are obligated to abide by *everything* that the law commands. The law continues to demand perfect obedience.

More briefly, Paul's words in Galatians 5:3 and Romans 2:13 may be considered. In Galatians 4, Paul has emphasized the freedom that believers enjoy in Christ; now as he comes to chapter 5, Paul warns his readers of the danger of giving up this freedom and submitting again to a yoke of bondage (5:1). In context, the yoke of bondage clearly in mind here is life under the Mosaic Law. Remarkably, Paul has just associated life under the Mosaic Law with life under paganism, referring to them by similar terms (4:3 and 4:8–9). From the perspective of the new covenant in Christ, a return to Moses or a return to paganism would be little different! Both would entail rejection of justification by faith and would thus leave but one alternative: justification by the law. And justification by the law is a hopeless prospect, again precisely because the law demands perfect obedience: "I testify again to every man who accepts circumcision that he is obligated to keep the whole law" (5:3).

In Romans 2:13, in the midst of his argument between 1:18–3:20 placing each and every person under the condemnation of sin, Paul writes: "For it is not the hearers of the law who are righteous before God, but the doers of the law who will be justified." This is a basic truth, but Paul is concerned here to show that, on account of sin, no person trying to fulfill this requirement by his own power will succeed (see especially Rom.

24. For helpful material on these issues in Galatians 3:10, see Das, *Paul*, chap. 6; Waters, *Justification*, 168–69; and Estelle, "The Covenant of Works."

3:19–20). At this point, with this most fundamental human predicament placed before us, we move to the next section.

The Righteousness of God, the Active Obedience of Christ

The human race finds itself in the most dire condition. God, in his bountiful goodness, had created man in covenant with him and promised him blessed, eschatological life upon condition of obedience to his law. Adam turned his back on that promise by disobeying that law and thereby left the human race a corrupt ruin. No one is able to keep the law perfectly but, in fact, all have become guilty in Adam and by their own sin add to that guilt every day. The holy judge of all the earth declares that he will not justify the guilty. Yet in his love for his people God sent his Son. Through his suffering, the Lord Jesus Christ endured his Father's wrath against sin and thereby cleansed his people from all their guilt. This is good news—necessary good news. But it is still only half of the good news. Those looking to God for salvation also need to hear the other half.

Why is this? As the previous section of this chapter seeks to make clear, the biblical teaching on Christ's obedience does not appear in a vacuum. From the beginning, God has required of all human beings perfect obedience to his law. Adam did not fulfill this demand on behalf of his posterity, and no sinner since then has been able to fulfill it on his own. Yet God has continued to remind his people of this demand and thereby to indicate that he will not simply overlook it. Those who read Scripture carefully would naturally *expect* their Messiah to satisfy this requirement on their behalf. Thus, when Jesus says that he must fulfill all righteousness (Matt. 3:15), when Paul announces that Christ was born "under the law" to redeem us (Gal. 4:4–5), and when the author of Hebrews proclaims that he "learned obedience" and was "without sin" (Heb. 5:8; 4:15), they surely have more in mind than simply passive obedience or active obedience merely in the sense of qualifying Christ to be an acceptable sacrifice. This theological background, which shows the *necessity* of Christ's active obedience if we are to be saved, must be recognized.

In addition to such general theological concerns, more specific exegetical considerations also demonstrate the truth and importance of Christ's active obedience. A key example is Paul's teaching on the righteousness of God. As discussed above, one of the elements of the New Perspective's critique of traditional interpretations of Paul is that the important Pauline phrase *the righteousness of God* refers to God's covenant faithfulness. New Perspective proponents have also argued that righteousness, when applied to human beings, indicates their covenant status.

The idea of righteousness is inevitably crucial for an understanding of justification. Not only does justification itself refer to a declaration of righteousness, but Paul also identifies the righteousness of God as the answer to the human plight caused by our inability to be justified by works of the law. Much traditional Reformed exposition of Paul and the doctrine of justification has seen a vital connection between the righteousness of God that justifies and the righteousness that is imputed to believers for their justification. More specifically, Reformed theologians have associated the righteousness of God with the obedience of Christ that is imputed to Christians and upon which the justifying verdict is rendered. The typical New Perspective understanding breaks this connection; it views the righteousness of God as not the sort of thing that can be imputed to another, because the righteousness of the judge is a very different thing from the righteousness of a plaintiff or defendant.

Paul's use of *righteousness* language is a large question and the subject of much recent scholarly debate; however, this chapter is not the forum for a detailed interaction with various writers' proposals. Another chapter in this volume pursues this discussion, and a number of other competent scholars have provided rigorous critiques of the New Perspective view of the righteousness of God.[25] In the remainder of this chapter, I offer an exegetical defense of the idea that the righteousness of God comes to be identified with the active obedience of Christ by the apostle Paul. By looking in particular at Romans, therefore, I hope to establish one important line of biblical evidence for the doctrine of active obedience.

What does it mean to be declared righteous, that is, justified? Is the Christian's righteousness simply a matter of his covenant status, as suggested by New Perspective proponents? Paul's use of *righteousness* language is not consistent with this claim, as is evident straightaway upon Paul's introduction of the righteousness theme in Romans. Immediately after announcing that the righteousness of God is revealed in the gospel (1:16–17), Paul writes that "the wrath of God is being revealed from heaven against all ungodliness and *unrighteousness* [ἀδικίαν] of men who by their *unrighteousness* [ἀδικία] suppress the truth" (v. 18). Paul, therefore, speaks of unrighteousness in moral terms, indicating that righ-

25. For example, see Stephen Westerholm, *Perspectives Old and New on Paul: The 'Lutheran' Paul and His Critics* (Grand Rapids, MI: Eerdmans, 2004), chap. 15; Mark A. Seifrid, "Righteousness Language in the Hebrew Scriptures and Early Judaism," in *Justification and Variegated Nomism*, vol.1, *The Complexities of Second Temple Judaism* (Tübingen: Mohr Seibeck/Grand Rapids, MI: Baker, 2001), 415–42. On Paul's use of righteousness language, see Mark A. Seifrid, "Paul's Use of Righteousness Language against Its Hellenistic Background," in *Justification and Variegated Nomism*, vol. 2; *The Paradoxes of Paul*, ed. D. A. Carson, Peter T. O'Brien, and Mark A. Seifrid (Tübingen: Mohr Siebeck/Grand Rapids, MI: Baker, 2004), 39–74.

teousness has to do with moral activity and not just covenant status.[26] Furthermore, when Paul speaks about the righteousness that does *not* justify, he speaks in moral terms and not in terms of being in or out of the covenant. For example, in Titus Paul says that we are justified by grace (3:7), "not because of works done by us in *righteousness* [δικαιοσύνη]" (3:5). Likewise, what does not justify is their own righteousness [τὴν ἰδίαν δικαιοσύνην] (Rom. 10:3) or "a righteousness of my own" [ἐμὴν δικαιοσύνην] (Phil. 3:9). In context this personal kind of righteousness is one that is pursued zealously, by doing (Rom. 9:31; 10:2, 5), by zealous efforts according to the law (Phil. 3:5–6). And again the verdict that "none is *righteous* [δίκαιος], no, not one" (Rom. 3:10), is demonstrated by the immoral behavior of all people (Rom. 3:11–18) and ends with the verdict that no flesh shall be justified [δικαιωθήσεται] by works of the law (Rom. 3:20).

The Pauline answer to the plight that no one is righteous and therefore that one's own righteousness cannot justify is the *righteousness of God* (δικαιοσύνη θεοῦ). This is evident in most of the passages referenced in the preceding paragraph. The great contrast with the unrighteousness of men (Rom. 1:18) is the gospel's revelation of the *righteousness of God*, such that the righteous will live by faith (1:16–17). The dramatic transition from Romans 3:20 to 3:21 is similar: no one is righteous and hence no flesh shall be justified by works of the law (3:10, 20), "But now the *righteousness of God* [δικαιοσύνη θεοῦ] has been manifested apart from the law, although the Law and the Prophets bear witness to it—the *righteousness of God* [δικαιοσύνη θεοῦ] through faith in Jesus Christ for all who believe" (Rom. 3:21–22). Likewise in Romans 10:3: those seeking to establish their own righteousness were those who did not submit to the *righteousness of God*, of which they were ignorant. Philippians 3:9 also makes such a contrast. Paul no longer wishes to have his own righteousness, but *the righteousness from God* (τὴν ἐκ θεοῦ δικαιοσύνην). Finally, a passage not mentioned in the previous paragraph but also speaking of the righteousness of God in the context of justification is 2 Corinthians 5:19–21.

Paul is clear, then, that the righteousness of God is the answer to our inability to be justified by our own righteousness. Nearly all of the passages cited above explicitly associate this righteousness of God with justification by grace through faith. Thus, if our problem is lack of righteousness, understood in moral terms, then the righteousness of God must provide the solution. What then is this righteousness of God and how does it provide for our lack of righteousness in justification? Two

26. See pertinent comments by Waters, *Justification*, 137, which consider inconsistencies in Wright's presentation at this point.

passages just mentioned, Philippians 3:9 and 2 Corinthians 5:21, speak very significantly of the righteousness of God for our justification coming to us "in Christ." The righteousness of God provides for our lack of righteousness only through Christ and his work. Christ mediates and communicates the righteousness of God.

Paul describes in more detail what this means in Romans 5:16–19. Here he speaks specifically of our righteousness as the obedience of Christ, the Second Adam. That Paul's concern in this pericope is with justification and the covenant of works is clear. In 5:16 he states that the gift brought δικαίωμα, justification, in contrast to κατάκριμα, condemnation. The references to Adam, transgression, the disobedience of the one, and death draw readers' minds to the covenant of works at creation. Verse 17 of chapter 5 begins with γὰρ (for), indicating that verse 17 explains what the justification mentioned in 5:16 entails. Paul says that those who reign in life through Christ are those who receive the gift of δικαιοσύνη: justification, then, according to Paul, consists in receiving δικαιοσύνη as a gift. A number of commentators understand this δικαιοσύνη as a reference to the Christian's status as righteous.[27] As considered above, however, our predicament in regard to righteousness concerns our moral uprightness, not our status *per se*. Paul speaks not of a gift of *justification*, which might indeed refer to a gift of the status of being righteous. He speaks instead of a gift of righteousness, a provision of the moral rectitude that we lack in ourselves. Given all that Paul says elsewhere, this gift of righteousness must be the righteousness of God in Christ, somehow bestowed upon us.[28]

Romans 5:18–19 confirms this interpretation. In 5:18, Paul says that justification of life comes through "one act of righteousness" (ἑνὸς δικαιώματος).[29] This "one act of righteousness," then, apparently defines what the "gift of righteousness" in 5:17 is—and this makes perfect

27. E.g., see Douglas J. Moo, *The Epistle to the Romans* (Grand Rapids, MI: Eerdmans, 1996), 339; Thomas R. Schreiner, *Romans* (Grand Rapids, MI: Baker, 1998), 286; and Leon Morris, *The Epistle to the Romans* (Grand Rapids, MI: Eerdmans, 1988), 237.

28. This is the view defended by Murray, *Romans*, 1:198.

29. This phrase presents two difficult issues of translation. First, on the definition of δικαιώματος as "act of righteousness" rather than "justification," as in 5:16, see Murray, *Romans*, 1:200–201. Morris, *Romans*, 239, takes the opposite view. Second, assuming the definition of "act of righteousness," whether the translation should read "one act of righteousness" or "the act of righteousness of the one" is grammatically ambiguous. The latter translation would seem to be supported by the widely accepted idea that 5:18 finishes the comparison begun in 5:12 but suspended through verses 13–17; the emphasis in 5:12 is on the one man who sinned rather than on the oneness of the sin. If this translation is adopted, the objection to taking this verse in support of the doctrine of active obedience considered in the next section is certainly weakened. I am willing to assume the former translation because 5:18 teaches active obedience one way or the other.

sense in light of the idea of righteousness as moral rectitude, considered above.[30] Paul then becomes most specific in 5:19: the righteous act that we receive as a gift of righteousness is none other than the obedience of the one. The many are constituted[31] righteous through the obedience of Christ. Hence, in summary, Paul asserts that a gift brings justification (5:16), this gift is a gift of righteousness (5:17), this gift of righteousness focuses upon one righteous act (5:18), and this righteous act is the obedience of the one man, Jesus Christ (5:19).

Perhaps the more likely reading of 5:18 contrasts the "one trespass" that brings condemnation with the "one act of righteousness" that brings justification.[32] Objectors note that reference to "one" act seems inconsistent with the idea that Paul was pointing to Christ's active obedience, and therefore they believe that the scope is limited to the crucifixion, understood, in their view, as his passive obedience.[33] A number of considerations, however, indicate that this reference proclaims the fullness of Christ's obedience and not the crucifixion alone. First is the implausibility of the objectors' own interpretation. Was the crucifixion itself really *one* act of Christ? Insofar as Christ submitted himself to this fate and interacted with his Father and those around him, the crucifixion was a series of actions rather than a single act. Also, if one desires to see the imputation of *passive* obedience taught in this passage, surely it must be admitted that Christ's passive obedience was no more a single act than his active obedience, since he suffered throughout his life and thereby learned obedience in order to become a perfect high priest (e.g., Heb. 2:10, 17–18; 5:7–10). To see Christ's active obedience in Romans 5:18 involves no more conceptual difficulty than seeing his passive obedience in general or the crucifixion in particular. There must have been some

30. This claim is in contrast to a number of commentators who do not associate the gift of righteousness with the one righteous act; e.g., see James D. G. Dunn, *Romans 1–8*, vol. 38a, *Word Biblical Commentary* (Dallas: Word, 1988), 283, though he does not explain his reasons for this conclusion.

31. On the forensic meaning of this term, see, e.g., Moo, *Romans*, 345. Murray, *Collected Writings*, 2:214–15, speaks of this in terms of union with Christ and therefore as richer than imputation, but also demands that the term be taken as strictly forensic. Schreiner, *Romans*, 288, does not so limit it.

32. On the different possible translations of this verse, see footnote 29 above.

33. Dunn, *Romans*, 283–84, is clear on this point; Moo, *Romans*, 344, and Schreiner, *Romans*, 287–88 agree tentatively. Wright, though rejecting the idea of active obedience, takes a somewhat broader view of Paul's reference than simply the crucifixion; see N. T. Wright, *The Letter to the Romans*, in vol. 10, *The New Interpreter's Bible* (Nashville: Abingdon, 2002), 529. Both Wright and Dunn say that Paul "almost certainly" does not speak of active obedience in this passage. Norman Shepherd, without any qualifications, restricts the reference in 5:18–19 to Christ's "sacrifice of atonement"; see "Justification by Faith in Pauline Theology," 88–89.

reason for Paul's emphasis on the oneness of Christ's righteous action other than the isolation of a single discrete event.

Much more plausible is Murray's suggestion that the one act ought to be seen as the whole of Christ's obedience in its "compact unity."[34] An initial consideration in support of Murray's interpretation is the analogy between Adam and Christ. In 5:18, this analogy is obvious and cannot be denied, as is the case in 5:15–19 more generally. What significance does this have for understanding the reference to Christ's obedience? Dunn argues that interpreting Christ's one act as comprehensive breaks the comparison to Adam,[35] but the opposite in fact seems to be the case. Paul, of course, establishes both similarity and dissimilarity between Adam and Christ in these verses. While the similarity seems to lie in the mode of representation by which Adam and Christ have brought death/condemnation and life/justification to the many, dissimilarity lies in the fact that Christ gained for us "much more" (5:17) than Adam lost.

But God required of Adam perfect obedience, not mere moral guiltlessness. Adam was born guiltless and continued in that state for a time, but God demanded a positive obedience to his law, the passing of a probationary test, for Adam to attain true life and judicial approbation. If Christ indeed came as the Second Adam to succeed where Adam failed, and brought in much more than Adam lost, then seeing simply passive obedience in 5:18 and surrounding verses seems radically insufficient. Christ's passive obedience brings no more than moral guiltlessness, a condition that Adam once enjoyed but that was not enough for life and justification. In context, the "righteous act" of Christ surely cannot be dissociated from the positive righteous obedience that Adam was required by God to accomplish in the garden.[36]

Other considerations also support Murray's suggestion that Paul refers to Christ's obedience in its "compact unity" in Romans 5:18. For example, if Paul did have Christ's death particularly in mind in 5:18, this hardly constitutes reason to eliminate active obedience from this passage. Christ's death may well have been at the forefront of Paul's thoughts. Paul and many other biblical writers speak of the cross as *the* great act of Christ's earthly ministry on our behalf, and the immediately preceding context provides an example of this (Rom. 5:8, 10). However, the crucifixion itself was part of Christ's active obedience, a supreme demonstration of his love

---

34. Murray, *Romans*, 1:200–202.

35. Dunn, *Romans*, 283–84.

36. This point needs to be affirmed, I believe, against Robert H. Gundry's claim, in regard to Romans 5:12–19, concerning "the absence of any contextual indication that Christ's obedience included a previous life of obedience to the law"; see Robert H. Gundry, "The Nonimputation of Christ's Righteousness," in *Justification: What's at Stake in the Current Debates*, ed. Mark Husbands and Daniel J. Treier (Downers Grove, IL: InterVarsity, 2004), 32.

for God and neighbor. In addition, the importance of the crucifixion can only be understood in the light of a number of other passages—Pauline and otherwise—that describe the cross as the *climax* of a course of obedience extending throughout his entire earthly life and encompassing his fulfillment of every aspect of the law.

The Gospels present such a picture of the relation of Christ's death with his previous ministry. Luke 9:51, for example, speaks of Christ fixing his face to go to Jerusalem (surely an allusion to Isa. 50:7). Little more than one-third of the way through this Gospel, Luke begins to portray specifically the death of Christ as the goal toward which his long course of obedience was pointing in the face of great temptation to divert from it. Christ's crucifixion was not an isolated act, but the climax of the whole.

Paul's own testimony on this point is perhaps best seen in Philippians 2:8. Here Paul writes that Christ became obedient $\mu\acute{\epsilon}\chi\rho\iota$ $\theta\alpha\nu\acute{\alpha}\tau\sigma\upsilon$, *unto* death. The text does not allow this obedience to be identified with or isolated in the crucifixion. Instead, as an obedience *unto* death, the crucifixion must be seen as the end or climax of a longer course of obedience. Where did this obedience begin? Whether the first action of Christ referred to in 2:7 ("he emptied himself," AT) refers to his incarnation or death,[37] the other two actions described here surely refer to the incarnation. Christ's obedience, then, began at the very inception of his human existence, and his death brought it to its dramatic completion.[38]

More generally Philippians 2:5–11 offers helpful confirmation of the idea at work throughout this section, namely, that Christ offered a true human obedience that was accepted by the Father and earned an eschatological reward. Verses 7–8 meditate upon Christ's obedience in his emptying himself, taking the form of a servant, being found in appearance as a man, and humbling himself. These verses climax with the affirmation that Christ became *obedient* ($\dot{\upsilon}\pi\acute{\eta}\kappa\sigma\varsigma$) "unto death, even the death of the cross" (KJV). Verses 9–11 proceed to reflect upon the Son's exaltation following his obedience. God exalted him and gave him the name above every name in order that every knee might bow before him and every tongue confess Christ as Lord.

Crucial for the present discussion is that Paul makes the exaltation the consequence of the obedience and the obedience the cause of the exalta-

37. On this point, see Robert B. Strimple, "Philippians 2:5–11 in Recent Studies: Some Exegetical Conclusions," *WTJ* 41 (Spring 1979): 247–68.

38. Moo, *Romans*, 344, and Schreiner, *Romans*, 278–88, also cite Philippians 2:8 as a parallel to Romans 5:18. They refer to the former to argue that Paul had Christ's death principally in mind in the latter, but they do not seem to appreciate the context into which Paul places Christ's death in Philippians 2. Gundry, "The Nonimputation," 26, 31–32, takes a view similar to that of Moo and Schreiner but specifically to refute the idea of active obedience.

tion. Paul does this by connecting the conclusion of his description of Christ's obedience in 2:8 and the beginning of his description of Christ's exaltation with the strong causal conjunction διό: Christ "was obedient unto death, even the death of the cross, *therefore* God exalted him" (AT). God exalted Christ on the basis of his obedience.[39] Despite claims to the contrary by Federal Vision proponents,[40] therefore, Philippians 2 provides further evidence that Christ fulfilled the original task given to Adam—perfect obedience to the law. That obedience meant his exaltation and, in turn, our justification.

Conclusion

The active obedience of Christ is not a peripheral issue but rather a crucial matter for the Reformed system of doctrine. It touches not only upon the completed work of our Savior and the doctrine of justification, but also upon the character of God himself and the most fundamental obligations of man created in his image. Reformed churches and theologians have affirmed the active obedience of Christ zealously since the Reformation and, despite its current gainsayers, this doctrine remains of central importance for biblical Christianity. It is not a matter that the church can safely lay aside. For the sake of the teaching of Scripture, the glory of Christ, and the peace and assurance of believers, Reformed Christians must renew their affirmation of this doctrine and take up its defense all the more clearly in the midst of the current controversies.

---

39. For further discussion of this passage in the context of similar issues, see David Van-Drunen and R. Scott Clark, "The Covenant Before the Covenants," in *Covenant, Justification, and Pastoral Ministry: Essays by the Faculty of Westminster Seminary California.*

40. See Lusk, "A Response," 137–38; and Jordan, "Merit Versus Maturity," 193. They claim that Philippians 2:9 does not permit the idea of Christ's meritorious earning of the reward, based upon the fact that Paul uses the word ἐχαρίσατο, which derives etymologically from the word for "grace," χάρις, to describe God's "giving" the name above every name to Christ. This argument commits what D. A. Carson calls the "root fallacy": "One of the most enduring of errors, the root fallacy presupposes that every word actually *has* a meaning bound up with its shape or its components. In this view, meaning is determined by etymology; that is, by the root or roots of a word." See *Exegetical Fallacies* (Grand Rapids, MI: Baker, 1984), 26–32. The precise meaning of the verb must be established in context, and the context of Philippians 2:9 is clearly one of "work rendered and value received." See Geerhardus Vos, *The Pauline Eschatology* (Grand Rapids, MI: Eerdmans, 1930; 1972), 275; and also Vos, "The Alleged Legalism," 398–99.

7

Covenant, Inheritance, and Typology

Understanding the Principles at Work in God's Covenants

R. FOWLER WHITE AND E. CALVIN BEISNER

Historians of doctrine call justification by faith alone—*sola fide*—the "material principle of the Reformation." Today, that doctrine, which continues under official Roman Catholic anathema, is under reappraisal and attack within evangelical circles and even within distinctly Reformed communities. Our saying so should not prompt you to look for articles in popular magazines or theological journals or on websites bearing titles like "Four Reasons Why I Renounce *Sola Fide*" or "A Biblical Critique of the Doctrine of Justification by Faith Alone." No, those who currently pose the greatest threat to *sola fide* do not explicitly reject the doctrine by name but affirm it while redefining its terms or, as the case may be, using traditional terms in non-traditional ways.

Sola fide and God's covenants. One area in which this redefinition has appeared is the doctrine of God's covenants, a doctrine to which, historically speaking, the Reformed doctrine of *sola fide* was directly conjoined. The importance of this conjunction should not be over-looked or underestimated. In point of fact, the apostle Paul himself makes this connection when he spells out his teaching on justification by faith in terms of the Abrahamic, the Mosaic, and the new covenants (Galatians 3–4; Romans 4; 2 Corinthians 3). Moreover, the apostle ties his exposition of justification explicitly to his doctrine of the two Adams (Romans 5), a fact that gave rise to such classic distinctives of covenant (i.e., federal) theology as the structuring of biblical revelation into the covenant of works and the covenant of grace and the doctrine of meritorious accomplishment in the covenant of works made with the first and Last Adams. Clearly, then, redefinition of the doctrine of God's covenants inevitably brings reformulation of the doctrine of justification.

Two streams of redefinition. And indeed just such a redefinition has emerged in two recent streams of research and publication. The one stream comes from those who promote the New Perspectives on Paul and the Mosaic Law, the other stream from those who support the effort initiated by the late John Murray to recast (reconstruct) classic covenant theology. As the available literature shows, each of these streams in its own way affects the way the conjunction of the doctrines of covenant and *sola fide* is to be interpreted.

A fresh exposition of God's covenants. We shall leave it to others to engage directly the crosscurrents that to one degree or another threaten to displace the Reformation doctrine of *sola fide*. This study has another purpose, namely, to provide a fresh exposition of God's covenantal deal-ings with man, one that conserves the classic features of historic cov-enant theology. In the process we hope to shed additional light on the relationship of the covenants of redemption, works, and grace with the Noahic, Abrahamic, Mosaic, and Davidic covenants by exploring that relationship in the light of the hermeneutic of typology. The impetus for this study comes from the typological shape given particularly by the apostle Paul to the relationship between Adam and Christ in Romans 5 and elsewhere. Our thesis is that two contrasting but compatible[1] prin-ciples of inheritance—namely, personal merit (i.e., merit grounded in the heir's own works) and representative merit (i.e., merit grounded in another's works)—are at work in each of these covenants and that these

1. As we hope to make clear, we construe the relationship between the principles as con-trasting but compatible because, agreeing with WCF 7.5–6, we affirm both the continuity of the one covenant of grace and the discontinuity between the administrations in the time of the law and in the time of the gospel. Both continuity and discontinuity should be accented as context requires, but neither should be accented at the expense of the other. The words *contrasting but compatible* are intended to express these two interests.

principles of inheritance have existed side-by-side through all of history (pre-fall and post-fall) until Christ, with the former always subserving the latter.[2]

The Covenant of Redemption: The Covenant of Works with Christ

Two principles of inheritance. The suprahistorical (eternal) covenant of redemption (e.g., John 4:34; 5:30; 6:38–40; Heb. 7:20–22, 28; 8:6; 10:7), which was established among God the Father, God the Son, and God the Spirit,[3] incorporated two contrasting but compatible principles of inheritance, one for the Son, the other for his elect seed. On the one hand, the everlasting inheritance of all things was promised and would be rendered to the Son (Heb. 1:2) as personally merited by his obedi-

2. We are aware that some writers object to the very concept and term *merit* in Christian soteriology, whether applied to sinners or to Christ. See Rich Lusk, "A Response to 'The Biblical Plan of Salvation,'" in *The Auburn Avenue Theology, Pros & Cons: Debating the Federal Vision*, ed. E. Calvin Beisner (Fort Lauderdale, FL: Knox Theological Seminary, 2004), 118–48, especially at 120, where Lusk writes, "when the Reformers threw out the medieval understanding of salvation, they should have gone the whole way and thrown out the antiquated concept of merit as well." See also James B. Jordan, "Merit Versus Maturity: What Did Jesus Do for Us?" in *The Federal Vision*, ed. Steve Wilkins and Duane Garner (Monroe, LA: Athanasius Press, 2004), 151–200. Convinced that these writers are mistaken, we uphold the concept of merit as biblically sound, implicit in, e.g., Romans 4:4: "to the one who works, his wage is not credited as a favor, but as what is due." See Richard A. Muller, *Dictionary of Latin and Greek Theological Terms Drawn Principally from Protestant Scholastic Theology* (Grand Rapids, MI: Baker, 1985), 190–192. John Calvin's bold remark, "'Merit,' an unscriptural and dangerous word!" (*Institutes*, 3.15.2, section heading) must be read in its context, 3.15 being titled "Boasting About the Merits of Works Destroys Our Praise of God for Having Bestowed Righteousness, as Well as Our Assurance of Salvation." Calvin's discussion in 3.15 makes it clear that he objects to *merit* as applied, particularly without careful qualification, to human works. Nonetheless, in that chapter and elsewhere he uses *merit* and *value* synonymously, and in 3.17.3 he writes, "of his own fatherly generosity and loving-kindness, and without considering their worth, [God] raises works to this place of honor, so that he attributes some value to them," while he titles 2.17 "Christ Rightly and Properly Said to Have Merited God's Grace and Salvation for Us" and there and elsewhere (2.7.8; 3.11.2; 3.15.6; 3.16.3) develops the notion of Christ's merit. (John Calvin, *Institutes of the Christian Religion*, 2 vols., trans. Ford Lewis Battles, ed. John T. McNeill [Philadelphia: Westminster Press, 1960], 1:356–7, 528, 726–7, 789, 793–94, 805–6.) The WCF undoubtedly takes the term and concept as legitimate; see 16.5; 17.2; 30.4. Turretin accepts the concept and term (see Francis Turretin, *Institutes of Elenctic Theology*, trans. George Musgrave Geiger, ed. James T. Dennison Jr. (Phillipsburg, NJ: P&R, 1992, 1994, 1997), 4.10.3; 8.3.16–17; 14.13.5; 17.5.1), while carefully qualifying its proper use in regard to works (17.5.1–45).

3. Though it is not our task to expound it here, our contention is that, to be truly intra-trinitarian, formulations of the covenant of redemption must take account of the work of all three Persons of the Godhead.

ence to his Father's will. On the other hand, the everlasting inheritance would also be rendered to the Son's elect seed (Isa. 53:10) as vicariously (representatively) merited for them by the Son's obedience and unilaterally imputed to them through faith in him. The Son was thus to obey his Father's will and thereby become the Heir of all things, including an innumerable seed who would become co-heirs with him. This covenant of redemption, being pre-creational, preceded and was archetypal of the covenant of works between God and Adam.[4] Indeed, Christ the Son in the covenant of redemption was archetypal of Adam in the covenant of

---

4. That the principle of inheritance by personal merit (meritorious works) originates not in the covenant of works but in the covenant of redemption refutes the objection that it is improper to posit merit on the part of the creature toward the Creator. The Father and the Son being equally God, it is proper to posit strict merit between them, and that is the case in the covenant of redemption. The covenant of redemption being archetype of the covenant of works, the merit principle in the latter is seen to be analogous, but not identical, to the merit principle in the former. The similarity between the two is that God (in the covenant of redemption, the Father toward the Son; in the covenant of works, the Trinity toward Adam) binds himself by his justice to reward a certain performance; the difference is that in the covenant of redemption the obligation is according to *strict justice* as between equals, the Father and the Son, and that covenant originates in *mutual agreement*, while in the covenant of works it is according to *covenantal justice* as between Superior and inferior (God and Adam), and that covenant is *sovereignly imposed* by the Superior (WCF 7.1: "The distance between God and the creature is so great, that although reasonable creatures do owe obedience unto Him as their Creator, yet they could never have any fruition of Him as their blessedness and reward, but by some voluntary condescension on God's part, which He hath been pleased to express by way of covenant."). N.b.: This distinction between strict and covenantal merit (and strict and covenantal justice) must not be confused with that between condign and congruent merit developed by medieval Roman Catholic scholastics. Condign merit was taken to be "full merit," i.e., merit fully equal to the reward rendered, while congruent merit was taken to be "half-merit," i.e., merit less than the reward rendered, the difference between reward and merit attributed to grace. (See Muller, *Dictionary of Latin and Greek Theological Terms*, s.vv. *meritum de condigno* and *meritum de congruo* [191–92].) The whole congruent/condign merit distinction makes sense only within the larger scheme of infusionist justification. It is alien to the construct of imputationist justification that defines Reformation (and especially Reformed covenantal) soteriology. Among other problems with the infusionist scheme, it saw merit as something "deserving of grace"—an oxymoronic phrase incompatible with the biblical doctrine of grace as favor contrary to ill desert. In contrast, our distinction is between strict justice, possible between equal persons, and covenantal justice, which may be established—by the latter's condescension to promise reward for particular behavior—between a dependent person and one on whom he depends, though the dependent person owed such behavior even in absence of the covenant. It is crucial for the understanding of our distinction to note that, in this context, said condescension is not grace, for, though condescension is favor, it is not favor *contrary to ill desert*, but favor *in the absence of positive merit or desert* (i.e., in the absence of the fulfillment of righteous requirements). Rather, the obligation provisionally embraced by the independent party is a matter of justice because, while by nature the dependent party has no claim on the independent, the independent party obligates himself by promise should the dependent party fulfill the covenanted condition. See Turretin, *Institutes of Elenctic Theology*, 8.3.1–2.

works. As Adam's archetype, Christ was truly, according to the covenant of redemption, the God-man wounded "*before* the foundation of the world" for the creation of His bride.[5]

The Covenant of Works with Adam: the Covenant of Creation

Two principles of inheritance. The covenant of works (Gen. 2:15–17), which was instituted by God with Adam, the type[6] of Christ, and in Adam with all his seed (Rom. 5:14; 1 Cor. 15:45–49), also incorporated two contrasting but compatible principles of inheritance, one for Adam, the other for his seed. On the one hand, there was the principle of personal merit according to which the reward of everlasting life[7] was promised and would be rendered to Adam as merited by his obedience, or the punishment of everlasting death was threatened and would be rendered to Adam as merited by his disobedience. On the other hand, there was the principle of representative merit according to which the reward of everlasting life would be rendered to Adam's posterity as vicariously merited for them by Adam's obedience and unilaterally imputed to them, or the punishment of everlasting death would be rendered to Adam's posterity as vicariously and unconditionally merited for them by Adam's disobedience and unilaterally imputed to them.

Commission and commandments in Genesis 2:15–17. As we distinguish the principles of inheritance at work in the covenant of works with Adam, we should also distinguish therein the commission of Genesis 2:15 and the commandments of Genesis 2:16–17. According to Genesis 2:15, having fashioned Adam from dust and placed him in the garden of beauty and purity for community with himself (and his bride), the

5. The gift of the bride in Genesis 2:18–25 actually must precede the benedictory commission of Genesis 1:28 in time, inasmuch as 1:28 presupposes man as male and female. So the man truly qualified to fulfill the commission in 1:28 is the man already wounded for the creation of his wife in 2:18–25. (The "man wounded" will later be revealed as "the Lamb slain" and at that "the Lamb slain before the foundation of the world.")

6. The correspondences in Romans 5 have Adam's post-fall situation in view, while the correspondences in 1 Corinthians 15 have his pre-fall situation in view. N.b.: As we use the terms here, *archetype*, *type*, and *antitype* are related thus: the archetype is the original and prefigures both type and antitype; the type both fulfills the archetype and prefigures the antitype; and the antitype fulfills both the type and, indirectly through it, the archetype.

7. In other words, the reward promised for obedience was immortality. As we shall expound more fully below, the life given to Adam at creation was indeed life in fellowship with his Creator God. But as the divine commandment in Genesis 2:16–17 necessarily implies, God made his retention of that life subject to probation and death. Thus, the life promised to Adam for obedience to the divine commandment of Genesis 2:16–17 was life in fellowship with the Creator God and no longer subject to probation and death; it was, in a word, immortality. It was, if you will, "life upon life."

LORD God commissioned Adam, literally, "to serve and to keep" (AT), that is, in context with the stipulations of Genesis 2:16–17, to serve the LORD his God and to keep his commandments.[8] The stipulations of Genesis 2:16–17 clearly differ from the commission of Genesis 2:15. In the commandments, the Creator set before his creature the alternative issues of life and death, good and evil (compare Deut. 30:15–20), and made Adam's retention of the life and virtue that he had received at his creation explicitly contingent upon his obedience. The imposition of the commandments, however, did not, indeed could not, invalidate the commission. Rather, by means of the stipulations, the LORD God placed Adam on probation, and his successful standing of that probation would enable him to pass from a state of *peccable* and unconfirmed holiness—*posse peccare* and *posse non peccare*—to a state of impeccable and confirmed holiness—*non posse peccare*.[9] In this way, God made it clear to Adam (and his bride) that the only man qualified to fulfill Genesis 2:15 would be one who had proven to be *non posse peccare* according to Genesis 2:16–17.[10]

We must recognize, therefore, the difference between stipulation and commission in the covenant of works. On the one hand, the stipulations (commandments) were conditional, bilateral, and hence violable, obligating Adam to "do this or die"; the commission, on the other hand, was unconditional, unilateral, and hence inviolable.[11] In addition, we must recognize that the violable bilateral stipulations of Genesis 2:16–17 stood

8. The Hebrew construction here involves two infinitives (as translated above) or two gerunds ("for serving and for keeping"). See, e.g., U. Cassuto, *A Commentary on the Book of Genesis, Part I: From Adam to Noah, Genesis 1–6:8*, trans. Israel Abrahams, (Jerusalem: Magnes Press, 1989), 122–23. Even if we interpret the commission in 2:15 more narrowly as a mandate to work and to keep (guard) the holy garden, we must still recognize that the garden was there for man to develop and to guard as the *umbilicus mundi* from which to pursue the broader mandate to rule and fill the earth (1:28). The wording of WLC 20, in which God is said to have appointed Adam to "dress" the paradisal garden, is, in its context, not at odds with this conclusion.

9. Gerhardus Vos, *Biblical Theology: Old and New Testaments* (Grand Rapids, MI: Eerdmans, 1948), 22–23. Importing the language of Paul in 1 Corinthians 15:45–49 into this consideration, the probation was designed to enable Adam to move from his first, natural, earthly, protological state to his second and last, spiritual, heavenly, eschatological state.

10. It would be such a man and no other who would secure his posterity against apostasy. Adam was not that man, as all agree. Christ the Last Adam, having persevered in knowledge, righteousness, and holiness during his humiliation, secured for his posterity the gift of perseverance, and that irrevocably. Even before his apostasy, Adam was a type of Christ.

11. The commissions (2:15 and 1:28) are comparable to the effectual words of God in creation (1:3, 6, 9, 11, 14, 20, 24, 26, 28): words that ensure their own fulfillment. The stipulations (2:16–17) are comparable to the commandments issued on Sinai (Exod. 20:1–17): words morally obligating but not effectuating their fulfillment.

alongside the inviolable unilateral commission of Genesis 2:15 to subserve its fulfillment, not to nullify it.[12]

The Covenant of Grace

Two principles of inheritance. The covenant of grace (Gen. 3:15, etc.), which was instituted by God with his people[13] through Christ as mediator, also incorporates two contrasting but compatible principles of inheritance, one for Christ, the other for God's people. On the one hand, the covenant of grace incorporates a principle of inheritance by personal obedience in that Christ's role as mediator in the covenant of grace is founded on his obedience to the Lord's will, his faithfulness in serving his God and Father and in keeping God's commandments. On the other hand, the covenant of grace incorporates a principle of inheritance by representative merit in that Christ administers to the elect the everlasting inheritance on account of his obedience imputed to them.

The covenant of grace distinguished from the covenant of redemption. As the preceding comments imply, it is important to maintain the distinction between the covenant of grace and the covenant of redemption. The historical (temporal) covenant of grace was enacted on the basis of the suprahistorical (eternal) covenant of redemption (see, e.g., Heb. 10:7–10). That is, it is Christ's obedience to his Father's will, as stipulated in the covenant of redemption, that entitles him to function as mediator of blessing (salvation) and curse (judgment) in the covenant of grace. His appointment as mediator in the covenant of grace is the reward for his obedience to the stipulations of the covenant of redemption. Furthermore, Christ's role in the covenant of grace also has as its standard the eternal intratrinitarian covenant of redemption. That is, as Christ administers the covenant of grace in history, he mediates both blessing and curse according to the covenant of redemption: he mediates blessing to his elect and as such functions as their Savior and Head; he mediates curse to the reprobate and as such functions as their Judge.[14] The distinction, then, between the covenant of grace and the covenant of redemption is important, as it illuminates the

---

12. The relationship between stipulation and commission in the covenant of works will emerge again in the relationship of the Mosaic covenant (the law) to the Abrahamic covenant (the promise). See p. 157.

13. That is, his church, composed of believers and their seed, living under the authority and sanctions of Christ the Lord.

14. It is striking to realize that, in a crucial sense, the blessings to the elect include the curses on the reprobate. That is, according to texts like Genesis 12:3 and Deuteronomy 28:1–14, the curses on the reprobate are actually among the blessings to the elect. Defeat for the reprobate is victory for the elect; death for the reprobate is life for the elect.

fact that the covenant of redemption forms the basis and the standard for the Son's administration of God's covenant of grace with his people.

The covenant of grace in history. In light of the preceding, it also becomes clear that the covenant of grace is the historical context for the outworking of the suprahistorical covenant of redemption. Indeed, as the following discussion will seek to expound, before Christ's incarnation, it pleased God, more often than not (particularly in the post-flood era), to administer the covenant of grace in history through the mediation of certain believers whom he constituted as types of Christ, namely, Noah, Abraham, and David. In those administrations (as distinct from the administration of Moses),[15] God condescended to count the exemplary works of faith by Christ's types both as the ground of their appointment as mediators and as the ground of their posterity's special earthly and temporal blessing.[16] Thus, it is useful to keep in mind that, as God accomplishes the outworking of the suprahistorical covenant of redemption in the historical covenant of grace, he does so especially, though not exclusively,[17] through a series of typological mediators and administrations.[18]

The Seeds of Adam and Christ and the Two Principles of Inheritance

The likeness between the seeds of Adam and of Christ. Recognition that two principles of inheritance (personal merit and representative merit) are at work in each of the covenants of redemption, works, and grace sheds light not just on the likeness between Adam and Christ but also on the likeness between their seeds. That is, the relationship of Adam's seed (the whole human race naturally born) to God in the covenant of works was like the relationship of Christ's seed (the elect) to God in the covenants of redemption and grace. For both Adam's seed and Christ's

15. It is noteworthy that, though Moses is clearly a type of Christ and a covenant mediator (e.g., 2 Corinthians 3; Heb. 3:1–6), God does not count his exemplary works of faith as the ground of his appointment as mediator nor as the ground of his posterity's special earthly and temporal blessing. Indeed, Moses entreats the Lord not to do this out of deference for his oath to Abraham, Isaac, and Jacob (Exodus 32).

16. N.b.: The exemplary works of faith by these mediators did not and could not be counted as the ground of either their own or their posterity's heavenly and eternal blessing. Only Christ's (active and passive) obedience was sufficient for that purpose. See further under "Noah, Abraham, and David as Types of Christ," 155.

17. The era most conspicuous for the absence of a mediator, except as Christ had been made known in Genesis 3:15, was the era from Seth to Noah.

18. We see here that, from the perspective of the covenant of grace, Christ is the antitype of Adam in the covenant of works. We saw above that, from the perspective of the covenant of redemption, Christ is the archetype of Adam in the covenant of works.

seed, the inheritance of eternal life is conditioned on the obedience of their representative and is, therefore, procured vicariously for the seed by the meritorious works of another.[19] The crucial difference between the two seeds is, of course, that Adam failed to fulfill the condition for his seed and thus failed, as their representative, to merit eternal life for them, while Christ fulfilled the covenantal condition for his seed and thus did, as their representative, merit eternal life for them and pay the penalty for which they were liable due to Adam's (and their own) demerit.

Christ's success and Adam's failure. A closer look at the covenant of grace discloses still further how the two principles of inheritance are applied to rectify the effects of Adam's failure in the covenant of works. According to the covenant of grace, Christ, by his perseverance in uprightness, fulfilled all the legal requirements of the covenant of works[20] not only for himself but also for his posterity (the elect). In addition, by his perfect sacrifice of himself, Christ paid the penalty for disobedience demanded by God in the covenant of works not at all for himself but only for his posterity. Accordingly, in the covenant of grace there is a triple[21] imputation: God imputes Christ's righteousness in fulfilling the covenant of works (his active obedience) to the elect; he imputes the guilt of the elect (because of their breaking of the covenant of works) to Christ in his suffering (his passive[22] obedience); and he imputes the penal satisfaction of his justice by Christ to the elect.

Noah, Abraham, and David as Types of Christ and Lesser Antitypes of Adam

Types of Christ after Adam. What can we say about God's covenants with Noah (Genesis 6),[23] Abraham (e.g., Genesis 12), and David (2 Sam-

19. The representative merit or demerit imputed to Adam's heirs in the covenant of works comes to them as a matter of covenantal justice. The representative merit imputed to Christ's heirs in the covenants of grace and redemption comes to them as a matter not of justice in their regard but of grace. As for Christ himself, his active and passive obedience did, in fact, merit, as a matter of justice in his regard, the heirs' remission of sins and acceptance as righteous in God's sight (their justification).

20. Recall that these same legal requirements are instanced in the covenant of redemption.

21. It is customary to speak of the imputation of Christ's righteousness, subsuming under this rubric the imputation of both his active and his passive obedience. Here, because some deny the imputation of his active obedience and only affirm the imputation of his passive obedience, we distinguish the two explicitly.

22. The term *passive* in this context denotes not "inactive" but "suffering."

23. We cite the pre-flood covenant of Genesis 6 and not the post-flood covenant of Genesis 9 because only the former involved the two principles of inheritance. The covenant of Genesis 6:18–21 involved the principles of personal merit for Noah and of representa-

uel 7; Psalm 89), particularly as administrations of the covenant of grace? As for Noah, Abraham, and David, they were covenant representatives whom God constituted as lesser antitypes of Adam in the covenant of works and as types of Christ in the covenants of grace and redemption. As such, their (exemplary) obedience to the commandments of God[24] brought earthly and temporal (not heavenly and eternal) blessings to them and to their posterity. The seeds of Noah, Abraham, and David, thus, were related to their representatives in their respective covenants in a way closely analogous[25] to the way the seeds of Adam and of Christ were related to their representatives in the covenants of works, grace, and redemption. That is, the seed received[26] the blessings not because of their own obedience but because of the obedience of their divinely appointed representative.

The obedience of types after Adam. Although the seeds of Noah, Abraham, and David received inheritance blessings by reason of their union with their representatives, those blessings were only earthly and temporal and were accompanied by temporal curses. Why? Because the obedience of Noah, Abraham, and David, on the basis of which a given inheritance was promised, was neither perfect nor perpetual—nor could it have been. Their obedience, though exemplary as works of faith, fell short of the perfect and perpetual obedience required to secure exemption from earthly and temporal curses and to obtain heavenly and eternal inheritance for themselves or their posterity. That is, God did indeed bless the seeds without imposing any condition on them, solely on the condition of these fathers' obedience, but these fathers' obedience was deficient as both active and passive obedience. None could satisfy the requirements of righteousness in the covenant of works that would result in the justification and eternal

tive merit for his house in that God promised Noah and his house the temporal blessings of deliverance from the first world and entrance into a new world as a temporal reward grounded on the exemplary obedience of the one man Noah (Gen. 6:8–9, 22; 7:1, 5). By contrast, the benedictory commission of Genesis 9:1–7 and the covenant of Genesis 9:8–17 were unilateral and unconditional toward Noah, his sons, their descendants after them, and every living creature with them in that, wholly apart from considerations of either personal or representative merit, God promised them the temporal blessing of protection against future universal judgment by flood.

24. Noah: Gen. 6:8–9, 22; 7:1, 5; Abraham: Gen. 22:16–18; 26:4–5; 35:11–12; Deut. 4:37–38; 7:6–8; 9:4–6; 10:14–15; David: 2 Sam. 7:5–16; 22:21–25.

25. We say the relationships were "closely analogous" and not "identical" because the sin of Adam and the righteousness of Christ were imputed to their respective seeds. No such imputation took place in the covenants of Noah, Abraham, or David.

26. We must distinguish between the seed's *reception* of blessings and their *retention* of them. This is the same distinction we made in the case of Adam: he received blessings at creation; he would have retained (and eternalized) those blessings by standing his probation. We develop this point later in the chapter.

life of their seeds. Neither could any of these lesser antitypes of Adam pay the penalty for violation of the covenant of works, either for himself or for his posterity, since they were sinners.

The deficiency of Noah, Abraham, and David meant that only the Last Adam, Christ himself, as the final and only perfect antitype of Adam in the covenant of works, could provide by his mediation of the covenant of grace the special heavenly and eternal inheritance blessings for his seed. And this Christ did by fulfilling the covenant of works (his active obedience) and by bearing the penalty for their sin (his passive obedience).

The Relation of the Mosaic Covenant to the Abrahamic Covenant

The relation is not genealogical. How was the Mosaic covenant (Exodus 24; Deuteronomy, passim) related to the Abrahamic covenant? For one thing, it differed from it in that it was not related genealogically to it.[27] That is, the seed who would be heir of the Abrahamic promise was to come from Israel, not through Levi (via Moses), but through Judah (via David). Though the Levitical order, of which Moses was a member (Exod. 2:1–10; 6:16–27), was instituted as an administration of the promise in shadow and type,[28] it was not intended to produce the true heir of the promise. Instead, the heir was to be from the tribe of Judah as well as from the Melchizedekal order (Hebrews 7), and the Abrahamic covenant was instituted to anticipate the true Melchizedekal (Genesis 14) and Judahite (Genesis 49) administration of the promise. Accordingly, at the arrival of the true Heir, the administration of Moses and the Levitical order must pass into obsolescence.

The relation is pedagogical: it exposes their spiritual inability. If, however, the Mosaic covenant was not related genealogically to the Abrahamic covenant, how was it related to it? It was related to it pedagogically. This pedagogical function of the Mosaic covenant is presuppositional to Paul's typological argument in Galatians 3–4 (see also 2 Corinthians 3).[29] As a part of his exposition, the apostle exposes a great irony in Israel's emancipation: the redemption mediated through Moses (i.e., Levi) to the

27. In other words, the Mosaic covenant was related mechanically, not organically, to the Abrahamic covenant.

28. When we say that the Mosaic covenant was an administration of the promise (albeit Levitical, not Melchizedekal), we are affirming that the old covenant was an administration of the covenant of grace—though only in shadow and type. Thus, "[t]here are not . . . two covenants of grace, differing in substance, but one and the same, under various dispensations" (WCF 7.6).

29. Cf. W. A. Gage, *The Gospel of Genesis: Studies in Protology and Eschatology* (Winona Lake, IN: Carpenter, 1984), 36–38.

nation had delivered them from *physical* bondage to *physical* freedom, but had left them, nonetheless, in *spiritual* bondage. They were no longer slaves to Pharaoh, but they remained slaves to sin.

The irony of Israel's redemption was compounded by another irony: the covenant mediated through Moses to the nation after their redemption required them, as a people still in bondage to sin, to obey God's law from the heart (Deut. 6:6)—something they could not do in their natural condition. Moreover, that covenant was powerless to deliver those slaves from their slavery (death) and provided them no enablement (life) to satisfy its requirements (Deut. 5:28–29; 29:4; Gal. 3:21). Hence, as Paul put it, Mount Sinai bore children who were to be slaves in bondage to sin (Gal. 4:24–25; cf. 4:1–3). Born beset with original sin as a result of the imputation of Adam's sin, Israel was not morally competent (i.e., they were not free) to serve the LORD God and to keep his commandments. In addition, these sons of Sinai boasted in the sons of Levi—their priesthood, their sanctuary, and their sacrifices—even though the Levites, weakened by sin and death, could offer only a ceaseless cycle of sacrifices that could never take away sins. Accordingly, Israel was disqualified from being that righteous seed who would render to God the perfect, personal, and perpetual obedience, active and passive, as required by the law, and the law proved to be a covenant of condemnation, bondage, and death (2 Cor. 3:6–14; Rom. 7:10–11) that shut the nation up under sin (Gal. 3:22) and curse (Gal. 3:10).

The relation is pedagogical: it teaches the need for faith in the true Seed. In the face of Israel's sin, then, the Mosaic covenant functioned as God's pedagogue to reveal the people's spiritual inability, though it could not relieve it (Gal. 3:21–24). The law, however, also did something else as God's pedagogue: it shut the people up to faith (Gal. 3:22–24) in the redemptive work (Gal. 3:13) of the one true Seed of Abraham (Gal. 3:19) from the tribe of Judah and the order of Melchizedek (Gen. 14:18–20; 49:10; Ps. 110:4; Heb. 7:4–14). He it would be who would qualify as the righteous Seed, and to the righteousness of God through faith in that Seed the Law and the Prophets bore witness (Rom. 3:21–22). Indeed, the Mosaic covenant bore its pedagogical witness to that Heir through the offices of prophet, priest, and king and the promises, prophecies, ordinances, and types ("shadows") related thereto. Together these testified to the person and work of the true Seed who would be a prophet greater than Moses, a priest greater than Levi, a king greater than David.

The true Seed will be the true Prophet (greater than Moses). Thus, the nation's bondage to sin meant that, though mediated by Moses, the law had to await the appearance of the true Moses (Deut. 18:15), the Prophet who would lead God's people to spiritual liberty and who, according to the promise of a better covenant, would write his laws on their hearts and thus provide them the enablement that Moses and the law could not (Jer. 31:31–33; Heb. 8:10; 10:16; cf. Deut. 30:6–10).

The true Seed will be the true Priest (greater than Levi). Moreover, the nation's bondage to sin meant that the law had to await the appearance of the Melchizedekal Priest, sinless and immortal, who would offer that one sacrifice of himself to take away sins and to bring an end to the ceaseless cycle of sacrifices for sin, thereby to purify the sons of Levi and constitute the true nation of priests (Mal. 3:1–4).

The true Seed will be the true King (greater than David). Furthermore, the nation's bondage to sin meant that the law had to await the appearance of the true David, the Judahite King born under the law yet without sin, who would conquer sin and death and thereby make his nation, called from all peoples of the earth, secure and pure for fellowship with God.

The true Seed will be the true Israel. Still further, the nation's bondage to sin meant that though given in grace to them, the law had to wait for its perfect fulfillment, the appearance of the true Israel, who though tempted would render to God the active and passive obedience that satisfied his law. To that one Seed and him alone the administration of the promise in its heavenly and eternal antitypes would belong. This would be the case because that one Seed of Abraham, who alone would indeed be Heir of the promise according to the works of the law, would be justified by the law before God and would become a curse for the transgressors of the law to redeem them from its curse.

Listening to God's pedagogue, then, the sons of Sinai could look, in the Spirit and faith, beyond Sinai with its earthly sanctuary built by man to behold and boast of the heavenly sanctuary built by God, thereby becoming the sons of Zion, together with all who were sons of Abraham by faith, instead of flesh (see, e.g., Ps. 46:4; 1 Kings 8:27; Isa. 66:1; Heb. 11:13–16).

The two principles of inheritance. While awaiting the arrival of that Heir, the two principles of inheritance continued to apply as follows. On the one hand, the nation's *reception* of the inheritance of Canaan was administered unconditionally and unilaterally according to the principle of representative righteousness enunciated in the Abrahamic covenant (see Gen. 22:16–18; 26:5 with Deut. 4:37–38; 7:6–8; 9:4–6; 10:14–15). Thus, Israel received the earthly and temporal blessings of residence in the land according to the exemplary obedience of Abraham, not an obedience of their own.

On the other hand, to drive home the message that the justification of sinners was, from beginning to end, by grace alone through faith alone—"from faith to faith" (Rom. 1:17) in Christ alone (Acts 4:12; Tit. 3:5–6)—the nation's *retention* of the inheritance of Canaan would be administered conditionally and bilaterally according to the principle of their works of personal (including corporate) righteousness enunciated in the Mosaic covenant (see Lev. 18:5 with Deut. 6:25; 30:15–20). In other words, Israel would keep or lose the *earthly and temporal blessings* of residence in the land according to their own obedience. In fact, as we shall expound more fully below, God would drive home the lesson of both principles by treating the nation according to their representatives' (especially the kings') conduct (e.g., 2 Sam. 12–24; 1 Chron. 21; Neh. 9:34–36; Isa. 43:27–28).

Given the nation's and their representatives' consistent failure, they ought thereby to learn that, if they were ever to receive and retain the *heavenly and eternal* blessings of rest in Abraham's promised homeland (Heb. 11:10, 14–16), they must find the obedience that satisfied the law in that one Seed from the tribe of Judah and from the order of Melchizedek who, greater than Abraham, could stand in their place, even becoming sin for them that they might be made the righteousness of God in him (2 Cor. 5:21).

In this light, we see more clearly how the bilateral, conditional, and hence violable Mosaic covenant (the Law) came in alongside (Rom. 5:20) the unilateral, unconditional, and hence inviolable Abrahamic covenant (the promise) to subserve (not nullify, Gal. 3:17) its fulfillment in the one true righteous Seed. Adapting the apostle Paul's idiom more completely, the Law of Moses was not contrary to the promise of Abraham but was added alongside it to increase transgression so that, where sin increased and reigned in death, even so grace might abound all the more and reign through righteousness to eternal life through that one Seed of Abraham who was to come. To him the law testified as God's pedagogue for the many sinful seed that they might be justified by faith in him, and only thus.

The Relation of the Mosaic (Old) Covenant to the New Covenant

One covenant of grace, two administrations. Our reference earlier to the replacement of the Levitical order by the Melchizedekal order raises the issue of the relationship between the Mosaic covenant and the new covenant. In summary, we affirm that, as for continuity, "[t]here are not . . . two covenants of grace, differing in substance, but one and the same, under various dispensations."[30] We also affirm that, as for discontinuity, the one covenant of grace "was differently administered in the time of the law, and in the time of the gospel."[31]

30. WCF 7.6.
31. WCF 7.5. More completely, the old covenant is simply the covenant of grace "in the time of the law," "administered by promises, prophecies, sacrifices, circumcision," etc., "all

Two administrations, one everlasting law of God. We must be clear that the two covenants do have their continuity. First, they are both administrations of the everlasting law of God (Jer. 31:31–33). That is, the old commandment of love for God and neighbor (Deut. 6:5; Lev. 19:18) is the new commandment as well (Matt. 22:34–40; John 13:34; 14:15; 15:10). The law taught at the beginning of the ages in Eden and thereafter at Sinai is the same law taught now at the end of the ages from Zion (1 John 2:7; 3:11–12 with Heb. 12:18, 22).[32] The tablets of the commandments housed in the tabernacle of Moses are the tablets of the commandments housed in the temple of Solomon. The words issued from the summit of Sinai and engraved on tablets of stone are the words placed in the ark at the summit of Zion and inscribed on tablets of flesh in the heart of the believer. The Law of Moses, as the law of love (Rom. 13:8–10), is the law of Christ. The ten words of Sinai are, thus, the ten words of Zion.

Two administrations, one everlasting gospel of God. As we indicated above, the two covenants also have continuity as administrations of the everlasting gospel of God. The ministries of word and deed under each covenant made known the gospel of God's sovereign saving grace. Israel's exodus and conquest are two examples of this continuity. The redemption of Israel-according-to-the-flesh from physical slavery in Pharaoh's kingdom was a typological revelation of the redemption of Israel-according-to-the-Spirit from spiritual slavery in Satan's kingdom of sin and death. When Israel under the law offered the Passover lamb—a lamb without fleshly spot or blemish—as a ceremonial reminder of their deliverance from Egypt, that annual event was exemplifying the gospel of Christ, who, as the true Israel and the greater Passover Lamb without spiritual spot or blemish (1 Cor. 5:7; 1 Pet. 1:19; John 1:29), poured himself out in death for his people (Isa. 53:12; Heb. 2:10–13; Rev. 5:6–9) and thereby brought about the new and true exodus (Luke 9:31; Matt. 1:21).

The entry of the first Israel into the earthly land of promise was also a typological revelation of the entry of the true Israel into their heavenly land of promise (Heb. 11:16; 12:18–24). Israel's exodus generation had the gospel of God's promise of rest in earthly Canaan preached to them. Even so, subsequent generations of the church, exemplified in David and

---

foresignifying Christ to come" (WCF 7.5), while the new covenant is simply the covenant of grace "under the gospel, when Christ . . . was exhibited," in which time the covenant of grace is administered in "the preaching of the Word, and the administration of the sacraments of baptism and the Lord's Supper" (WCF 7.6; cf. Heb. 7–9, 12:24; Matt. 26:28 [Mark 14:24; Luke 22:20]; 1 Cor. 11:25; 2 Cor. 3:6), so that "There are not therefore two covenants of grace, differing in substance, but one and the same, under various dispensations" (WCF 7.6).

32. The "mountain of God" motif was present in Eden (Ezek. 28:14, 16), and thus the law of God issued therein was given at that site.

his generation (Psalm 95) and in the author of Hebrews and his read-ers (see Heb. 4:1–13; 12:25–29), have had the gospel of God's promise of rest in the new Canaan (new earth) preached to them. The lessons taught in the exodus and the conquest were taught more generally in the ministries of word and deed in both the Mosaic covenant and the new covenant, and in them we can see that each covenant made known the same gospel of God.

The new administration better than the old. The continuity of the two covenants ought not, however, to obscure their discontinuity. Whereas the old covenant proved to be a covenant of condemnation, bondage, and death, the new covenant is a covenant of justification, liberty, and life (2 Cor. 3:6–14; Rom. 5:16–20; 7:10–11). Whereas the old covenant was a pedagogical covenant of shadow that made known the gospel of God's sovereign saving grace in the sufferings and glory of the Messianic Seed to come (Luke 24:26–27, 44–47), the new covenant is a covenant of reality in which the pedagogy of the old covenant has reached its historical realization in the antitypes associated with the new covenant ministry of the Messiah. Whereas the old covenant was enacted on the violable oath of Israel to the LORD (Exod. 20:18–21; Deut. 5:2–5), the new covenant is a covenant enacted on an inviolable oath of the LORD to Jesus, the One who kept what the many violated (Heb. 7:20–22, 28; 8:6). Taken together, these developments leave little room for wonder that the Scriptures say of Jesus that he "has become the guarantee of a better covenant" and "has obtained a more excellent ministry, by as much as he is also the mediator of a better covenant, which has been enacted on better promises" (Heb.7:20, 22; 8:6).

Two administrations of the Abrahamic promise. In light of what we have said above, it becomes clearer that the two covenants are, in fact, two contrasting but compatible administrations of the Abrahamic promise (Gal. 3:15–20; cf. 4:24–26). The old covenant administered the promised earthly and temporal typological inheritance according to "the righteousness of the law," that is, according to the personal (including corporate) righteous works of the seed of Abraham (Exod. 19:4–6; Lev. 18:5; Deut. 6:25; 30:15–20). Of this truth, the apostle could hardly have been clearer: "the Law is not of faith; on the contrary, 'He who practices them shall live by them'" (Gal. 3:12 NASB); and again, "For Moses writes about the righteousness which is of the law, that the man who does those things shall live by them" (Rom. 10:5 KJV). The apostle's point is that the one Seed of Abraham to whom the inheritance was promised was the Man who would satisfy the law's demands. Until such a Man was sent by God, the law justified no one according to his own works, and so the many seed of Abraham came under the law's curse and forfeited the earthly and temporal inheritance (Gal. 3:10–11).

Justification and inheritance before Christ. Yet, while waiting for God's Man to come, none needed to despair of either justification or inheritance. They needed only to follow in the footsteps of father Abraham to find a righteousness better than their own and an inheritance better than Canaan. After all, Abraham believed God and it was imputed to him as righteousness (Gal. 3:6; Rom. 4:9–12), so that he became an heir of the promised heavenly and eternal antitypical inheritance (Heb. 11:16) according to "the righteousness of faith" (Rom. 10:6; Phil. 3:9; cf. Heb. 11:7), that is, according to the imputed righteousness of his one righteous Seed. Likewise, as by faith Abraham had found a righteousness better than his own and an inheritance better than Canaan, so by faith could his many seed.

Justification and inheritance after Christ. In the fullness of time, God did at last send his own Son to become the Man who would satisfy the law's requirements and would redeem the many unrighteous seed of Abraham from the law's curse, having become a curse for them. Enacted on Christ's obedience, the new covenant continued and brought to culmination the historical administration of the Abrahamic promise according to the principle of imputed representative righteousness, even as it brought to conclusion (obsolescence) the historical administration of that promise according to the principle of personal righteousness. Consequently, as many in Israel as believed as father Abraham had believed would themselves receive and retain a better inheritance always and solely on the same basis as he did, namely, Christ's righteousness imputed to them through faith (Rom. 10:4–10; Gal. 3:10–14).[33] And, what is more, with the enactment of the new covenant, the principle of representative righteousness according to which Abraham and the remnant of Israel[34] were justified would also be applied to all the nations.

33. At this juncture we gain greater clarity on two important points. First, though the Mosaic and the new covenants administered the Abrahamic covenant according to two contrasting principles (the first, personal merit; the second, representative merit), the two principles were compatible in that they both bore witness to the one true Heir of Abraham. The first bore witness (in type) to him as the one Man who would be justified by the works of the law, and the second bore witness (in antitype) to him as the One whose works of the law will justify the many who have faith in him. Second, the error of Paul's opponents was not that they misinterpreted Moses by mistakenly believing that he had written of the righteousness of the law. No, in fact, Moses had so written. Their error was that they did not listen to Moses when he contrasted the righteousness of the law with the righteousness of faith. They misapplied the righteousness of the law to the reception and retention of the heavenly and eternal inheritance, when that righteousness applied only to the retention of the earthly and temporal inheritance. In other words, the error of Paul's opponents was that they sought the heavenly and eternal inheritance by the righteousness of the law, neglecting the fact that that inheritance was only attainable by the righteousness of faith (cf. Rom. 9:30–10:11).

34. Of course, even before the enactment of the new covenant, justification according to the principle of representative righteousness did not apply exclusively to Abraham and the remnant

The Relation of the Mosaic Covenant to the Covenant of Works with Adam

If the Mosaic covenant subserved the Abrahamic administration of the covenant of grace as we have described, how was the Mosaic covenant related to the covenant of works with Adam? To answer this question, let us begin by considering the similarities and differences between Israel and Adam.

Israel like Adam. As it was with Adam at his creation, so it was with Israel at its creation: unilateral, unmerited divine benediction[35] marked the start of the nation's history. There can be no doubt that Adam was created and commissioned in a state of benediction. He was blessed to be fruitful and to rule the earth (Gen. 1:28) as well as to serve the LORD his God and to keep his commandments (Gen. 2:15). Likewise, Israel, the national son of God, was fruitful and multiplied according to the blessing of the God of Abraham, Isaac, and Jacob, and, as a result, the land of Egypt was filled with them (Exod. 1:7 with Gen. 1:28). Similarly, Israel's king, also the son of God (2 Sam. 7:14; Ps. 2:7), was appointed to rule the nations of the earth, again according to the blessing of the God of the fathers (Gen. 49:10 with Gen. 1:28).

Israel unlike Adam. Yet Israel also was unlike Adam. Whereas Adam was blessed to rule and multiply while in a state of virtue (upright), Israel was blessed to rule and multiply while in a state of sin (fallen). How, then, are we to account for Israel's blessedness? Strikingly, the nation's blessed state is traced not to the nation itself, but to a representative. Moses made it clear to Israel that they were the fulfillment of God's promise to bless Abraham with seed, and their king was the fulfillment of his promise to bless Abraham with rule, as a reward for his exemplary obedience (Deut. 4:37–38; 7:6–8; 9:4–6; 10:14–15; cf. Gen. 22:16–18; 26:4–5; 35:11–12). Moreover, in those same texts, Moses also declared to Israel that they were to receive the blessings of exodus from Egypt and entry into Canaan,

---

in Israel. There were remnants in the earth before Abraham (e.g., Abel, Noah) and also from outside of Israel (e.g., Rahab, Ruth) who became heirs according to the righteousness of faith.

35. Adam's state of benediction before the fall was unmerited (unconditional and unilateral) but it was not gracious, because Adam had no sin and hence no demerit. Conversely, Israel's state of benediction at her redemption from Egypt was unmerited (unconditional and unilateral) and gracious, because they indeed had sin and hence demerit. The term *grace* presupposes the state of sin and demerit brought about by the fall. To speak of the original covenant with Adam as gracious materially alters the meaning of the term *grace* as it develops in Scripture. Grace is not simply favor in the absence of positive merit or desert, that is, in the absence of the fulfillment of righteous requirements. Grace is favor in the presence of demerit or negative desert, that is, in the presence of the transgression of righteous requirements. Thus, to teach that the Adamic covenant did not differ in substance or principle from the covenant of grace is to compromise the Scriptural doctrine of grace.

not because of their own merits, but because of the merits of the fathers, principally Abraham. Simply put, they were to receive these blessings initially despite their sin and for the fathers' sake.

Our point is that Israel was like Adam insofar as the nation, with their king, was the blessed son of God by the unconditional and unilateral benediction of the LORD. Israel was unlike Adam, however, insofar as Adam was blessed in his original state of sinlessness, while the nation, with its king, was blessed despite its original state of sinfulness and according to the principle of representative righteousness. Beyond the analogy of their blessedness at their creations, however, the correspondences between Adam and Israel are still more extensive.

Benediction and commission to Israel. We introduced the point earlier that, having been created in God's image and placed in the garden of beauty and purity for community with his Creator and his bride, Adam received divine benediction and commissions in Genesis 1:28 and 2:15. In Genesis 2:16–17, however, the LORD God gave stipulations to Adam, and according to those commandments he would retain the life and virtue he had received at his creation. In this way, God made it clear to Adam and his bride that the man qualified to fulfill Genesis 1:28 and 2:15 would be one who had proven to be *non posse peccare* according to Genesis 2:16–17. The violable bilateral stipulations of Genesis 2:16–17, therefore, stood alongside the inviolable unilateral commissions of Genesis 1:28 and 2:15 to subserve their fulfillment, not to nullify them.

The state of affairs just described for Adam is, *mutatis mutandis*, applicable to Israel, reflecting the relationship of the Mosaic covenant (the law) to the Abrahamic covenant (the promise). Having formed Israel as a new creation (Deut. 32:11–14 with Gen. 1:2; 2:1–3) and having promised to place the nation in the garden land of Canaan (e.g., Num. 24:5–6), the LORD gave to Israel, as He had given to Adam, a special commission in the form of commandments. The LORD their Redeemer commanded Israel to imitate his holiness in their character and conduct (Lev. 19:2). In his commandments, the LORD set before Israel the alternative issues of life and death, prosperity and adversity, victory and defeat, possession and dispossession. He also made those issues explicitly dependent on the nation's own righteousness and unrighteousness (e.g., Deut. 30:15–20 with Lev. 18:5). By giving Israel the law, then, God placed the nation, blessed but sinful, on probation in the land, and their successful standing of that probation would enable them to learn obedience (Deut. 5:1; 6:1–2) and thus pass from the minority status of children, in which they did not differ from slaves, into the majority status of sons.

Benediction and commission to Israel's king. After the same fashion, having established the son of David as Israel's king and having appointed him to inherit the nations, the LORD also commanded him to rule his people and their enemies according to his law (Deut. 17:18–20; 2 Sam. 7:14; Ps. 89:30–32). In his commandments, God commanded the king to imitate his holiness and set before him the alternative issues of accession and deposition, victory and defeat, prosperity and adversity, life and death. He also made those issues explicitly dependent on the king's own righteousness and unrighteousness (2 Sam. 7:8–16; 22:21–25). In this way, the LORD placed Israel's king, like the nation, on probation that he too might learn obedience and thus pass from his minority into his majority.

The probation and the identity of Abraham's true Seed. By these probationary measures God made it clear to Israel and their king that the seed of Abraham, one or many, to whom the everlasting inheritance was promised had to be a righteous seed, a seed who rendered to God an active and passive obedience that was perfect, personal, and perpetual. This seed would alone be the true Israel and the true David. Of this truth Mounts Ebal and Gerizim stood as perpetual reminders: the blessings of God would be the consequence of man's obedience (Deut. 28:1–14); conversely, the curses of God would be the consequence of man's disobedience (Deut. 28:15–68). For this reason, the apostle could and had to write, "The Law is not of faith; on the contrary, 'He who practices them shall live by them'" (Gal. 3:12 NASB).

Adam and Israel in Romans 5. To improve our understanding of the relationship between the covenant of works with Adam and the Mosaic covenant, it is valuable to turn to Romans 5 to consider the correspondence between Adam and Israel necessarily implied in that passage. The historical frame of the correspondence is set by the phrases "until (the) Law" (Rom. 5:13 NASB) and "from Adam until Moses" (Rom. 5:14 NASB) and "the Law came in alongside" (Rom. 5:20 AT); thus, the eras before and after the law's introduction are in view. Indicative of the Adam-Israel analogy is the apostle's willingness to use the same terms to describe both "the transgression of the one man"—Adam—and "the transgression" multiplied in "the many"—including Israel under the law (Rom. 5:20 with 5:15–16, 18). This common language and the explicit references to Moses (Rom. 5:14) and the law (Rom. 5:13, 20) confirm for us the trajectory of Paul's reflections: like Adam, Israel was presented with divine law, which in turn occasioned transgression for both.

We need also, however, to notice a difference between the two. Israel did not, unlike Adam, receive that law in the state of *posse non peccare,* but in the state of *non posse non peccare.* While Adam had been created without original sin, Israel had been created beset with original sin as a result of the imputation of Adam's sin. As we observed above, Israel was born in bondage to sin and was not morally competent to serve their God and to keep his commandments. So it was with their king as well (Ps. 51:5). The people and the king, then, were disqualified from being that righteous seed who would render to God the active and passive obedience that satisfied his law's requirements. Only such a Seed would be the true Israel and the true David, born under the law in a state of *posse non peccare*. But he would also be more: he would be the Last Adam, born of a woman yet without sin, indeed in a state of *non posse peccare*.

How, then, was the Mosaic covenant related to the covenant of works with Adam? The Mosaic covenant was a republication of the covenant of works modified to be compatible with the covenant of grace. Specifically, the covenant of works was modified in the Mosaic covenant by limiting the application of the principle of personal merit to the *retention* (vis-à-vis *reception*) of earthly and temporal (i.e., typological) blessings by Israel and their king. Granted the failure of both Adam and Israel, they ought thereby to learn the common lesson from their respective (pedagogical) probations that, if they were ever to receive and retain the heavenly and eternal blessings, they must find them in that one Seed of Abraham, born of woman, born under the law, who had proven to be *non posse peccare* according to the covenant of works first published in Eden and then republished (with modifications) in the Mosaic covenant at Sinai.

Conclusion

The two principles of inheritance. Two contrasting but compatible principles of inheritance are at work in the covenants of redemption, works, and grace and in the Noahic, Abrahamic, Mosaic, and Davidic covenants. The principles of inheritance by personal merit and by representative merit have existed side-by-side through all of history (pre-fall and post-fall). In the course of history, the principle of personal merit was enunciated in bilateral, conditional, and hence violable commandments (stipulations), while the principle of representative merit was enunciated in unilateral, unconditional, and hence inviolable benedictory commissions, with the former always subserving the latter.

Temporal blessings and curses with an eye to Christ. In the historical context just described, the temporal blessings as rewards for obedience and the temporal curses as punishments for disobedience, of both the lesser antitypes (Noah, Abraham, and David) and their seeds, not only express the principle of inheritance by personal merit but also go beyond it to express the principle of inheritance by representative merit. How do temporal blessings and curses express these principles? When considered apart from Christ and the typological revelation of his person and work before his incarnation, even the best of a sinner's works are but filthy rags and so merit not reward but punishment, while the worst of a sinner's works merit punishment far beyond that meted out for them in this world.[36] God condescended to our weakness, however, and dispensed temporal blessings and curses to certain believers and their seed according to the principles of personal and representative merit. Such covenantal transactions were to the better for us because by them, he foreshadowed to us the benefits of Christ's administration of the covenant of grace, the most basic of which benefits was justification by faith. Consequently, throughout Scripture (in both Testaments) and under all administrations of the covenant of grace before Christ, we find temporal blessings promised or curses threatened and then dispensed according to the principles of inheritance both by personal merit and by representative merit, all with an eye to their administration in antitypical fullness through Christ's mediation.

The yoke of the law and the yoke of grace. Taken together, the application of the two principles of inheritance typifies the eschatological blessing obtained by Christ for himself and his seed through his satisfaction (fulfilling the terms of the covenant of redemption) of both the requirements and the penalty of the covenant of works with Adam. Christ having fulfilled the law as a covenant of works, believers are no longer under the yoke of the law (Gal. 5:1, 18), but under the yoke of grace (Matt. 11:28–30; Rom. 6:14–15; Gal. 5:18). This yoke of grace is not antinomian, however. Rather, it uses the law lawfully according to the gospel (promise), e.g., 1 Timothy 1:8. That is, the yoke of grace uses the law for instruction in righteous character and conduct (e.g., Gal. 6:7–8; Matt. 6:33), but not for justification according to a principle of inheritance by personal merit inasmuch as, according to the gospel, Christ fulfilled that principle and thereby made it obsolete. Moreover, having himself persevered in righteousness and holiness during his humiliation, Christ also secured for believers the gift of perseverance, and that irrevocably. Therefore, just as the imputation of Christ's own righteousness renders the heavenly and eternal inheritance irrevocable for believers, even so the gift of perseverance makes the good works of believers, done in obedience to God's commandments, inseparable from that gracious imputation as the fruits and evidences of justifying faith.

---

36. As Calvin explained, "I . . . admit that what the Lord has promised in his law to the keepers of righteousness and holiness is paid to the works of believers, but in this repayment we must always consider the reason that wins favor for these works. Now we see that there are three reasons. The first is: God, having turned his gaze from his servants' works, which always deserve reproof rather than praise, embraces his servants in Christ, and with faith alone intervening, reconciles them to himself without the help of works. The second is: of his own fatherly generosity and loving-kindness, and without considering their worth, he raises works to this place of honor, so that he attributes some value to them. The third is: He receives these very works with pardon, not imputing the imperfection with which they are all so corrupted that they would otherwise be reckoned as sins rather than virtues." Calvin, *Institutes*, 3.17.3.

The two principles of inheritance and Christ. Two particularly note-worthy instances of the operation of the two principles of inheritance appeared in the covenant of works with Adam and the covenant of Moses. In each case, the conditional did not, and indeed could not, nullify the unconditional, but instead subserved it. The only man qualified to fulfill the commissions of Genesis 2:15 and 1:28 would be one who had proven to be *non posse peccare* according to the commandments of Genesis 2:16–17. Likewise, the only Seed of Abraham to whom the inheritance was promised was the Man who satisfied the law's demands. Thus, Moses (the law) stood in the same relation to Abraham (the promise) as Genesis 2:16–17 (the commandments) stood in relation to Genesis 2:15 and 1:28 (the commissions). As this study indicates, the conditional (violable) and unconditional (inviolable) words of God are compatible because, and only because, both words anticipate Christ—or, better, because Christ, as the archetypal Man wounded and Lamb slain before the foundation of the world, anticipates them. Hence, we have the mystery of Christ in Genesis 1–2 and the explication of the Christ-Adam typology in Romans 5 and elsewhere.

Epilogue

The cooperation of Biblical Theology and Systematic Theology. In addition to its lessons regarding the relationships among the theological and historical covenants, this study yields several benefits. It demonstrates that biblical theology and systematic theology can work hand in hand, as they do here.[37] They are not, as often assumed by post-Enlightenment advocates of either theological method, rivals but co-laborers in the church's quest for increasing understanding of the Scriptures.[38]

A common thread in current reappraisals and attacks on sola fide. As valuable as this realization may be, it is a subsidiary and academic benefit

37. The labors of biblical theologians Geerhardus Vos and Meredith G. Kline are distinguished by their sensitivity to the interests of systematic theology. We gladly acknowledge their pervasive influence on the method and content of this study.

38. "The great divide in the understanding of Scripture and, therefore, in the way in which the formulation of doctrine and, indeed, the construction of theological system was conceived cannot be placed between the Reformation and the era of orthodoxy—and it has nothing to do with the adaptation of scholastic method by the Protestant orthodox. Rather, as identified in the rise of higher criticism and in Gabler's address on the distinction between biblical and dogmatic theology, the great divide arose as a result of the historical dimension that the late seventeenth and early eighteenth century added to the critical dimension of Reformation and post-Reformation exegesis." Richard A. Muller, *Post-Reformation Reformed Dogmatics: The Rise and Development of Reformed Orthodoxy, ca. 1520 to ca. 1725*, 4 vols. (Grand Rapids, MI: Baker, 2003), 2:524.

that is exceeded by the value of this study as a backdrop against which to assess the efforts under way in evangelical and Reformed circles to redefine the doctrine of God's covenants or to use key traditional terminology in non-traditional ways. We submit that there is a thread common to the crosscurrents of reflection that are questioning the accuracy of classic Protestant reading of Paul and classic covenant theology. That common thread is the misapplication of the two contrasting principles of inheritance that are at work, and compatibly so, in God's covenantal dealings with man. That misapplication, while initially appearing benign, actually proves malignant in those cases where faith is not consistently contrasted with the law (the works thereof) as the means of justification and obtaining the heavenly and eternal inheritance.[39] In such instances we can be sure that the historic doctrine of *sola fide* has been loosed from its moorings in the historic doctrine of God's covenants and, in the process, has been reformulated into another gospel—which is to say, no gospel at all.

39. In other words, there is a danger in misapplying the two principles of inheritance, and it is the danger of falling into the error of Paul's opponents. See n. 33.

8

Why the Covenant of Works Is a Necessary Doctrine

Revisiting the Objections to a Venerable Reformed Doctrine

JOHN BOLT

Disagreeing with one's own teachers or colleagues in public is always a bit awkward; it should never be done casually. It is therefore out of deep respect for two honored former teachers, one of whom also became a valued colleague and mentor, that I will take issue with them in this essay.[1] Both Anthony Hoekema, former professor of systematic theology at Calvin Theological Seminary, and John Stek, emeritus professor of Old Testament at Calvin Seminary, are on record as challenging the classic Reformed doctrine of the covenant of works.[2] Since both have deserved reputations as thoughtful, careful scholars who do not dismiss

1. See, for example, my tribute to Professor Stek in the contribution to his festschrift: J. Bolt, "The Necessity of Narrative Imagination for Preaching," in Arie C. Leder, ed. *Reading and Hearing the Word: From Text to Sermon (Essays in Honor of John H. Stek)* (Grand Rapids, MI: Calvin Theological Seminary and CRC Publications, 1998), 203.
2. Anthony A. Hoekema, *Created in God's Image* (Grand Rapids, MI: Eerdmans, 1986), 117–21; John H. Stek, "Covenant Overload in Reformed Theology," *Calvin Theological Journal* 29 (1994): 12–41.

tradition lightly, this challenge needs to be taken seriously. Upon further reflection, however, I find myself unable to follow them and compelled rather to reaffirm the doctrine. In this chapter I shall first restate the doctrine in its classic form, then summarize Stek's and Hoekema's objections along with similar ones from contemporary Reformed theologians,[3] and finally indicate my own reasons for rejecting the challenge.

Definition

For an initial definition of the covenant of works one can hardly improve on the simplicity and confessional clarity of the Westminster Confession of Faith (1647; chap. VII, §2): "The first covenant made with man was a covenant of works, wherein life was promised to Adam; and in him to his posterity, upon condition of perfect and personal obedience."

The biblical "proof" provided by the Confession is primarily that of Galatians 3:12: "The law is not of faith; rather, 'The one who does them shall live by them.'" The passage quoted in the Galatians verse is Leviticus 18:5. The Confession authors also cite Romans 10:5 where the same Leviticus passage is quoted by Paul, and the important Adam/Christ parallel in Romans 5:12–20. Finally, to remind us that disobedience to law results in curse and judgment, the *Confession* takes note of Galatians 3:10 and the probationary command given in Genesis 2:17.

From this summary evidence the doctrine's basis and purpose is clear. God's relationship to humanity from the outset was a legal, covenantal

---

3. Others in the confessional, Reformed/Presbyterian tradition include Herman Hoeksema, John Murray, and G.C. Berkouwer (see Hoekema, *Created in God's Image*, 119). The critique of the covenant of works more broadly, as a legalistic imposition incompatible with the gospel of grace, was largely inspired by Karl Barth (see *Church Dogmatics*, translated by Geoffrey Bromiley [Edinburgh: T & T Clark, 1956], 4:1, 54–66) and includes such scholars as James B. Torrance, Holmes Rolston III, and David N. J. Poole. For helpful summaries of the literature on this see Richard J. Muller, "The Covenant of Works and the Stability of Divine Law in 17th-Century Reformed Orthodoxy: A Study on the Theology of Herman Witsius and Wilhelmus à Brakel," *CTJ* 29 (1994): 71–101; Lyle D. Bierma "Law and Grace in Ursinus's Doctrine of the Natural Covenant: A Reappraisal," in *Protestant Scholasticism: Essays in Reassessment*, ed. Carl R. Trueman and R. S. Clark (Carlisle: Paternoster, 1999), 96–110. As always, I am indebted to my colleague Richard Muller for ongoing, stimulating theological conversation and especially for helpful hints on the Reformed tradition and recent scholarship regarding the covenant. While considerations of space and potential accessibility to their works by readers, along with my personal relationship with and respect for my teachers, led me to focus on Hoekema and Stek, their challenges, thankfully, are also free from the various tendentious theological agendas characterizing much of the contemporary discussion about covenant of works. Both are scrupulously concerned with nothing more than articulating a clear and consistent biblical theology of covenant, and for that reason their case against the doctrine of the covenant of works deserves honest consideration.

relationship in which obedience was demanded and to be rewarded, disobedience proscribed and under sanctioned curse and punishment: "Obey and live; disobey and die."

It is worth noting here that the biblical basis for the doctrine in the Confession does not rest on a dubious translation of Hosea 6:7: "Like Adam, they have broken the covenant—they were unfaithful to me there"(NIV).[4] The doctrine of the covenant of works cannot be bound to a straightforward biblicism in which a doctrine may be affirmed only if it is explicitly stated as such in a biblical text; Reformed orthodoxy also acknowledges the validity of aspects of "the whole counsel of God" that may be "deduced" from Scripture "by good and necessary consequence" (WCF 1.6). This is also Calvin's approach when considering the "unbiblical" doctrine of the Trinity. Heretics, according to Calvin, "rail at the word 'person,' or . . . cry out against admitting a term fashioned by the human mind."[5] To insist that we must follow the rule that confines us "within the limits of Scripture not only [with respect to] our thoughts but also our words" is to impose an "unjust law." Nothing should prevent us "from explaining in clearer words those matters in Scripture which perplex and hinder our understanding, yet which conscientiously and faithfully serve the truth of Scripture itself, and are made use of sparingly and modestly and on due occasion." Calvin concludes by warning us not to find fault with new words when "they render the truth plain and clear."

To consider only one more example of a classic understanding of the covenant of works in the Reformed tradition, here is the fuller definition from the popular work of Dutch Reformed theological piety, Wilhelmus à Brakel's *Our Reasonable Service*:

> The covenant of works was an agreement between God and the human race as represented in Adam, in which God promised eternal life upon condition of obedience, and threatened eternal death upon disobedience. Adam accepted both this promise and this condition.[6]

Brakel's argument follows in three steps, corresponding to the three parts of his definition.[7]

---

4. I do find it amusingly ironic that the NIV translation, in which John Stek played a major role, does translate the kᵉʾādām of Hosea 6:7 as "like Adam" and relegates the more likely translation, "at Adam" or even "like men," to a footnote. The NRSV translates "at Adam."

5. John Calvin, *Institutes of the Christian Religion*, Library of Christian Classics, vol. 20, ed. John T. McNeill, trans. Ford Lewis Battles (Philadelphia: Westminster, 1960), I.xiii.3. The passages cited further in this paragraph are found in this section.

6. Wilhelmus à Brakel, *Our Reasonable Service*, trans. Bartel Elshout (Ligonier, PA: Soli Deo Gloria, 1992), 1:355. Page references that follow in the text are to this work.

7. This definition of "covenant of works" flows naturally from the generally accepted understanding of *covenant*, for example, as given by Herman Witsius: "A covenant of God with

1) God gave a law to man.
2) Adam had the promise of eternal felicity.
3) Adam accepted the promises and conditions of the covenant.

While the first two points are relatively straightforward—Genesis 2 does point to a command and consequences—it is more difficult, as Brakel himself acknowledges,[8] to demonstrate the truth of the third. Still, this is crucial since Adam as covenant partner must also agree to the covenant. Brakel attempts to demonstrate this indirectly, beginning with noting that there are times in Scripture when only the promises of the covenant are mentioned though the full covenant reality, involving both parties, is really in view. He refers to the promise of Genesis 3:15 where "there is not one word mentioning Adam and Eve's acceptance of this covenant" (364).[9] In addition, Adam's sinlessness meant that he could do no other; in fact since Adam and Eve evidently refrained from eating from the tree prior to the fateful conversation with the snake, their obedience indicated acceptance of the covenant. If these reasons do not sound entirely convincing—and they do not fully persuade me—Brakel's other reason (third in his own order) is remarkable in its direction. He observes that even sinful people acknowledge deep down in their souls that God's law is holy, just and good.[10] If this is so for postlapsarian sinners, how "much more could man in his perfection not do otherwise than accept both condition and promise" (365).

What is remarkable is the easy move beyond biblicism to appeal to general human experience as a way of explaining a biblical doctrine. Brakel, of course, does not ignore explicit biblical reference. His final "proof" is an appeal to Hosea 6:7. Brakel engages in a lengthy discussion to demonstrate that the Hebrew *adam* should be translated as a proper name and not as the generic *men*. He does not consider the translation *at Adam*.

---

man, is an agreement between God and man, about the way of obtaining consummate happiness; including a commination of eternal destruction, with which the contemner of the happiness, offered in that way, is to be punished." (*The Economy of the Covenants between God and Man*, trans. By William Crookshank, 2 volumes [London: R. Baynes; Aberdeen: J. Maitland; Glasgow: T. Lochhead; Edinburgh: T. Nelson, 1822; rpt. 1990, Escondido, CA: The Den Dulk Foundation], I.i.9); on the close relationship between Brakel and Witsius, see R. Muller, "Witsius and Brakel," esp. 80n.12.

8. "My response is that even though it is not expressly stated in Scripture, it can nevertheless be clearly deduced from it" (ibid., 364).

9. An even stronger example is the covenant with Noah in Genesis 9 where there is no explicit acceptance by Noah and the covenant is with "all living flesh" including, undoubtedly, living creatures incapable of speech and covenantal response.

10. Brakel does not but he could have referred to Romans 2:14 ("Gentiles who do not have the law, do by nature the things of the law . . .").

The contemporary interpreter of Scripture is unlikely to be impressed with Brakel's case for the covenant of works. There are two important points, however, that must not be overlooked. In the first place, as Herman Bavinck has noted, the notion of a covenant (of works) with Adam is not an innovation with the Reformers; it dates back to the church fathers and Augustine.[11] Furthermore, the understanding of Hosea 6:7 as providing exegetical warrant for a creation covenant with Adam is equally venerable. In appealing to this passage the sixteenth- and seventeenth-century defenders of a covenant of works were simply reflecting and articulating a longstanding exegetical consensus.[12]

We therefore make a serious error when we dismiss the notion of a covenant of works simply on the basis that it fails to meet the standards of modern biblical exegesis. Even if true, and the point is debatable, the case for the doctrine never depended solely on the exegesis of a few "proof texts." Richard Muller summarizes the point this way:

> The Reformed theologians of the sixteenth and seventeenth centuries who raised and developed the issue of the covenants [of *works* and of grace] did not understand their exegetical starting point to be the text of Genesis chapters two and three or such texts as Hosea 6:7 ("like Adam [or man] they have transgressed the covenant") and Job 31:33 ("If I covered my transgressions as Adam"). [Rather] the doctrine was a conclusion drawn from a large complex of texts . . . [and] it was, moreover, a conclusion largely in accord with the exegetical tradition.[13]

Bearing that in mind, we are now in a position to consider the recent objections to the doctrine as stated by Stek and Hoekema.

The Challenge

John Stek contends that the Reformed theological tradition has "overloaded" the covenant notion as "a systematically useful way of construing the God-humanity relation." The result, he believes, is that covenant became part of a constellation of "theological constructs" that over the course of time "came to have . . . a probative force of their own, even when at times these constructs strained and constrained the biblical data

---

11. Herman Bavinck, *Reformed Dogmatics*, vol. 2, *God and Creation*, ed. John Bolt, trans. John Vriend (Grand Rapids, MI: Baker, 2004), 567; also in H. Bavinck, *In the Beginning: Foundations of Creation Theology*, John Bolt ed., John Vriend trans. (Grand Rapids, MI: Baker, 1999), 201.

12. Bavinck clearly points to this (ibid., 357, 201); the point is underscored and vigorously argued in detail by Richard Muller, "Witsius and Brakel," 89–91.

13. Muller, "Witsius and Brakel," 89–90.

to their limits and beyond."[14] He takes issue with claims such as that of Herman Bavinck that the metaphysical distance between God and humanity makes a covenant necessary for communion between them.[15] Not only does he consider this an abstraction from the biblical narrative which is then arbitrarily imposed upon Genesis 1–2, but Stek also contends that it is "misguided" to define covenants as *relationships*. Instead they are kingdom "commitments made under self-maledictory oaths" in the specific crisis circumstances of "situations fraught with uncertainties" promising "that certain specific future actions would be carried out."[16] Covenant, Stek insists, is not "the central theological category for synthetic construal of the God-humanity relationship."[17]

Not only does Stek take issue with the Reformed theological tradition, specifically disagreeing, *inter alia*, with G. Spykman, L. Berkhof, and Herman Hoeksema, but he also summarizes in some detail the extensive twentieth-century biblical-theological efforts by such theologians as Walter Eichrodt, Meredith Kline, O. Palmer Robertson, William Dumbrell, and Thomas McComiskey to make covenant a central biblical concept. Stek concludes that it is all unconvincing. What is wrong, according to Stek, is the method of trying "to establish an abstract definition of covenant and then [to] look for instances of the defined concept."[18]

What Stek objects to is a method that fails to restrict theological concepts to explicit and specific biblical warrant. This becomes more apparent when he singles out for exceptional praise the late theologian John Murray of Westminster Theological Seminary in Philadelphia. He notes that "Murray agreed with the tradition that after God created humankind in his image, he, 'by a special act of Providence, established for man the provision whereby he might pass from a state of contingency to one note of confirmed and indefectible holiness.' And he also agreed that this provision involved a condition, a promise, and a threat. But he declined to call this divine administration covenant."[19]

Why? Because Murray wants to restrict the term *covenant* to the way it is explicitly used in scriptural texts. Stek so appreciates Murray's turning "back to Scripture (and the early Reformed confessions) rather than

14. Stek, "Covenant Overload," 16.

15. Stek cites this passage from Bavinck's *Gereformeerde Dogmatiek*, vol. 3 (Kampen: Kok, 1918), 211: "If religion is to be a true communion between God and humankind as distinct rational and moral agents and be a relationship in which rights are duly honored along with obligations, then this can come about only as God stoops down to humankind and enters into covenant with them."

16. Stek, "Covenant Overload," 36.

17. Ibid., 25.

18. Ibid., 21.

19. Ibid., 15.

continuing with the tradition," that he provides us with a lengthy quote from Murray, adding in a footnote that similar sensitivities lead Murray to reject the notion of a *pactum salutis* or *covenant of redemption*:[20]

> Scripture always uses the term covenant, when applied to God's administration to men, in reference to a promise that is redemptive or closely related to redemptive design. Covenant in Scripture denotes the oath-bound confirmation of promise and involves a security which the Adamic economy did not bestow. . . . [Moreover] the Adamic [administration] had no redemptive provisions, nor did its promissory element have any relevance within a context that made redemption necessary.

What is noteworthy here is that Stek does not challenge the *content* of the Adamic situation—a provisional situation under law and sanctions leading to life or death—but only the use of the word *covenant* to describe it. His objection is methodological: terms like *covenant* should not be used where Scripture does not use them and it is "misguided" to abstract from other texts that speak of covenant in order to formulate a definition that is then arbitrarily, in an *a priori* manner, imposed on a text such as Genesis 1–2. It is this theological construal and alleged imposition to which Stek objects in the Reformed tradition's espousal of a covenant of works.

Anthony Hoekema shares Stek's (and Murray's) objections to the covenant of works[21] and provides four reasons for rejecting the term:

1) The term *covenant of works* "does not do justice to the elements of grace that entered into the 'Adamic administration.'"
2) "The Bible does not call this arrangement a covenant."
3) "There is no indication in [the] early chapters of Genesis of a covenant oath or covenant ratification ceremony."
4) "The word *covenant* in Scripture is always used in the context of redemption."

(Though Hoekema acknowledges: "with the possible exception of Hosea 6:7.")

With Stek (and Murray), Hoekema also follows the methodological principle of restricting covenant terminology exclusively to that used by Scripture itself. Yet, he does go further than Stek in addressing the *content*

---

20. Ibid., 15.n.14; the reference which Stek provides is, "The Plan of Salvation," in *Collected Writings of John Murray* (Edinburgh and Carlisle, PA: Banner of Truth, 1977), 2:130.

21. "Though not necessarily agreeing with all the objections mentioned by these three authors [G. C. Berkouwer, H. Hoeksema, J. Murray], I share their conviction that we ought not call the arrangement God made with Adam and Eve before the Fall a 'covenant of works'" (*Created in God's Image*, 119).

of the Adamic administration. His conclusion sneaks up on the reader as something of a surprise: "Though we should not, therefore, read the opening chapters of Genesis as a description of a 'covenant of works' between God and Adam before the Fall, we must indeed maintain the doctrinal truths that lie behind the concept of the covenant of works."[22]

These doctrinal truths include Adam as federal head of the human race, the reality of a probationary command, death to all through his disobedience, and as a type of Christ. It is not clear, and Hoekema does not adequately explain, why the term *covenant* at least should not then be used, if not *covenant of works*.

Herman Hoeksema also objects to any covenant of works with Adam but for quite different reasons. Hoeksema begins with clearly affirming that "the original relation between God and Adam is called a covenant relation."[23] In fact, "even though the first three chapters of the book of Genesis do not mention the covenant, there can be no doubt that the relation between God and Adam was such a covenant relation."[24] This does not depend, according to Hoeksema, on a single text such as Hosea 6:7:

> But all of Scripture proceeds from the truth that man always stands in covenant relation to God. All God's dealings with Adam in paradise presuppose this relation; for God talked with Adam and revealed Himself to him, and Adam knew God in the wind of the day. Besides, salvation is always presented as the establishment and realization of God's covenant.[25]

Hoeksema objects particularly to the notion that Adam would have achieved something higher through obedience. He affirms the covenantal character of the relation between God and Adam but categorically rejects any notion "that God gave to Adam the promise of eternal life if he should obey that particular commandment of God." In fact, had Adam not fallen, he "might have lived everlastingly in his earthly state. He might [even] have continued to eat of the tree of life and live forever; but everlasting earthly life is not the same as what Scripture means by eternal life." Furthermore, the idea "that Adam would have attained to this higher level of glory, that there would have come a time in his life when he would have been translated, the Scriptures nowhere suggest."[26]

22. Ibid., 121.
23. Herman Hoeksema, *Reformed Dogmatics* (Grand Rapids, MI: Reformed Free Publishing Association, 1966), 214.
24. Ibid., 220.
25. Ibid., 221.
26. Ibid., 217.

All this smacks too much of merit and reward in Hoeksema's judgment. And finally, perhaps at the core of Hoeksema's objection, the notion of a covenant of works "presents the covenant relation as something incidental and additional to man's life in relation to God. It is a means to an end, not an end in itself."[27]

And here we come to the heart of the matter for Hoeksema. He does not conceive of covenant as a *legal* relationship but as one of "friendship and intimate fellowship": a matter of "walking with God."[28] It is, Hoeksema insists, not something incidental to the image of God in the created Adam but essential to it. Adam stood in covenantal relation to God "by virtue of his creation . . . after the image of God" and not "by way of an agreement." The covenant with Adam "is not essentially an agreement, but a relation of living fellowship and friendship. It was given and established by Adam's creation after the image of God."[29] For Hoeksema, Adam's connection to his posterity is primarily organic rather than legal though he does not deny Adam's federal headship, even acknowledging that "God created the whole human race in Adam as a legal corporation, represented by our first father."[30]

The full and rich measure of Hoeksema's understanding of the covenant with Adam can only be seen in the light of his discussion of the *pactum salutis* or counsel of redemption. Hoeksema sees covenant as the very essence of the Godhead itself: "Now the Scriptures teach very clearly that God is in Himself a covenant God." This is so not because of creation and the covenantal God-creature relation but eternally in God himself: "He is the covenant God in Himself. And he is the God of the covenant, not according to an agreement or pact, but according to His very divine Nature and Essence."[31] With the Adamic covenant serving as the image of God's own inner-trinitarian covenant between Father, Son, and Holy Spirit in the course of redemption, Hoeksema's understanding of covenant is indistinguishable from election. What he shares with the other two critics of covenant of works discussed earlier in the essay is an insistence on the redemptive character of covenant. Hoeksema's understanding of the covenant removes all notions of conditionality and human responsiveness found in the traditional understanding of covenant;[32] covenant and

27. Ibid., 219.
28. Ibid., 221–22.
29. Ibid., 222.
30. Ibid., 277; cf. 223.
31. Ibid., 322.
32. See, for example, Hoeksema's critique of his own teacher William Heyns on the conditionality of the covenant, *Reformed Dogmatics*, 442, 696–700.

election are finally identical. In Hoeksema's own words: "Soteriology is theology in the deepest sense of the word."[33]

Assessment of the Critique

The critique of the covenant of works doctrine that we have summarized above is first of all characterized by what could be called a methodological biblicism. This critique does much more than merely pay lip service to Calvin's solemn warning "not to attempt with bold curiosity to penetrate to the investigation of [God's] essence, which we ought more to adore than meticulously search out, but for us to contemplate him in his works whereby he renders himself near and familiar to us, and in some manner communicates himself."[34] It claims rather to retreat from all theological formulations that do not arise directly from the biblical text itself but are abstracted from the larger narrative and then imposed on a particular passage. Methodological biblicism is wary to the point of rejection with respect to the procedure of drawing inferences by "good and necessary consequence from Scripture" (WCF 1.6). We need to consider (1) whether the accusation that the doctrine of covenant of works is an unwarranted imposition on the Genesis text is in fact valid, and (2) whether the definitions of covenant proposed by critics of the doctrine are not themselves abstractions from data which are then imported into the biblical text. A full evaluation requires attention to specific matters of biblical exegesis and interpretation as well as to overall theological coherence and integrity with respect to the complete narrative of biblical salvation-history. In this essay we can only sketch the argument in broad outline.

John Stek's charge that Reformed theology had "overloaded" on the covenant concept prompted quick and extensive response from Craig Bartholomew two issues later in the *Calvin Theological Journal*.[35] Bartholomew picks up from Gordon Spykman's *Reformational Theology* the term *covenantal deconstruction* which Spykman uses to protest the removal of covenantal ideas from the creation story.[36] Spykman is convinced that "covenantal relationships are given in, with, and for all created reality." Those who shift the origins of the biblical covenant from Adam to Noah and/or Abraham, he notes, do not deny that Adam functions in

33. Ibid., 445.

34. John Calvin, *Institutes of the Christian Religion*, I.v.9.

35. Craig Bartholomew, "Covenant and Creation: Covenant Overload or Covenant Deconstruction?" *CTJ* 30 (April 1995): 11–33.

36. Gordon J. Spykman, *Reformational Theology: A New Paradigm for Doing Dogmatics* (Grand Rapids, MI: Eerdmans, 1992), 261. The quotations that follow in this paragraph are from 260–61.

some sense as the representative head of the human race. But this "then raises the questions: If Adam was not the covenant head of mankind, what then was the nature of his headship? And if it was not a covenant he broke, how then shall we describe the relationship which he broke?" In addition, the mere lack of an explicit use of the Hebrew word *berith* in Genesis 1–2 is a weak argument from silence and insufficient reason to deny the covenantal character of the passage. In a direct challenge to the kind of definition of covenant that Stek utilizes, namely that covenant is defined, among other things, by an oath-ceremony, Spykman wonders if this is not a case of "reading a more explicit feature of later redemptive covenant renewals back into the preredemptive covenant given with creation." It also "runs the risk, moreover, of shifting the norm for biblical interpretation from the *analogia Scripturae* to an exaggerated reliance on extrabiblical archeological sources (for example, the Hittite 'suzerainty treaties')."

Spykman, in my judgment, raises the right questions. Stek, we recall, objects to any method that attempts "to establish an abstract definition of covenant and then [to] look for instances of the defined concept" and believes that the traditional covenant of works doctrine does just that.[37] Leaving aside for now the rhetorically prejudicial formulation "abstracting from"—one could more favorably (e.g., with Spykman) speak of the *analogia Scripturae*—has Stek not done just that when he defines *covenant* in terms of "commitments made under self-maledictory oaths" in the specific crisis circumstances of "situations fraught with uncertainties" promising "that certain specific future actions would be carried out"?[38] This too is an abstraction which is then "imposed" on the text of Genesis 1–2 in order to rule out the presence of covenant there. What is more unsettling for Stek's argument methodologically is that in the first instance in Genesis where the word *berith* is explicitly used, namely with Noah in Genesis 6:18 and Genesis 9:9, there is no self-maledictory oath explicitly mentioned either, in fact the *language* of covenant initiation is altogether absent. Stek deals with this absence by calling attention to the rainbow "as a divine war-bow drawn and aimed at heaven."[39] This observation is taken from Delbert Hillers's historical study of the covenant idea,[40] and Stek notes that though "his proposal appears not to have been picked up by others, he was surely right."[41]

37. Stek, "Covenant Overload," 21.
38. Ibid., 36.
39. Ibid., 28.
40. See "Covenant Overload," 28 n.59; the reference is to Delbert Hillers, *Covenant: The History of a Biblical Idea* (Baltimore: Johns Hopkins, 1969), 102.
41. Ibid.

I have no quarrel with Stek's conclusion; I think that the rainbow sign is likely best understood as an implied self-maledictory oath. My objection here is to the methodological inconsistency of a biblicistic insistence on explicitly "sticking to the text" and not using the analogy of Scripture along with "good and necessary consequence," in order to reject the doctrine of a covenant with creation, only then to use the exact same approach to rescue one's own definition when it doesn't fit the text, strictly taken. In addition, as Craig Bartholomew, following William Dumbrell, demonstrates, the Noahic covenant renewal in Genesis 6 and 9 "is the perpetuation of an existing covenant and not the institution of a new one"; it is, in fact, "the renewal of God's purposes as set out in Genesis 1. Noah is a second Adam; through him human beings are told to be fruitful and multiply and to exercise dominion over the earth. The inclusion in [Genesis] 9:1 and 9:7 makes this motif unavoidable."[42] Bartholomew concludes: "Genesis 6 and 9 point us back to Genesis 1 and 2 as the basis for the Noahican covenant."[43]

Stek, recall, also claimed that covenants functioned only in redemptive situations of crisis and were used to shore up the promise of commitment. He also challenged the notion that covenants had anything to do with relationships of love, friendship, and communion.[44] Here Bartholomew effectively dismantles Stek's case, noting that the very people Stek appeals to as sources for information about extrabiblical covenants (e.g., Weinfeld, Mendenhall, Herion, Kulleveettil) do find major relational elements in covenant. In the biblical narrative, marriage in particular serves as a case in point. Bartholomew concludes:

> It does seem, therefore, that Stek works with a reductionistic understanding of covenant that undermines the relational element in the semantic range of the word, and this prevents him from seeing the constitutive and regulative relational aspects of the divine covenant.[45]

Bartholomew adds to his argument by a closer look at the Abrahamic, Sinaitic, and Davidic covenants, also noting that creation and creation-regained motifs feature prominently in Jeremiah and Isaiah's "covenantal promises about the future in God's purposes."[46] To all this we could add that the ubiquitous biblical "prophetic" pattern—obedience yields blessing; disobedience draws down curse—is a covenant condition. Since this pattern is applied by way of a "natural law" presumption to the Gentile

42. Bartholomew, "Covenant and Creation," 17.
43. Ibid., 18.
44. Stek, "Covenant Overload," 25.
45. Bartholomew, "Covenant and Creation," 22.
46. Ibid., 19.

nations too by prophets such as Isaiah, Ezekiel, Amos, Jonah, Nahum and Habakkuk, we must, with Herman Hoeksema,[47] link covenant obligation to the *created* image of God in all people. It is the sanctions of the covenant (of creation) based on the created image of God that must be regarded as fundamentally prior to the specific sanctions applied to the redeemed people of God. Otherwise there is no way to make sense of Paul's claims in Romans 1 and 2.[48] For our purposes we have more than enough to raise significant questions about Stek's repudiation of the covenant of works or covenant with creation to call the rejection itself into question.

Once the biblicist argument and the exegetical issues have been dealt with, disposing of the further objections of Hoekema (and Murray) is easier. Both Hoekema and Murray reject the notion of a covenant of works on grounds similar to Stek's (absence of *berith* in Genesis 1 and 2, covenants are redemptive only, and no self-maledictory oath present) but then go on to insist that, notwithstanding these factors, we must continue to hold to some idea of Adam's federal headship of the human race. Hoekema even insists:

> Though we should not, therefore, read the opening chapters of Genesis as a description of a "covenant of works" between God and Adam before the Fall, we must indeed maintain the doctrinal truths that lie behind the concept of the covenant of works. We must, for example, insist that Adam was indeed the head and representative of the human race that was to descend from him; that he was given a 'probationary command' to test his obedience, that his disobedience to that command brought sin, death, and condemnation into the world; and that he was therefore a type of Christ, our second head, called 'the last Adam' in I Corinthians 15:45, through whom we are delivered from the sad results of the first Adam's sin."[49]

Herman Hoeksema goes even further. Though he has his own specific doctrinal reasons for not accepting any idea of a covenant of works—Hoeksema rejects any elements of conditionality in covenant—even he speaks forthrightly and clearly about a creational covenant with Adam: "However, even though the first three chapters of the book of Genesis do not mention the covenant, there can be no doubt that the relation between God and Adam was such a covenant relation."[50] This all seems to me like a lot of unnecessary evasive dancing, so much exegetical "rope-

47. Though, admittedly, in a different way and with a different outcome from Hoeksema's.

48. For the stimulus to pursue this line of thought I am indebted to conversations with my Calvin Seminary student assistant David Sytsma.

49. Ibid., 121.

50. Hoeksema, *Reformed Dogmatics*, 220.

a-dope."[51] I have no problem with calling the original creation covenant with Adam something other than "covenant of works." In fact, like the ill-chosen term "common grace," simply referring to the "covenant with Adam" or "covenant of creation" seems preferable. What is not negotiable, in my judgment, is the doctrine of Adam's federal headship of the human race. And that is directly tied to the larger question of a unity in salvation history.

Our last two citations from Hoeksema above (n.49, 50) indicate the reason that this is so crucial when they mention the Adam/Christ parallel. If we deny the covenant of creation with Adam we unravel the tapestry of God's redemptive plan in Christ. Specifically we alter our understanding of the work of Christ in salvation. Wilhelmus à Brakel already pointed this out clearly in the late seventeenth-century:

> Acquaintance with this covenant [of works] is of the greatest importance, for whoever errs here or denies the existence of the covenant of works, will not understand the covenant of grace, and will readily err concerning the mediatorship of the Lord Jesus. Such a person will readily deny that Christ by His active obedience has merited a right to eternal life for the elect. . . . Whoever denies the covenant of works, must rightly be suspected to be in error concerning the covenant of grace as well.[52]

With that last point, having established at least the reasonable exegetical *possibilities* of a covenant of creation with Adam, we come to what is for me the primary *theological* reason for maintaining a doctrine of covenant of works.

Maintaining the Covenant of Works Doctrine: Its Legal Character

It is important, in my judgment, to protect and maintain the fundamentally legal/forensic character of the Creator-creature relation while at the same time not *reducing* it to a legal one. Covenant is both legal (obedience, blessing, sanctions) and gracious (assuming here a suzerainty-vassal treaty structure based on the intrinsic sovereignty of the Creator God) in character. Creation itself must be understood as evidence of grace and favor because creation is not necessary but contingent; its very existence is based on a posture of divine grace or undeserved favor. (Note that *grace* here is understood broadly as divine gratuity as such. That is

---

51. For the uninitiated this is a reference to heavyweight champion boxer Muhammed Ali's term for evading the heavy-duty punches of his great rival Joe Frazier.

52. Brakel, *Our Reasonable Service*, I:355; I am indebted to my colleague Richard Muller for this reference; Muller, "Witsius and à Brakel," 76n.3.

to say, as long as we are clear that we not speaking of a gracious, loving act of forgiveness *after* the fall, rooted in God's gracious act of election, we can speak of creation as an act of *grace*. Grace is thus a gift, it is unnecessary, not required, even unexpected. Creation's utter contingency is an important reminder that existence itself is gratuitious; we *are* but we *need* not be.) I believe that much of the opposition to *covenant of works* is terminological (this is particularly true of Karl Barth and Hoeksema). Hence I propose a different set of terms for the ideas included in a covenant of works.

However, we first need to be reminded that the critical biblical piece of evidence that has to be taken into account is the Adam-as-legal-representative/Christ-as-legal-representative parallel developed by Paul in Romans 5 (and 1 Corinthians 15). Paul's discussion of justification in Romans is part of the legal-courtroom field of metaphor that is at the heart of an orthodox (Anselmian) doctrine of the atonement. Thus, dropping the covenantal notion in the creation stories threatens the classic views of the atonement and of salvation. Our legal status before God was changed by the sin of the first Adam as humanity's representative and by the redemptive work of the Second Adam. In addition to being faithful to Scripture, a system of theology should be coherent and not internally contradictory.

With that I now submit my proposed changes in nomenclature. First, I suggest that as a basic distinction we simply speak of:

a) The covenant with Adam = covenant of creation (law; gracious law);

and

b) The covenant with Abraham = covenant of redemption (grace; lawful grace)

This leads us to note the complementary truth in a coherent system of Reformed theology of the twofold perspective that:

law is gracious
and
grace is legal/forensic.

Maintaining the Covenant of Works Doctrine: Its Relational Character

In the preceding section I did not engage the position of Herman Hoeksema on the legal, forensic character of the covenant and work of Christ.

Hoeksema's position is distinct in that while he rejects the notion of a covenant of works, his fundamental reason is a theological one where he does not define covenant in terms of a *legal* relationship but as a *friendship* relationship.[53] For Hoeksema, introducing legal conditionality into covenant understanding undermines the sovereign grace of God in election. Covenant is really about God's electing work unto communion with humanity. If Stek denies relationality by underscoring the legal dimension of covenant, Hoeksema's rejection of all conditionality in covenant undermines its legal, forensic character.

In my judgment Hoeksema is wrong about covenant conditionality but that is a larger topic than can be treated here.[54] At the same time, I believe that Hoeksema is right about the relational dimension of the Adamic covenant and also right in hinting that the Sabbath is the preeminent sign of this relationality and communion.[55] Hints, unfortunately, is indeed all that they are, but Hoeksema's theological instincts, I believe, are right on target here and reflect some of the profoundest convictions and insights in the Reformed theological and confessional tradition. For the biblical notion of Sabbath has to do with resting in God, communion with God, God's dwelling with us, with tabernacle and temple, with Shekinah and glory, with holiness and beauty.[56]

It is the indwelling Holy Spirit that transforms us, makes us holy, sanctifies us. God alone is intrinsically holy; created things and persons become holy when sanctified by the presence of the Holy Spirit. Thus God's people are holy, the Jerusalem temple is holy, and the church is

53. According to Hoeksema, the covenant with Adam "is not essentially an agreement, but a relation of living fellowship and friendship. It was given and established by Adam's creation after the image of God" (*Reformed Dogmatics*, 222).

54. Peter Lillback's discussion of conditionality in Calvin's understanding of the covenant is an excellent introduction to the issues and to the vast literature of an intense scholarly debate. See Peter A. Lillback, "The Continuing Conundrum: Calvin and the Conditionality of the Covenant," *CTJ* 29 (1994): 42–74.

55. My treatment of this theme is also necessarily schematic. The most significant influence on my thinking about Sabbath themes was and is an essay by my Ph. D. mentor Herbert Richardson, "Toward an American Theology," in *Toward an American Theology* (New York: Harper and Row, 1967). This essay, one of the most creative and seminal pieces of theology I have read, also directed my attention back to Jonathan Edwards who continues to stimulate my theological reflection on Sabbath, glory, beauty, holiness, and the work of the Holy Spirit. Similar themes, albeit developed in a panentheistic direction, can be found in Jürgen Moltmann, *God in Creation: A New Theology of Creation and the Spirit of God*, trans. Margaret Kohl (San Francisco: Harper & Row, 1985). I have developed some of these themes further in an essay, "The Characteristic Work of the Holy Spirit: Sanctification, Sabbath Glory, Beauty," *Stulos* 3 (1996): 3–13.

56. See my essay "The Characteristic Work of the Holy Spirit: Sanctification, Sabbath Glory, Beauty" for a fuller elaboration of these themes. The paragraph that follows is adapted from that essay.

holy because God dwells in them and by his presence sanctifies them. Holiness is the ultimate goal of the new creation as well: God's dwelling is with humanity, and his presence so sanctifies all that there is no need of a temple or sun or moon—God himself *is* its light (Rev. 21:3, 23, 23). For this reason it has been suggested[57] that we should think of creation itself as being fashioned *for* the indwelling of the Holy Spirit. Meredith Kline puts it this way: "The Glory-Spirit was present at the beginning of creation as a sign of the *telos* of creation, as the Alpha-archetype of the Omega-Sabbath that was the goal of creation history."[58]

Similarly, human beings are created in the image of God. "God created man in the likeness of the Glory to be a spirit-temple of God in the Spirit."[59] We can state this somewhat more simply in this way: "God created the world for Sabbath holiness." It is the Sabbath structure of creation itself that makes the incarnation possible, and for Richardson, necessary. "The mere time and space of the Sabbath is the formal and material precondition for God's personal coming. By his personal coming God sanctifies the Sabbath. The Sabbath is, so to say, the world's aptitude for the incarnation."[60]

For Richarson, following Jonathan Edwards, this means that the question *cur deus homo*? must be placed in the larger framework of the question *cur creatio*? Christ's redemption must not be seen in light of God's purpose for the sixth day of creation (creation of humanity) but in view of God's purpose for the seventh day—the glory of the Sabbath. "Now, the Sabbath Day was created by God, so that He Himself might enter into the world and sanctify it by His personal presence. In this way He makes the world holy."[61] Jürgen Moltmann agrees with this conclusion: "The inner secret of creation is the *indwelling of God*, just as the inner secret of the sabbath of creation is God's rest."[62] Sabbath glory was thus God's goal for the creation. "God created the world for his glory, out of love; and the crown of creation is not the human being; it is the sabbath."[63]

Thus in conclusion, since the chief end of humanity is to glorify God and enjoy him forever (WCF), it can be said that—in this sense only—"man was created for the Sabbath." Since the Sabbath is the holiness gift—the sanctification fruit—of the Holy Spirit, we are justified in speaking of the

---

57. In addition to Richardson whose argument is being rehearsed here, see Meredith Kline, *Images of the Spirit* (Grand Rapids, MI: Baker, 1980).

58. Ibid., 20.

59. Ibid., 21.

60. Richardson, "Toward an American Theology," 126.

61. Ibid., 130.

62. Jürgen Moltmann, *God in Creation*, trans. Margaret Kohl (San Francisco: Harper & Row, 1985), xiii.

63. Ibid., 31.

Holy Spirit as the Telos and Perfecter of all creation, a truly divine person
no less than its Creator and Redeemer. To this we could add yet one more
covenant indicator in Genesis 1–3, the sacramental significance of the two
trees in the Garden of Eden. Are they not best understood sacramentally
as *signs* of the *covenant:* trees as *signa,* covenant as *res?*

Still another angle on the characteristic work of the Spirit is provided
by considering it under the rubric of beauty. The link between the Spirit
and beauty was affirmed already in the early church by Clement of Al-
exandria and the Cappadocians, recurs in Calvin's consideration of common grace, and is developed into a full theology of beauty by Jonathan
Edwards and more recently by Russian Orthodox theologians Sergei
Bulgakov and Paul Evdokimov as well as the Roman Catholic Hans Urs
Von Balthasar.[64] The basic claims are:

> that the Spirit of God communicates God's beauty to the world, both
> through Creation, in the case of natural beauty, and through inspiration, in
> the case of artistic beauty; that earthly beauty is thus a reflection of divine
> glory, and a sign of the way in which the Spirit is perfecting creation; and
> that beauty has an eschatological significance, in that it is an anticipation
> of the restored and transfigured world which will be the fullness of God's
> kingdom. (2)

We conclude this quick survey of Sabbath theology with a citation from
Jonathan Edwards that not only links beauty and holiness with sabbatar-
ian glory, but also with the Holy Spirit's formative role in the creation
story itself.

> It was made especially the Holy Spirit's work to bring the world to its
> beauty and perfection out of the chaos; for the beauty of the world is a
> communication of God's beauty. The Holy Spirit is the harmony and ex-
> cellence and beauty of the deity, as we have shown. Therefore, 'twas His
> work to communicate beauty and harmony to the world, and so we read
> that it was He that moved upon the face of the waters. (95)

With this background established, Hoeksema's brief and cryptic comments in his discussion on the covenant with Adam in creation carry all
the more weight. For Hoeksema the covenant relation is not "incidental, a
means to an end," but rather "a fundamental relationship in which Adam
stood to God by virtue of his creation; [it was] a relation of living fellowship and friendship. . . . From the very first moment of his existence . . .

---

64. For a quick historical overview see Patrick Sherry, *Spirit and Beauty: An Introduction
to Theological Aesthetics* (Oxford: Clarendon, 1992), chap. 1. Page references which follow in
the text, including citations from other sources, are to this work.

Adam stood in that covenant relation to God and was conscious of that living fellowship and friendship which is essential to that relationship. He knew God and loved him and was conscious of God's love to him. He *enjoyed* the favor of God. He received the Word of God, walked with God and talked with Him; and he *dwelled in the house of God* in paradise the first."[65] As God's covenant friend and representative "office-bearer in all creation" Adam was given a task as God's co-worker for which his reward was the Sabbath-like "pure delight of it in the favor of God."[66] Hoeksema picks up similar Sabbath-like language when he describes Adam's priestly role to "dwell in God's house and consecrate himself and all things to Him."[67] Hoeksema notes that covenantal imagery—and we might add Sabbath imagery—is found through Scripture even where the word *berith* is not explicitly mentioned.

> Enoch and Noah walked with God (Gen. 5:24; Gen. 6:9). To walk with God is an act of friendship and intimate fellowship. Abraham is called the friend of God (Isa. 41:8; James 2:23). The tabernacle and temple foreshadowed the truth that God dwells with his people under one roof, in the same house, as a friend with his friends. This covenant relationship is centrally realized in the incarnation of the Son of God: "And the Word was made flesh, and dwelt among us" (John 1:14).

Hoeksema concludes:

> Indeed, all Scripture presents the covenant relation as fundamental and essential. If the work of redemption and the work of creation are related to each other, there can be no doubt that Adam in this state of integrity stood in covenant relation to God. [68]

Yes. Indeed!

65. Hoeksema, *Reformed Dogmatics*, 222, emphasis added.
66. Ibid., 223.
67. Ibid.
68. Ibid., 221.

9

The Reformation, Today's Evangelicals, and Mormons

What Next?

GARY L. W. JOHNSON

What is an evangelical? The label has been subjected to intense scrutiny over the last few decades, with the word becoming more and more elastic with each passing year. Those most often identified with the kind of Reformed evangelicalism as espoused by the old Princeton School insist that the term must have not only a direct link to the Protestant Reformation, but also clear-cut theological boundaries.

Oxford theologian Alister McGrath, although sympathetic with these Reformed concerns, admits that this approach is unacceptable. Why? "It is a simple matter of fact that any theologically rigorous definition of *evangelicalism* tends to end up excluding an embarrassingly large number of people who regard themselves, and are regarded by others, as Evangelicals."[1] Instead, as argued by respected evangelicals like Donald Dayton (who writes out of an Arminian tradition), the term should be defined in other ways (with the not so subtle suggestion that the Reformed

---

1. Alister McGrath, *Evangelicalism &The Future of Christianity* (Downers Grove, IL: InterVarsity, 1995), 54.

folks should now be perceived as being on the periphery given the way evangelicalism is presently constituted).[2]

Clark Pinnock, the most prominent proponent of open theism, tells us that *evangelical* is to be defined "more sociologically than precisely theologically."[3] In other words, people may claim to be *evangelical* and do so without specific affirmation of theological tenets that have historically characterized evangelicalism. Doctrines that have historically been deemed essential to evangelical identity are now being discarded by many of today's evangelicals like yesterday's newspaper, with little or no loss of status in today's evangelical community. Penal substitution, for example, once a critically important feature of evangelical theology, is now openly disdained and considered detrimental by a growing number of today's evangelicals.[4]

If we complain that this is not a doctrine that should be up for negotiation, we are chastised and told that we should not expect that any precise theological definition (and certainly no doctrinal litmus test) will find favor with the big tent model that is so much in vogue with evangelicals, so we must settle for a theologically vague and imprecise definition. The term, we are repeatedly told, must be defined in such a way as to gain wide acceptance across today's evangelical landscape. Following the lead of the British historian David Bebbington, Wesleyan scholar Kenneth Collins recently attempted to describe the major features of evangelicalism in terms of four key characteristics. Taken together, these four things constitute

2. Donald Dayton, *Discovering an Evangelical Heritage* (New York: Harper & Row, 1976), 20. In another book he echoes the sentiments of folk singer Bob Dylan ("the times they are a changing"), and as such the older way of defining evangelicalism "calls into question the continuing usefulness of the label *evangelical* as a historical and theological category.)"; cf. *The Variety of American Evangelicalism* ed. Donald W. Dayton and Robert K. Johnston (Eugene, OR: Wipf and Stock Publishers, 1997), 251. Reformed historian D. G. Hart has taken a similar position, contending that evangelicalism needs to be relinquished as a religious identity because it does not exist. In fact, it is the wax nose of twentieth-century American Protestantism. Despite the vast amounts of energy and resources expended on the topic, and notwithstanding the ever-growing volume of literature on the movement, evangelicalism is little more than a construction. See his *Deconstructing Evangelicalism: Conservative Protestantism in the Age of Billy Graham*, (Grand Rapids, MI: Baker, 2003). More recently, Dayton's fellow-Arminian Roger Olson accused Calvinists across the board, especially those who follow the Old Princeton men, of misrepresenting and distorting what evangelical Arminianism teaches. See his *Arminian Theology: Myths and Realities* (Downers Grove, IL: InterVarsity Press Academic, 2006).

3. Clark Pinnock, "Evangelical Theologians Facing the Future: An Ancient and a Future Paradigm" *Wesleyan Theological Journal* 33 (Fall 1998): 8.

4. Kenneth J. Collins, *The Evangelical Movement: The Promise of American Religion* (Grand Rapids: Baker, 2005). David Bebbington, Evangelicalism in Modern Britain: A History from the 1730s to the 1980s (London: Unwin Hyman, 1989). Bebbington's description of evangelicalism in the words of John Stackhouse "enjoys the approval of most historians and theologians who study evangelicalism," Evangelical Landscapes: Facing Critical Issues of the Day (Grand Rapids: Baker, 2002), 163. I am going to argue in this assessment of Millet's book that Collins and Bebbington's definition of evangelicalism is badly in need of substantial revision.

what it means to be an evangelical: the normative value of Scripture, the necessity of conversion, the cruciality of the atoning work of Christ, and the imperative of evangelism.[5] Well now, is everybody happy? We finally have a definition that *everyone* across the broad spectrum of evangelicalism can agree on—or can we?

It's All in the Family

Along comes Keith Fournier, who writes a book that is then published by an evangelical publisher, carrying glowing endorsements from high-profile evangelicals,[6] and guess what? He can subscribe to this definition of what it means to be an *evangelical*. There's only one problem. Fournier is *not* a Protestant (which, at one time, was used interchangeably with the

5. Steve Chalke, a high-profile advocate of what calls itself the *Emergent Conversation*, recently launched a frontal assault on the doctrine of penal substitution calling it, among other things, a form of "cosmic child abuse." See his *The Lost Message of Jesus* (Grand Rapids, MI: Zondervan, 2003). This has become a common refrain amongst embrangling emergent types, including their leading spokesman, Brian McLaren; cf. his "A Radical Rethinking of Our Evangelistic Strategy" *Theology News & Notes* (Fuller Theological Seminary, Fall 2004), where he says, "bona fide evangelicals (such as Mark Baker, Joel Green, and N. T. Wright) are suggesting that the gospel is not atonement-centered, or, at least, not penal-substitutionary-atonement-centered." He has also gone on record describing penal substitution: "presents a God who is incapable of forgiving. Unless He kicks somebody else." See his *The Secret Message of Jesus: Uncovering the Truth That Could Change Everything* (Grand Rapids, MI: Zondervan, 2005) Joel Green and Mark Baker co-authored the book *Recovering the Scandal of the Cross: Atonement in New Testament & Contemporary Contexts* (Downers Grove, IL: InterVarsity, 2000). This book is even more truculent than Chalke, declaring, for example, "Undoubtedly the widespread popularity of penal substitutionary atonement is built in part on the base of human fear of God, combined with the perceived necessity of placating an emotion-laden God ever on the verge of striking out against any who disobey his every will" (53). B. B. Warfield could well have been speaking of Green and Baker's book when he wrote a review of a similar-type book by Yale professor George Stevens: "We shall not profess to have found the volume pleasant reading. The polemic tone in which it is cast from beginning to end, strident from the commencement, finishes by becoming rasping. It is not obvious that the opinions thus endlessly controverted have been sympathetically appreciated. It is not even obvious that the trouble has been taken thoroughly to understand them. Certainly they are not always stated in their completeness; and they are not seldom refuted in mere caricature. The reader acquires an unpleasant feeling as he proceeds in the volume that the language of scorn, rising even to vituperation, is now and again depended upon to do the work of argument. Dr. Stevens does not like the doctrine of 'penal satisfaction.' Not liking it, he is entitled to argue against it, and (if he can) to refute it. It may be questioned, however, whether its refutation is advanced by declaring that it makes God a Shylock (410) whose most distinguishing characteristic is "his appetite for revenge" (331 *et seq.*). See *The Works of Benjamin B. Warfield: Critical Reviews X* (Grand Rapids, MI: Baker), 128.

6. *A House United: Evangelicals and Catholics Together: A Winning Alliance for the 21st Century* (Colorado Springs: NavPress, 1994); hereafter cited in text. I reviewed this in *Reformation & Revival: A Quarterly Journal for Church Leadership* vol. 5, No. 1. Winter 1996, 155–64.

label *evangelical*). Fournier passionately claims to be an evangelical who just also happens to be a loyal, theologically dedicated, Roman Catholic. He freely admits that he submits, without reservation, to all the dogmas that his church espouses, and yet claims that he can be both evangelical and Roman Catholic without contradiction in terms, logic, theology, or history (34). His book, written with the assistance of William D. Watkins (a Dallas Seminary graduate), is aimed at evangelicals. He exhorts his target audience to lay down their weapons and to scale the great wall of division and embrace each other once more as fellow members of the same church family. Evangelicals and Catholics together, as seen in the subtitle of the book, need to form an alliance and stand shoulder to shoulder in the battle for our nation's soul.

This appeal struck a responsive chord with many evangelicals. But Fournier's clarion call to arms to fight against the forces of moral decadence, along with his personal (and no doubt sincere) testimony, is really secondary to Fournier's real objective. The book had an apologetical thrust. It constitutes a full-fledged and unabashed defense of the dogmas of Rome. It was carefully packaged, but make no mistake—the design and intent of the author was to convince *today's evangelicals* that, doctrinally speaking, the Reformation was dead wrong and that Rome's gospel is the pure gospel. We are told throughout this book that Rome has always been faithful to the gospel, and that Protestant concerns are traceable to misunderstanding, or distortion (208). Roman Catholic distinctives are defended at every turn—the role of Mary, the papacy, the whole sacerdotal system—all of it is set forth in living color, with no apologies. According to him, an evangelical is one who knows Christ as Savior and Lord and tells others about him (34). If this is all it takes to be considered one of today's evangelicals, we should prepare ourselves to be accosted by evangelical Mormons or Moonies, each clamoring to be recognized as such. And why not? They can easily subscribe to Fournier's definition, (as well as that offered by Collins and Bebbington).

The burgeoning men's movement known as Promise Keepers ran into this problem. It was inevitable and unavoidable. Even though Promise Keepers stresses spiritual, moral, ethical, and sexual purity, it does not put an emphasis on doctrinal purity. Listen to the words of Bill McCartney, the founder of Promise Keepers: "Promise Keepers doesn't care if you're Catholic. Do you love Jesus? Are you born of the Spirit of God?" Randy Phillips, one-time president of Promise Keepers, has stated that doctrine does not matter when it comes to the differences between Roman Catholics and Protestants: "What we care about is do you love Jesus, and are you born again by the Spirit of God? And so, if you have been born again by the Spirit of God, then whatever the labels are should not divide us.

So from that standpoint, all men are welcome, whether you're Baptist, Pentecostal, or Roman Catholic. If you are in the Body of Christ, then you should certainly be welcome."[7] But it was not simply a question of labels. If that is the case, then the official position of the Church of Latter-day Saints should not be a concern. If individual Mormons claim they love Jesus and are born of the Spirit, why should they be excluded? As it turned out, Mormons were showing up in large numbers at Promise Keepers rallies and this created a very awkward situation. Which brings me to the subject alluded to in the title.

Distant Relatives?

Along comes Robert L. Millet, who writes a book that is published by a recognized evangelical publisher, carrying glowing endorsements from high-profile evangelicals including a foreword and afterword by Richard Mouw, president of Fuller Theological Seminary.[8] Millet, like Fournier, is not a Protestant . . . or a Roman Catholic. He is a Mormon and a professor in the Religious Studies Department at Brigham Young University. He is described by the evangelicals associated with this book as a gracious, honest, sincere and passionate man of faith. Mouw portrays him not only as a close friend, but as a person of great integrity (it was Mouw who encouraged Millet to write this book and arranged for Eerdmans to publish it [viii]). Mouw, who admits a certain degree of nervousness in his appreciation for what Millet has written nonetheless, with true evangelical ethos, finds Millet's personal testimony very compelling:

As an Evangelical Christian I want more than anything else that people— whatever disagreements I might have with them on other matters—know Jesus personally, as the heaven-sent Savior who left heaven's throne to come to the manger, and to Gethsemane, and to Calvary, to do for us what we could never do for ourselves. I also know that having a genuine personal relationship with Jesus Christ does not require that we have all our theology straight. All true Christians are on a journey, and until we see the Savior face-to-face, we will all see through a glass darkly. (182)

7. Cf. my chapter "The Eclipse of The Reformation in the Evangelical Church: Much Ado about Nothing?" in *Whatever Happened to The Reformation?* ed. G. L. W. Johnson and R. Fowler White (Phillipsburg, NJ: P&R, 2001).

8. Robert Millet, *A Different Jesus? The Christ of the Latter-Day Saints* (Grand Rapids, MI: Eerdmans, 2005); hereafter cited in text. I wrote a shorter review of this book for *Modern Reformation* (vol. 15, no. 2, March–April 2006).

What would move a self-described evangelical Calvinist like Mouw to
embrace Millet, a dyed-in-the-wool Mormon, not only as a good friend
but also as a fellow Christian (evangelical)? He says in his afterword that
he personally is convinced "that Bob Millet is in fact trusting in the Jesus
of the Bible for his salvation" (183).

Millet uses very evangelical-sounding words and phrases to convey
his convictions, all of which Mouw says he takes at face value (180).
He speaks of "trusting" only in Jesus for his acceptance with God (177)
or "I love the Lord," and "how completely I trust him" (43) and of his
"heartfelt acceptance of Jesus" (140). He also sounds a lot like your
typical garden-variety evangelical when it comes to accenting the love
of God. He says:

> Our God is the God of all creation, an infinite, eternal, and omni-loving
> Being who will do all that He can to lead and direct, to bring greater light
> into the lives of His children, to save as many as will be saved. He is the only
> true God and thus the only Deity who can hear and respond to the earnest
> petitions of His children. He is the God of the Catholics, the Protestants,
> the Buddhists, the Hindus, and all those who seek to know and love and
> offer praise and adoration to the true and living God. I have been a Lat-
> ter-day Saint all my life, but I do not in any way believe the Almighty loves
> Latter-day Saints any more than He loves Anglicans, Jehovah's Witnesses,
> Unitarians, Jews, or Muslims. He loves us all, and is pleased with any and
> every halting effort on our part to learn of Him, serve Him, and be true to
> the light within us. (63; see also 95)

Much of what passes for *today's evangelicalism* would joyfully concur
with a hearty *Amen*!

Real Issues

Millet's book, however, deals with more than just his personal testimony
about how much Jesus means to him (and I don't doubt his sincerity).
Like Fournier who was totally committed to *all* the theological distinc-
tives of Roman Catholicism, so Millet is unapologetic in his defense of
Mormon theology. To begin, he explicitly rejects the cardinal doctrine of
the Trinity, candidly admitting that Mormonism believes in "Three distinct
Gods" (70) who are "three distinct personages, three Beings, three separate
Gods" (141). In layman's language this is polytheism, pure and simple.
He acknowledges that if an acceptance of the doctrine of the Trinity is
essential to being a Christian, then of course Latter-day Saints are not
Christian, for they believe that the doctrine of the Trinity as expressed in

modern Protestant and Catholic theology is the product of the reconciliation of Christian theology and Greek philosophy (171).

This is a rather incredible claim coming from someone who should know better. He demonstrates throughout the book that he is widely read in evangelical literature and does not hesitate to tell us so (41).[9] He actually acknowledges that Karl Barth was the most important theologian of the twentieth century (164), but he seems totally unaware that Barth completely demolished that old worn-out canard in his *Church Dogmatics*. Furthermore, in concert with Christian theologians down through the centuries, Barth argued that the whole of Christianity stands or falls with the doctrine of the Trinity. But Millet cannot critically disengage himself from his Mormon presuppositions, even given his admiration and respect for someone with the theological stature of a Karl Barth.[10]

True to standard Mormon claims, Millet vigorously contends that after the first century, the authority and power to act in God's name "was lost" (Millet, 40) until it was recovered in the early nineteenth century by Joseph Smith. This refrain is played over and over again (41, 65, 69). Only Mormons possess the fullness of the gospel (162, 169), and of course, Joseph Smith is given exalted status as *the* Prophet and Apostle of God, and his chosen instrument for restoration of the gospel and the *true* church of Christ (58, 158).

Will the Real Jesus Please Stand Up?

This brings us to the crux of the matter: who is the Christ of Mormonism? Despite Millet's insistence that his Jesus is the same one that we met in the pages of the New Testament, it is the *other* Scriptures of Mormonism that define him. This Jesus was born "as we all were, the spirit children of the Father" (20). This Jesus is a spirit brother of Lucifer (21). This Jesus is the Christ of Joseph Smith and is considered absolutely foundational to Mormonism (39). It is conceded that the Christ of "traditional" Christianity and the Christ of Mormonism are *very* different, and in substantial ways. Why? Because the Christ of orthodox Christianity is rooted in theological creeds, while the Christ of Mormonism "comes from the witness of a prophet—Joseph Smith" (174). Contrary to Millet's claim that Christ is the central figure in the doctrine and practice of Mormon-

9. He cites and at times interacts with such prominent evangelical representatives as F. F. Bruce, D. Bloesch, D. A. Carson, John MacArthur, J. I. Packer, John Stott, and especially C. S. Lewis.

10. One does not have to be a Barthian to appreciate Barth's prodigious scholarship, especially in the field of historical theology, where he demonstrated a comprehensive grasp of the whole range of Christian theology that is second to none.

ism (80), Joseph Smith, by his later admission, holds that place of honor (158). In fact, without Joseph Smith, there is no Mormonism (151). The Jesus of Mormonism is distinctively the Christ of Joseph Smith. The two cannot be separated.[11]

Likewise, the gospel of Mormonism is radically different from the gospel that evangelicals have historically embraced. *Sola fide*, the material principle of the Reformation and the doctrine Luther rightly called "the article by which the church stands or falls" is outright rejected (Millet, 100). In its place is erected an elaborate system of "principles" (24), which are described in Millet's words as "obedience to Laws essential to salvation" (22). I am inclined to think that evangelical Arminians like Thomas Oden and I. Howard Marshall will no doubt respond with considerable consternation to Mouw's suggestion that the Mormon understanding of salvation by obedience to principles and laws, etc., is similar to that put forth by the theological descendants of John Wesley (181).

Millet has no hesitancy in declaring that Mormonism rejects any concept of total depravity (84) as well as the critically important doctrine of original sin (86). In fact, Millet presents what only can be called a full-blown Pelagian concept of grace (this is woven through the book (21, 26, 53, 65, 69, 84, 87, 95, 97, 103). Like Pelagius, Millet (quoting from 2 Nephi 31:19 and Moroni 6:4) says, "We must work to our limit, and *then* (emphasis added) rely upon the merits, mercy, and grace of the Holy One of Israel (69). Like Pelagius, Millet underscores Mormon belief that children are born innocent (87). Like Pelagius, Millet teaches the Mormon doctrine that all human beings have "the (innate) capacity" to be saved (95), and to "strive to do what we *can do*" (emphasis in original) to secure salvation (97). The effects of the fall, in his words, only "*tend* (emphasis

---

11. The situation that confronts evangelicals when dealing with Mormonism is not unlike that which John Owen encountered when dealing with Socinianism, as Carl Trueman points out. "It is worth noting at this point that, to a large extent, Owen's refutation of Socinian theology is simply a restatement of the orthodox christological framework and presupposes the validity of his defense of eternal generation, etc. The problem is fundamentally that of the relationship of doctrine to exegesis. Owen and the Socinians are interpreting the relevant biblical texts within two totally different theological frameworks and therefore arriving at totally different conclusions, a point which indicates that it would be inaccurate to interpret the Protestant notion of *sola Scriptura* in such a way as to regard it as a sufficient safeguard in and of itself to safeguard the church against heresy in the seventeenth-century context. In fact, Owen's defense of orthodox Christology in the face of the radically biblicist attacks of the Socinians clearly depends upon setting the notion of *sola Scriptura* and scriptural exegesis within the ongoing Catholic theological tradition. This is not to deny that the Scriptures do not possess normative authority for Owen when he comes to formulate doctrine, but simply to point out that this must be seen as standing in positive relation to the doctrinal and exegetical tradition. It is the Socinians' radical break with the tradition that makes the theological results of their exegesis so heterodox." *The Claims of Truth: John Owen's Trinitarian Theology*, (Carlisle, PA: Paternoster, 1998).

added) to entice humankind away from God" (103). Like Pelagius, Joseph Smith, the central figure in Mormonism, taught that there is no transfer, or imputation, of Adam's sin and guilt to his posterity (87).

This is so central to Mormonism that it is listed as one of the thirteen Articles of Faith of The Church of Jesus Christ of Latter-day Saints (185). The critically important Creator/creature distinction is likewise discarded. The distance between God and man, he says, "is still tremendous, *almost* (emphasis added) infinite" (144). Millet *graciously* allows for some sort of salvation for non-Mormons (48), but *only* Mormons who have been baptized by the "proper authority" will gain entrance into "the highest heaven" (49). Joseph Smith, we are later told, had God reveal to him "the concept of three main divisions in the afterlife—in descending order (in terms of the greatest eternal reward), the Celestial Kingdom, Terrestrial Kingdom, and Telestial Kingdom, each of which is a Kingdom of Glory" (107).

Next-Door Neighbors

Throughout Millet's book he seeks to make common cause with groups across the broad evangelical landscape—especially those identified with the pentecostal-charismatic wing of evangelicalism. Because Mormonism insists on additional *inscripturated* revelation, Millet tries to show how compatible this is with the claims of many evangelicals: "The acceptance of modern and continuing revelation, including the addition to the scriptural canon, is one of the distinctives of Mormonism and thus one of the reasons those of other faiths are prone to describe the Latter-day Saints as non-Christian. And yet, how radical is the idea of modern revelation?"

Roman Catholics certainly believe that God has directed and will continue to direct the church through the "working out" of church practice and tradition—based upon holy Scripture—and that an ongoing form of heavenly guidance comes through such means as papal encyclicals. People in the pentecostal and holiness movements within Protestantism believe that spiritual gifts, such as the speaking and interpretation of tongues, is one means by which Deity communicates his will to individuals and groups. And what of evangelicalism? Of my hundreds of evangelical acquaintances, every single one believes that God can and does hear his or her prayers, respond to his or her petitions, and in some cases send an answer through a kind of spiritual illumination that I can only describe as inspiration or revelation (15). Millet's attempt to equate "spiritual illumination" (or divine providential guidance) with "inspiration" or "revelation" is disingenuous. He clearly makes such a distinction when he tried to have statements of Smith and Young (see below) dismissed as being "uninspired" despite *their* claim to the contrary!

Scriptura Sacra Locuta, Res Decisa Est?

The Reformers claimed that once the Holy Scripture has spoken, the issue is decided. But it does not hold true for Millet. Not surprisingly, *sola Scriptura* is likewise rejected. What is disappointing is that Millet appeals for support to two erstwhile evangelicals in order to cast suspicion on this essential evangelical distinctive (15, 56, 76). The Bible, we are told, does not contain what it once did (46). This is a standard Mormon re-tort—the Bible has been corrupted (cf. I Nephi 13:25, 28).[12] Naturally the notion of biblical inerrancy is completely rejected (Millet, 37, 45), while the absolute truthfulness and trustworthiness of the *Book of Mormon*, is wholeheartedly affirmed (151). However, Millet says, "We do not believe in prophetic or apostolic infallibility" (*xiv*).

Does this mean that Millet is willing to admit that the Mormon scrip-tures contain theological errors? Hardly. Millet is concerned here with those kinds of embarrassing statements that Mormon prophets like Joseph Smith and Brigham Young made "off the record," so to speak—things like Smith's claim that the moon was populated by people who dressed like Quakers, or Young's equally absurd declaration that the Sun was inhabited—or even more embarrassing, Brigham Young's doctrine of "Adam-God."[13] Millet labels these kinds of things "extraneous" (Millet,

12. For extended analysis cf. R.V. Huggins, "Joseph Smith and the First Verse of the Bible," in *The Journal of the Evangelical Theological Society* (vol. 46, no. 1, March 2003): 29–52.

13. Based on the teachings of Joseph Smith, Brigham Young taught that Adam, the first man, was actually *our* God—the father of our spirits, the father of Jesus in the flesh—who impregnated the *Virgin* Mary (in which case there is no *virgin* birth, cf. with Millet's statement, 74), came here from another planet with a resurrected body, and that Mormons, when they become gods, will actually do so by becoming *Adams*. For extensive documentation, see *Where Does It Say That? Photo Reprints That Expose Mormonism's Deception* compiled by B. Witte (Scottsdale: COUP, 1973), 32–39. It is this kind of material that Millet labels "anti-Mormon propaganda" (140). Even Mouw speaks negatively of "anti-cult stuff" (*x*). Journalist Jon Krakauer in his *New York Times* bestseller points out: "Because the Mormon leadership is so obsessed with controlling how the Mormon past is interpreted and presented, histories sanctioned by the LDS Church tend to be extensively censored. In 1997, for example, the church released a manual (published in twenty-two languages, and designated as required reading for virtually every Mormon adult) titled *Teaching of the Presidents of the Church: Brigham Young,* in which this great Mormon leader was deliberately portrayed as being monogamous despite the fact that few scholars, Mormon or otherwise, would dispute that Young was actually married to at least twenty women, and was probably married to more than fifty. Even a cursory survey of other LDS-sanctioned publications will reveal a similarly disturbing sanitization of the historical record. Journalists and historians who publish versions of Mormon history that deviate from

xv), and as such, have no bearing on Mormon doctrine, which is restricted to the *official* standards of the LDS Church.

But Millet finds himself in a bit of a bind with this kind of distinction. In a genuine attempt to be irenic and sensitive to Christians outside the camp, Millet feels constrained to put the best spin possible on Joseph Smith's claims that God personally told him, in reference to *all* other churches that "*all* their creeds were an abomination in his sight; that those professors were *all* corrupt" (emphasis added)—a very harsh indictment and something Millet tries mightily to soften. He appeals to other statements that Joseph Smith made that imply that other Christian churches are really not all that bad—they have *some* truth—but these remarks are *not* part of the official standards—and despite the "spin," Millet knows it. This is simply window dressing put up for appearance's sake.

Millet reluctantly concedes that given the inspired status of Smith's revelation, "Latter-day Saints cannot jettison what they believe to be the language of the Lord to Joseph Smith in 1820 in order to allay bad feelings, or court favor" (64). In light of this admission I am left wondering what Richard Mouw had in mind when he commends Millet for helpfully showing "that Joseph Smith, himself, says things about mainstream Christianity that do not fit well with a thoroughly nasty interpretation of his *abomination* statement" (182).

Although Millet is forthright in admitting that he has "no desire whatsoever to compromise, or concede one whit on doctrine in order to minimize differences, or court favor in anyway" (166), he is nonetheless anxious that evangelicals come to view Mormons simply as Christians with their own particular "tradition" (*xv*, 41–42). In Mouw's mind (despite his cautious reservations), Millet seems to have succeeded. Mouw views their differences "not in terms of an unbridgeable gap of being, but in the language of *more* and *less*" (182, emphasis added). The astonishing thing about this statement of Mouw's is that he earlier declared that he is *not* the least bit inclined to accept the historical claims of the *Book of Mormon* or that Joseph Smith was a prophet (179). But the two cannot be separated, as Millet adamantly maintains (151).

Millet briefly addresses issues that in the last few years have cast serious doubts about the credibility of the *Book of Mormon* and Joseph Smith. Two of these require special mention: First, modern advances in the study of human DNA have conclusively shown that native Americans are of Asiatic ancestry and not, as the *Book of Mormon* teaches, of Jewish ancestry. Second, the recent discovery of the Joseph Smith papyri demonstrated that

the unremittingly expurgated versions put forward by the church are routinely and vigorously attacked, *ad hominem*, as I have been attacked for writing *Under the Banner of Heaven* (New York: Anchor Books, 2003), 364.

Smith's translation of the Book of Abraham (which is part of Mormon scripture) was a hoax—the document was an excerpt from an Egyptian book of the dead. Press reports of this proved extremely embarrassing to Mormons, but evidently not to Millet. Both of these legitimate concerns are summarily dismissed as having no merit (153–57).

Can I Get a Witness?

Millet closes by once again seeking to establish his *evangelical* credentials by means of his personal testimony. He relates a conversation he had with "two prominent" evangelical theologians. After discussing their differences, one of the two evangelicals asked, "Okay Bob, here's the question of questions—the one thing I would like to ask in order to determine what you really believe."

"I indicated that I thought I was ready for his query, though I readily admit that his preface to the question was a bit unnerving.

"He continued, 'You are standing before the judgment bar of the Almighty, and God turns to you and asks, "Robert Millet, what right do you have to enter heaven? Why should I let you in?"'

"It was not the kind of question I had anticipated. (I had assumed he would be asking something more theologically theoretical. This question was theological, to be sure, but it was poignant, practical, and extremely penetrating.) For about thirty seconds I tried my best to envision such a scene, searched my soul, and sought to be as clear and candid as possible. I looked my friend in the eye and replied, 'I would say to God: I claim the right to enter heaven because of my complete trust in reliance upon the merits and mercy and grace of the Lord Jesus Christ.'

"My questioner stared at me for about ten seconds, smiled gently, and said: 'Bob, that's the correct answer to the question'" (178).

The impression Millet wishes to leave is that this totally satisfied the two evangelicals about the genuineness of his profession. But it didn't. How can I say that? I know one of these theologians. David F. Wells, a personal friend, relayed this story to me. As it turns out he was one of the two men. The other was fellow faculty member at Gordon-Conwell theological seminary, Haddon Robinson (who asked Millet that question). They did *not* drop the matter, nor were they completely satisfied with Millet's answer. They both continued to press him about his distinctive Mormon beliefs, particularly those centered around his Mormon christology and soteriology. Unlike Mouw, Wells and Robinson were *not* convinced that Millet's beliefs were distinctively *Christian*, despite his sincere testimony.

Conclusion

Not too long ago, respected social historian Christian Smith made this important observation:

> Evangelicals operate with a very strong sense of boundaries that distinguish themselves from non-Christians and from non-Evangelical Christians. Evangelicals know who and what they are and are not. They possess clear symbolic borders that define the frontiers beyond which one is not an Evangelical. The implicit distinction between "us," and "them," is omnipresent in Evangelical thought and speech, so much so that it does not often in fact draw itself much attention. Yet it subtly and profoundly shapes evangelical consciousness and discourse. No good Evangelical operates without this distinction in their cultural toolkit.[14]

This appears to be the case no longer. Our postmodern makeup with its demands for tolerance—this has taken on an entirely different meaning than it once did. More and more, it is used as a synonym for *acceptance*) especially when it comes to distinctively religious matters. Senior evangelical statesman Donald Bloesch warned that "In our striving for church unity, we must not lose sight of our mandate to counter doctrinal error, for nothing subverts the cause of unity more than a latitudinarianism which signifies giving up on real church unity in favor of mutual tolerance."[15]

Millet and the evangelicals like Mouw want very much to engage in civil discourse, or in Mouw's words, "We feel we can differ theologically with people without being disagreeable in any sense" (173). I agree—*unless* that implies that any criticism of Mormon claims to be distinctly Christian is automatically ruled out of bounds and labeled "anti-Mormon propaganda." Mouw rightly recognizes that these disagreements have "profound implications" (182). One of us (either historic evangelicalism as defined by the Reformation or Mormons) is preaching a false gospel. They are not the same gospel. However, Mouw does not consider Millet's Jesus "another Jesus" (2 Cor. 11:4) and his Mormon gospel "another gospel" (Gal. 1:6). I do.

Richard Mouw has, over the years, shown himself to be a confessional Calvinist who conscientiously identifies with the likes of Abraham Kuyper, Herman Bavinck, Louis Berkhof, G. C. Berkouwer, and the late Anthony

---

14. Christian Smith, *American Evangelicalism: Embattled and Thriving* (Chicago: University of Chicago Press, 1998), 125.

15. *The Future of Evangelical Christianity: A Call for Unity amid Diversity* (Colorado Springs: Helmers & Howard, 1988), 152. Bloesch specifically mentions avowed "anti-Trinitarian" cults (10) that include Mormonism (86).

Hoekema.[16] This makes it all the more surprising that he would, even with guarded qualifications here and there, leave his fellow Christians the mistaken impression that someone could come to saving knowledge of Christ through Millet's Mormon gospel. Did he bother to consider the impact this could have on those Christians who would best be described as God's little ones and subject to being tossed to and fro by false doctrine (Eph. 4:4)? Mouw expressed concern about violating the ninth commandment by not giving Millet a fair hearing. Perhaps equal concern should be given to Jesus' words in Matthew 18:6.

After a careful reading of Millet's book, I am *more than ever* convinced that Millet's Jesus would not be recognized by our evangelical forefathers (like a Calvin, a Wesley, or a Spurgeon) and that Mouw would think otherwise is inexplicable. Having said that, I am forced to admit that developments over the last few decades in what goes by the name *evangelical* would make it difficult *not* to allow Mormons in under the big top of today's evangelical circus (after all, if antitrinitarian "oneness Pentecostals" like T. D. Jakes and the rebarbative "Word of Faith" prosperity teachers are considered members of today's evangelicalism, then why not Mormons like Millet?). In fact, given the present state of today's evangelicalism and the tendency to let people define for themselves what it means to be an evangelical, this morphosis is not all that surprising.

What next? Along comes minister Louis Farrakhan who writes a book, published by an evangelical publishing house, endorsed by a number of today's high-profile evangelicals, telling us about how meaningful Jesus is to the Nation of Islam . . .

16. I mention the late professor of theology at Calvin Theological Seminary, Anthony Hoekema, because he wrote one of the most devastating critiques of Mormonism. See his *The Four Major Cults* (Grand Rapids, MI: Eerdmans, 1963).

Afterword

A Change in the Audience, Not in the Drama

R. ALBERT MOHLER, JR.

Writing in 1933, the philosopher Alfred North Whitehead observed that every generation of humanity assumes "that each generation will substantially live amid the conditions governing the lives of its fathers and will transmit those conditions to mould with equal force the lives of its children." Yet Whitehead also observed: "We are living in the first period of human history for which this assumption is false."[1]

Whitehead's observation had mostly to do with larger intellectual currents and the world of science. Nevertheless, Whitehead's important observation is also directly relevant to theology and the life of the church. For too many theologians, the current assumption seems to be that the received tradition must be wrong and that it must be corrected, even if this means reversing the entire theological trajectory.

As the authors of this volume make clear, the evangelical doctrine of *sola fide* is now threatened by reformulation and doctrinal revision. In particular, the New Perspective on Paul and Pauline theology and the Federal Vision theology indeed represent a repudiation of the tradition received from the Reformers. Of course, the proponents of these two theological perspectives argue that their corrective is drawn directly from Scripture itself—and from a fresh reading of the critical passages of debate. The

1. Alfred North Whitehead, *Adventures of Ideas* (New York: First Free Press, 1967), 92–93.

key issue is the correct interpretation of the critical passages in debate. Thus, the argument is inescapably exegetical and hermeneutical.

The challenge is clear. Interpreters such as Krister Stendahl and E. P. Sanders argue that the evangelical tradition has seriously and tragically misconstrued the meaning of crucial Pauline texts. Moreover, Sanders argues that evangelicals have misinterpreted Second Temple Judaism, an error that has led to a warped theological trajectory and a misunderstanding of Paul's message. As the argument is pressed further, the proponents of the New Perspective argue that the Protestant Reformers distorted Paul by presenting his argument against the background of Jewish legalism and attempts at self-righteousness—a view of Judaism which Sanders disavows. Thus, the Reformers corrupted Paul by reinterpreting his theology in terms of forensic and legal categories—which were supposedly foreign to Paul's own thought.

The shocking dimension of this claim is best seen in the perspective of history. Are we to think that a tradition of interpretation, forged over centuries of theological controversy and spanning a millennium and a half of theological development, is now to be understood as based in a gross misinterpretation?

This amounts to an incredible claim of contemporaneity over continuity. Furthermore, these proponents fail to acknowledge that what they propose as the central thrust of Paul's understanding of justification—that it is about one's status in the covenant community, not the forgiveness of sin—finally leaves us with nothing better than another form of semi-Pelagianism. In other words, those arguing for the New Perspective have not escaped the bonds of tradition; they have simply come out on the wrong side.

This volume also was bold to take on the proposal usually known as the Federal Vision or, less formally, as the Auburn theology. As T. David Gordon argues, the Auburn theologians offer an incisive and much needed critique of contemporary evangelicalism. Nevertheless, the Auburn theology represents a *rejection* of historic federal theology and the imputation of Christ's righteousness. Gordon is surely right when he asserts that the Auburn theology is essentially reactionary. "Its very strength is its weakness; its keen perception of the errors of individualist, pietist, revivalist, and dispensationalist evangelicalism has driven it to make statements that are nearly as erroneous in the opposite direction." As a matter of fact, these statements may be even *more* erroneous in terms of a direct rejection of imputation and an undermining of *sola fide*.

I must agree with Richard D. Phillips and C. F. Allison that the doctrine of imputation stands at the very foundation of our salvation. Richard Phillips is surely right when he summarizes: "The doctrine of Christ's imputed righteousness should be upheld because of its biblical affirmations.

It should be treasured by believers because of the assurance it gives of an entrance into God's glory that is held upon by the joined demands of the mercy and justice of God. But there is another consideration, for which this great doctrine must be demanded with great zeal and defended at great cost, namely, the honor and glory of the Lord Jesus Christ" (97).

Each of the chapters in this volume is a worthy addition to the scholarly literature in this debate. Taken as a whole, the book is an arsenal of theological arguments in defense of the gospel.

So, why is *sola fide* now the focus of so much doctrinal compromise and controversy? Justification by faith is indeed *articula stantis et cadentis ecclesiae*—the article on which the church stands or falls. By this historic and crucial measure, evangelicalism in its contemporary form is largely falling—and falling fast.

In order to understand why this is so, one must assume that a good many who claim to be evangelicals now want to affirm something other than evangelical theology. The passage of centuries since the Reformation and the post-Reformation debates has now become the environment for a reckless and irresponsible spirit of innovation and theological change to enter evangelical ranks. With its doctrinal commitments undermined by a managerial worldview, therapeutic concerns, and an incredible superficiality, the evangelical church is highly susceptible to such calls for innovation. In this way, various theological proposals have gained ground in the most unexpected places. The Federal Vision is gaining influence among Reformed evangelicals who should be *least* likely to move in the direction of Trent rather than Geneva and Wittenberg. The New Perspective threatens to become dominant in some circles and within some theological faculties where such proposals would have been unthinkable just a few years ago. How has this happened?

Writing of theological and intellectual change in a very different context, Charles Hodge once observed, "When a drama is introduced in a theater and universally condemned, and a little while afterward, with a little change in the scenery, it is received with rapturous applause, the natural conclusion is, that the change is in the audience and not in the drama." This is a very important insight. Hodge's concern was the change in evangelical responses to Darwinian evolution. He was right—the change was in the audience. Similarly, we can detect that many of today's evangelicals now demand a new drama, a new theology. To some extent, this is a reaction to a failure in evangelical demonstration. In other cases, it appears that a sense of theological fatigue has set in, prompting some to look for theological formulations that demand a lower level of defense in light of current controversies. Whatever the case, a new audience demands a different drama.

This is precisely the case with respect to the theological proposals considered in this volume. The drama of the gospel has not changed, but the audience for evangelical theology *has* changed—and not for the better. The emergence of these new systems of thought, neither of which is as new as its proponents suggest, indicates a dangerous and potentially fatal weakening of evangelical conviction and doctrinal discernment. Judged by Scripture, these new proposals create more problems than they solve.

We can only hope and pray that contributions like this important volume can help to awaken evangelicalism to its doctrinal peril. Otherwise, nothing genuinely evangelical will remain of evangelicalism.

Index of Subjects and Names

Scripture Index